A Dollar the Hard Way

A Dollar the Hard Way

Growing Up in Tough Times in the Ozark Foothills

Stories by Kestner Wallace

WOMBLE
MOUNTAIN
PRESS

A Dollar the Hard Way:
Growing Up in Tough Times in the Ozark Foothills
Copyright © 2005 by Kestner Wallace

A Womble Mountain Press book

Library of Congress Control Number: 2005904749

ISBN-13:   978-0-9770080-1-8
ISBN-10:   0-9770080-1-0

FIRST EDITION

Acknowledgement is made to the *Springhouse Magazine*, in which most of these short stories were previously published over the last twenty-one years.

For information, contact:
>   Womble Mountain Press
>   womblemtnpress@nc.rr.com
>   919-622-2635

Publisher's Cataloging-in-Publication
(Provided by Quality Books, Inc.)

Wallace, Kestner.
    A dollar the hard way : growing up in tough times in
the Ozark foothills / Kestner Wallace. – 1st ed.
    p. cm.
    LCCN 2005904749
    ISBN 0-9770080-1-0

    1. Wallace, Kestner. 2. Depressions–1929–Illinois
–Saline County. 3. Saline County (Ill.)–Social life
and customs. 4. Saline County (Ill.)–Biography.
I. Title.

CT275.W25257A3 2005
977.3'04'092   QBI05-600082

Jacket and book design: MaryBeth Hill/mbdesignstudio
Illustrations: Angela L. Williams/Villanelle Productions

For my beloved wife, Evelyn

Preface

This book, a compilation of short stories written by Kestner Wallace over more than twenty years, is somewhat unusual in that the author had no involvement in the book's production. In an effort to create an unforgettable 85th birthday surprise for my father, the man who "already has everything [he] needs," I have compiled his stories in an order that made sense to me. Dad may well have done it differently and made other changes in the process, but lack of input is an unfortunate side effect of a complete surprise. Any faults or omissions thus lie with me.

I want to thank my brother, Ray, who acted as local co-conspirator to obtain vital information, such as a title, from our unsuspecting father, by asking key questions posed in the form, "if you were ever to have a book . . . ." Many friends stepped forward to make the book a reality: Harrison Hahn, Becky Davis, and Carolyn Crumpacker, who typed up the older stories created before computers transformed our lives; Miriam Baer, Diane Divine, and Belinda Smith, who read every word and shared their helpful suggestions and compliments; Angela Williams of Villanelle Productions, who created the delightful illustrations for each story; the endlessly creative MaryBeth Hill, of mbdesignstudio, who designed and produced both the book and the dust jacket; Carol Majors, of Publications Unlimited, who magically appeared just when most needed to help shepherd the book through to completion; and Peggy Vincent and Carla Daniel, attorney and accountant respectively, who patiently advised me on business matters.

...

Undoubtedly my father would like to acknowledge the ongoing support and encouragement of Gary DeNeal, long-time editor of the *Springhouse Magazine*, who has published nearly all of these stories in the twenty-two years of the magazine. He would also want to thank his dear wife, Evelyn, and all of the other people who have shared his life and enriched his stories in his eighty-five years in Southern Illinois.

I hope that you enjoy these stories as much as I have. Reading them as a whole has given me the greatest appreciation for my father. What a gift to have these stories to cherish forever.

LeAnn Wallace
Raleigh, North Carolina
July 2005

Contents

Oh, Brother!

My brother, Byrum, and I did our first digging for oil back in 1929, when he was seven and I was nine. At that time, just prior to and during the Depression of the '30s, many landowners in Southern Illinois escaped reality by dreaming of striking oil or locating a vein of fluorspar. The flame of hope was fanned by oil speculators who paid from twenty-five cents to five dollars per acre per year for land leases. In those days, some of the oil drilling was done with very modest equipment, and prospecting for spar was indeed simple, since the veins run perpendicular and often reveal tantalizing signs near the surface.

Byrum and I just had to know that our chances of success were remote, but we buried our doubts with hope and fantasy. Our drilling equipment consisted of a hoe, a long-handled shovel, and a post-hole digger.

Late one fall afternoon, we started our wells about ten feet apart, behind our smoke-house. Our digging was to be a secret until we struck oil.

We took our digging seriously at first, but after an hour or so, we began to horseplay and toss shovelfuls of dirt into the other's well when we could do so unobserved.

1

Therefore, as chore time drew near, our wells were only 30 inches deep.

Byrum went along with my suggestion that he would do all of our evening chores while I continued with our two wells—keeping them even in depth. While he was gone, I poured some coal oil—later known as kerosene—into his well.

When he returned, he found me on my hands and knees with my head in my well. Naturally he wanted to know what I was doing. My casual reply was, "Just smelling to see if any oil has seeped in."

Byrum wasted no time in dropping down for a good sniff. He sprang up like a Jack-in-the-box and dashed into the house as if he were possessed, screaming at the top of his lungs: "I've struck oil! I've struck oil! I've struck oil!"

Byrum's exuberant announcement of his strike was too much for Dad's nerves, so he exclaimed: "You shut up that audacious screaming and get out of here before I strike the seat of your pants!"

Byrum soon knew what I had done, but somehow he didn't think it was as funny as I did. Our oil venture over, we decided that we should return the dirt to our wells to prevent some person or animal from getting an injury.

Three or four years after our oil adventure, Byrum and I decided we should open our own fluorspar mine just south of the house where we had made molasses the previous year. We laid our plans carefully by casually discussing them so Dad could hear us. He had worked in a mine in Hardin County around 1890, when holes for blasting were made with hand iron and a sledgehammer. We reckoned that after we hit solid rock, which was often near the surface, he could give us a little supervision in putting off a few shots of

dynamite to check the formation. If we found it unprom-
ising, we would give up the venture, but if the prospect
was good, we would turn it over to someone equipped
for mining for a percent.

Byrum and I decided that we had just about talked
the subject to death and should get started mining. We
took a root-cutting, grubbing hoe and two long-handled
shovels and started out to pinpoint the spot. We were
driven by the sun to a spreading oak tree in the vicinity
of where we planned to dig.

Being somewhat influenced by the often-quoted statement "Spar is where you find it," we decided that digging
in the shade would be better than digging in the sun. Next
we had to decide on which side of the tree to dig. Again
we put on our thinking caps. Vaguely we recalled there
was a "rock candy" spar lead that crossed Williams Hill
and ran from a southwest to a northeast direction toward
Sulphur Springs near the Old Stone Face.

We decided that the west side of the tree would put
us on target. Byrum and I began to laugh at the same
time. In what appeared to be the logical spot to locate
the shaft, a cow had relieved herself, making a mound
that looked like third base on a baseball diamond.

As I was about to spend five seconds in removing
our obstacle with as much care and dignity as possible,
Byrum lit up with an inward pleasure and said, "Don't
touch it! I have an idea." Pleased with his display of happiness, I decided to go along with whatever he had in
mind, since he was a perfect example of a good-natured,
cooperative brother.

What he had in mind came as a surprise that I men-
tally labeled as "tom-foolery." He told me that he had a
four-inch firecracker that he had saved from Christmas.
He excitedly explained that we could locate it in the

middle of the mound, then watch from a safe distance and get some idea what blasting was all about. My smile of approval sent Byrum running for his firecracker.

Just after he left, our gaited work mare, Old Lil, came browsing by, followed by her mule colt. Seeing her reminded me of an experience that Byrum and I had had involving Old Lil. It was as follows:

In the hallway of our log barn, Byrum was mounted to take a ride when I asked him for a ride to the house about 300 yards away. He nodded his willingness for me to get on behind him and reined Old Lil toward where I was standing on one foot about four logs high, with the other foot and leg extended to get on behind him. He lacked a little being close enough for me to mount. So he turned and came in just right from the other direction.

My mind wasn't on mounting properly. I failed to switch legs and loaded on behind Byrum facing Old Lil's tail instead of her head. I decided that for a short distance, it might not be too bad.

As Lil left the barn prancing, an overhead two-by-wide caught the back brim of my straw hat and changed its position from firmly on the top of my head to firmly over my face—wedged just above my forehead and under my chin, and obstructing my vision.

Lil's squatting and prancing caused me to take a vise grip with both hands near the base of her tail. I attempted a death clamp with my legs around Lil's middle section, but my feet slipped back to where her mule colt got his dinner. That was an unforgivable no-no.

She went immediately into what I thought was a wild gallop. Since Byrum wasn't saying anything, I thought he was pleased with her performance and what I was experiencing was natural for a fellow on a horse backwards and blind-folded. After a bit, I was expecting to hear a "Whoa, whoa, hold up" from Byrum, indicating that we had arrived. It didn't happen. I identified with the man who had been tarred and feathered and ridden out of town on a rail. His comment was: "If it weren't for the honor of it, I'd rather be walking."

With me, it was "to heck with my reputation as a rider." I released my feet and leg clamp and slid off Lil's tail and landed on my two feet. Gracefully? Perhaps not. I straightened my hat and to my surprise, we were just outside the barn entrance. Lil had been bucking all the time—not galloping.

Byrum was soon back with his firecracker. He had about a foot length of twine string tied to the regular firecracker fuse. He explained that it represented the longer fuse used in setting off dynamite.

He placed the firecracker in the center of the mound and pressed it down until only the top and the fuse were in view. He even had a forked stick that he stuck in the ground and laid the fuse on it to keep it high and dry.

Then he handed me two matches and said, "If you fail to light the twine fuse with these two, I'll light it with this match."

Filled with a double dose of confidence, I carelessly struck one of the matches. It flashed, flickered, fluttered, and went out. Then with greater care, I hovered near the end of the twine fuse and cupped my hands around the second lighted match while approaching the string. Suddenly it took on a crimson glow without bursting into flame.

Byrum, in what appeared to be impatience with my slowness, lit his match. Without my seeing him, he touched it to the short original fuse. Suddenly I heard the sizzling, hissing sound of a burning fuse. I was in the process of leaping to my feet when the blast occurred. Byrum told me later that he got the impression that I was lifted into the air by the blast. I'll spare you the details, but you can take my word for it. I was plastered. There was a blinding, stinging splatter like you wouldn't believe. I feared my eyesight was injured.

In a contrite voice, Byrum asked if I was hurt. I ventured a look at him. In spite of my appearance, I rejoiced that I could see clearly and that Byrum was spotless. He was most helpful in racing to the house to get me a bar of soap, a towel, and a change of clothes. He went with me over to the swimming hole, and in a short time, I was clean and ready for dinner.

In the afternoon we began our digging. Two hours later, we were on solid rock. Neither of us breathed a word about blasting. Now, even after all these years, a small area similar to a sunken grave marks the spot.

Immediately after reliving the above account, and while writing on the first handwritten page, the phone rang. It was my brother Byrum—friendly, kindhearted, and likeable. Before learning why he called, I briefed him on what I had begun to write: the oil well, the bucking experience, and the mining. Then I asked if he wanted to add or delete anything.

I imagined the twinkle in his eye and heard the soft laughter in his voice as he answered, "No additions. No deletions. But try to squeeze in somewhere that my pulling off the firecracker deal helped me to get more than even with you for putting coal oil in my oil well."

Reflections of the Past

Alvin Sadler lived about three miles from the small country church where he preached back in 1927. The good church folks, along with neighbors and friends, called him Brother Alvin. He was lank and lean and about six feet tall, but even with his large frame, his weight was only about one hundred eighty pounds. His natural dark complexion was made darker by his work as a farmer and woodsman. Brother Alvin's hands were hard and calloused from not wearing gloves. His hair was black with perhaps a little gray showing. He combed a wisp of hair down on his forehead to his eyebrows and then gave it an artistic twist to the side and upward.

Brother Alvin demanded respect for various reasons. He had a reputation of being honest, truthful, and hard working. He did a better job providing for his family than many under similar circumstances. His farm, like others in southern Saline, Pope, and Hardin counties, was unproductive and stood in need of restoration. It barely produced enough to feed three or four cows and a few hogs, keep a small flock of hens in production, and feed his team of farm mules that doubled for transportation.

Brother Alvin loved his neighbors and friends and never passed up an opportunity to lend a helping hand. He also had a good sense of humor. If anyone poked fun at him, he gave them the benefit of the doubt as to whether or not it was humor or smart-mouthing. People just seemed to know that he wasn't a man with whom to trifle. If he asked someone if they'd had their plow cleaned lately, it was all the warning that they were going to get. They could clean up their act or put up their dukes.

Most regrettable for Brother Alvin was the fact that he had no formal education. He could neither read nor write. He admitted it quite freely and didn't pretend or make excuses. He just did the best he could under unfortunate circumstances. In his generation his lack of an education wouldn't have been so critical had it not been for the fact that he felt the Lord's calling for him to preach.

Brother Alvin's wife, Mandy, was a praiseworthy mother, grandmother, neighbor, and friend. She, too, was uneducated and not able to be very much help to Brother Alvin in his pastoral work. However, the angels in Heaven surely took notice of how she helped make a garden, can and preserve fruit and vegetables, help cure and smoke meat, and make and can sausage.

Brother Alvin's church held church services only once a month on the fourth Sunday morning and Sunday night. That gave him a great deal of time to work on the two sermons. He always had more on his heart, as he expressed it, than he had time to present. He nearly always ran past noon on Sunday morning. That turned out to be a big joke, and no one seemed to mind. Laughingly they would comment that he got so blessed that he couldn't find a place to stop.

...

One Sunday in late spring the church people were beginning to gather for church. Suddenly things began to happen. A few people were standing around in front of the church. An airplane flew over. It was quite high and looked very small. It held people's attention until it was out of sight.

About that time Brother Willie drove up in a Model T Ford. That caused excitement also. Brother Willie got out of the T Ford without paying much attention to those standing around. He raised the hood on one side and took a look. Naturally, all the people gathered around. He couldn't see what he wanted to see from that side, so he raised the hood from the other side also. Really there wasn't anything wrong with the T Ford, but the people had a chance to take a good look.

As they began to back off from looking at the car engine, Brother Alvin and Mandy, their son and his wife, and their daughter and son-in-law came up in a farm wagon drawn by a pair of white-nosed, yellow-bellied mules. The mules looked like tough scudders, because they arrived in a lively trot. Brother Alvin and Sister Mandy were riding high on a spring seat. The others were sitting, covered with quilts, on a thick layer of straw in the bed of the wagon.

A number of the men raised their hands in greeting and called out a pleasant "Good morning." One man inquired of the others what they thought Brother Alvin's text would be.

A boy six or seven years old, who wasn't missing anything, immediately took it upon himself to oblige them by going around behind the church, where Brother Alvin was tying his mules to a tree, to inquire about the text. We will call this kid, "Little Willie." He walked up and sounded off.

"Good morning, Brother Alvin. It is a fine morning isn't it? What is going to be your text this morning?"

That brought a friendly laugh from Brother Alvin's clan. The question didn't seem to be resented by Brother Alvin, nor was it ignored.

"I hope you will like my sermon. My text, Lord willing, will be 'The Walls of Jericho Came Falling Down.'"

"Thank you, Brother Alvin. I can hardly wait to hear your sermon."

Little Willie hurried back around to report what he had learned, but he couldn't report immediately because there were two buggies coming in from opposite directions. Each buggy was drawn by a fine, bay brood mare. Each mare had a long-legged mule colt dancing along beside its mother. The men were admiring the mule colts. One fellow said that they would make a good matched team. They all agreed.

Brother Tom chided, "Brother Joe, I'll bet you five dollars, as well matched as those colts are, they are not from the same jack."

"Brother Tom, if it weren't Sunday and we weren't standing in front of the church, I would take you up on that."

After a little more talk and observation, they agreed that one was out of Sam DeNeal's jack and the other was out of Joe Travelstead's jack. Their conclusion was confirmed by their owners.

As soon as Little Willie thought that the time was right, he proudly announced, "Brother Alvin's text will be 'The Walls of Jericho Came Falling Down.'"

Brother Tom humorously replied, "Let us rush on in so the walls can start falling."

Brother Alvin invited Brother Andrew to come up and lead the singing. He could start a song in the correct pitch by using what he called a tuning fork. Brother Andrew did a good job. He shared equal time with what almost appeared to be three groups, the men and women's "Amen" corners on opposite sides of the preacher's stand and those out front. The congregation responded well to Brother Andrew's insistence that they put their heart and soul in the singing. After a prayer by Brother Lew, Brother Andrew led the group in three or four verses of "Give Me That Old Time Religion," which put the people in a good mood for a testimony meeting led by Brother Joe.

When all seemed to be finished, Brother Alvin got up slowly, took off his coat and tie, turned up his sleeves a couple of turns, and commented, "I'm getting ready to go into action for the Lord. When I fight for the Devil, I usually take my coat off, that is, if I have time. I should do as much for the Lord."

That brought some smiles and some "Amen's."

Brother Alvin proceeded. "I'm no better educated this month than I was last month when I preached to you. Again, as before, my request is that you pray for me as I attempt to preach. My wife tells me that the congregation needs to do some good hard praying for me at least twice in every sermon, once to get me started and once to get me stopped. I'm more concerned in getting started than getting stopped. I wouldn't care if I got started some time and preached till Jesus comes."

At this point a woman known for her quick impulsive remarks threw up both hands and exclaimed, "Lord, have mercy."

Her remark was overshadowed by some good hefty "Amen's" from the men. Had he not kidded the woman about it later, people would have thought that he didn't hear her.

Brother Alvin continued, "Mandy is by me like a neighbor boy was about his first train ride. This boy's Pa took him down to Golconda to go on his first train ride. The boy was surprised at the size of the train. He had never seen anything to ride in or on any bigger than a farm wagon. He got on the train along with his Pa.

"The first thing off the bat, this little boy remarked, 'I doubt if this train ever moves out of its tracks.'

"They had a while to wait and every two or three minutes he repeated, 'I doubt if this train ever moves out of its tracks.'

"After a while in the midst of a lot of clanging and banging and huffing and puffing, the train started to move. A few miles down the tracks, the train was moving along at a pretty good clip. The little boy looked up in wild excitement and shouted, 'Pa, it is going, but I doubt if they will ever get it stopped.'

"That little boy didn't happen to be me because I didn't see a train until I was sixteen years old.

"I ain't going to say I'll get started. One thing I do know—I'm going to do a lot of clanging and banging and huffing and puffing trying.

"Now before we get away from the subject of doubting, I would like to sound a warning lest we tread the path and walk in the shoes of a doubting Thomas. Do you recall the words of doubting Thomas? His words were, 'I ain't going to believe that this is Jesus unless I can put my hand in his pierced side and see the nail prints in his hands.'

"We have not seen Jesus, but we believe in him. We believe he is the Son of God. We believe that Jesus died on the cross for you and me. This firm belief in our hearts, to me, is 'faith.' Without faith it is impossible to please God. Lord, give us more faith is my prayer for all of us.

"Making mention of faith brings me one step closer to my text, 'The Walls of Jericho Came Falling Down.' Had Joshua not used faith, the walls of Jericho would probably still be standing.

"At least now, Brother Willie, Little Willie knows I wasn't lying to him when I told him the subject of my sermon. But what Little Willie doesn't know is that I don't stick very close to my stated subject or text. I just let the Good Lord lead me and I say what he puts on my heart and mind. He has been giving me lots of sermons over the past month. I've been preaching a different one to myself every day. Now I'm not absolutely sure which one he wants me to use.

"Now, Sister Florence, don't get all excited. You have my word of honor that I'll not try to preach all of them today.

"Brothers and Sisters, I'm still praying that the Lord will send us a good preacher here. I promised to stand in for a couple of months until you can find someone. Since a year has passed, I have a sneaking feeling that you have quit trying to find anyone else. Here is my reply to that. If you are pleased and the Lord is pleased, I'm tickled to death.

"Friends and neighbors, as I have sojourned with you this past year, I have learned in my humble way of trying to serve the Lord, the closer I draw to the Lord, the closer he draws to me. Many times I have moved away from my Lord and lost the joy of my salvation. But he has never gone away from me. Each time when I returned, I found the same welcome and experienced the same joy that the Prodigal Son received when he returned to his father.

"Over the past month I have hewed out several railroad crossties with a broad ax. I seemed impressed to see how perfect a set of crossties I could make one morning. I took pieces of timber and turned them into square pieces by hewing them on four sides. The quality of my work pleased me. The edges of the square corners were smooth and as straight as an arrow. However, I was a little surprised at myself for taking the extra care when it really didn't make any difference.

"The Lord impressed this thought on my mind as I admired my work. 'Preach the way you hew. Preach it straight. Hew to the line.' I said out loud, 'Lord, I ain't been this happy since you called me to preach.' I was 'pert nigh' happy enough to shout. To be perfectly honest with you, I did shout. I said, 'Praise the Lord forever. I'm going to serve you till I die.'

"I wasn't working too far from the house. As I went in for dinner I felt like I was walking on air. Mandy said that I looked like a rooster walking on hot ashes coming across the field. The Good Lord blessed me again at the dinner table. Mandy had a good dinner. I was hungry. After we returned thanks, I spooned deep into the bean dish and sure enough there was a big chunk of ham meat. That didn't surprise me very much. It just pleased me and made me thankful for a good wife. The thing that touched my heart was God's message, 'Dig deep in my Word; there you will find spiritual food.' That message, my friends, is for you as well as for me because you are better qualified to dig in the Word than I am."

At this point in Brother Alvin's sermon a big flying bug came in an open door or window. It went up and down three or four pews on the women's side of the church and gave them a big scare. The women's excitement amused the men. As a result, Brother Alvin completely lost the attention of his congregation. For a little while the big, black, hard-shelled bug that the women thought was a bumblebee stole the show. It flew from one side of the church to the other banging from wall to wall. Brother Alvin stopped preaching and joined the others in being amused. It wasn't too long until the bug flew out the door.

Now with the congregation's attention turned back to Brother Alvin he continued.

"I do believe that bug was as hard-headed as I was before I became a Christian. If he hadn't been flying around with his eyes closed, he could have gone out one of the six windows or two doors. We will lay the bug business to one side by saying he was stupid.

"Now let us stop and think how much we are like the bug at times. We bang our heads against the wall so to speak. We worry about the future. We worry about the past. We worry about too much rain. We worry about not enough rain.

"Most of us have meat in the smokehouse for the present. We have hogs in the pen for next year, but we worry ourselves silly about what we are going to do for meat year after next. We are a heap like the woman who said that she felt bad even when she felt good for fear she would feel worse the next day.

"Let me tell you, Brothers and Sisters, what we should do. We should follow the words of that grand old hymn, 'What a Friend We Have in Jesus.' That song tells us that we bear many burdens we should take to the Lord and leave them."

Brother Alvin made a very impressive talk on three or four verses of "What a Friend We Have in Jesus." In fact, he really got turned on. If his wife, Mandy, had been praying that he would get started, she probably eased off in hopes he wouldn't go too far past noon time.

Brother Alvin's white shirt began to show signs of perspiration brought on by his vigorous movement in the pulpit and his vigorous arm-waving. He stopped to get his breath for a couple of seconds and to wipe his face with a white handkerchief.

Brother Andrew started the song Brother Alvin had been preaching about, "What a Friend We Have in Jesus." The group joined in almost immediately. That was a life-saver for Brother Alvin because he needed a little break to cool off and get his breath. He enjoyed the song very much. Starting a song during a sermon was in keeping with the custom of the day. They called it letting the Lord have his way.

Brother Alvin was surprised when he looked at his watch and saw it was after noon. He made the following comment.

"Brothers and Sisters, while I was carried away in the spirit the time went by quickly. I hardly said anything I planned to say. Perhaps another time I can preach on the 'Walls of Jericho.'"

When Brother Alvin asked if anyone wanted to say anything, several expressed their appreciation for a good sermon and a good service.

When Brother Willie came out to go home, Little Willie was sitting under the wheel of the Model T Ford. He was making a buzzing noise with his mouth and fighting the wheel like he was going fast on a rough road. Big Willie motioned Little Willie over from behind the wheel.

Brother Tom walked up and said, "Brother Willie, you get in and I'll twist her tail for you."

Brother Willie set his hat on firmly so it wouldn't blow off. Little Willie sat on his cap so he wouldn't lose it. He proudly left out beside his father and went up the road with his hair blowing back.

Little Willie could hardly wait for the car to stop to get out and run into the house and report to his mom.

He exclaimed, "You will never believe all that happened. Just as we got to church an airplane was going out of sight. It was about the size of a buzzard.

"There must have been something wrong with the car when we got to church. Eight or ten men fixed whatever was wrong with it in no time at all. I could tell it was fixed because Dad looked pleased.

"Two buggies came up each pulled by a mule with two little jacks following them. One belonged to Sam DeNeal and the other belonged to Joe Travelstead.

"I found out before anyone else that Brother Alvin was going to preach on the Bridge of Jerusalem came Falling Down.

"He told about a little boy riding from Golconda to Thacker's Gap on a train without stopping.

"Sister Florence fainted, or almost fainted when Brother Alvin said he was going to preach 'til Jesus comes.

"A bug flew in the church with a head as big and hard as the preacher's and scared the women and made the men laugh and caused Brother Alvin to stop preaching.

"When the bug flew out Brother Alvin got started real good. He preached 'til he was sopping wet. People listened like they believed what he was saying. Brother Alvin said everyone had plenty of meat to eat except a woman who feels bad when she feels good because she has lost the joy of her salvation.

"Mom, if you ask me, I believe he prayed that message down from Heaven. At least that is what Sister Mandy said.

"Mommie, Mommie can I go back tonight? Can I? Can I? The bridge is sure enough going to come down tonight."

Country Boy

In the summer of 1930, when I was almost ten, my dad asked me if I could take a plowpoint out to George Turner, a blacksmith, and get it sharpened. I told him I didn't see "how in the world" I could because I didn't have any idea where George Turner lived. He took care of that fast. He said, "I'll tell you 'where in the world' he lives and how to get there."

We lived about three miles southeast of Rudement on Route 34. George Turner lived a little more than a mile northwest of Rudement. I was to turn right at the first crossroad. He lived in the first house on the left.

The chore wasn't beyond my ability, but I dreaded finding a new location and meeting a strange person. However, Dad gave me little choice.

Dad made a carrying handle for the plowpoint by running a piece of bailing wire through the center of a piece of a corn cob. Then he ran the wire through the hole in the plowpoint that was used to hold it to the plow. In weight it was like carrying a small pail of water.

Dad gave me 15 cents to pay for the sharpening. Soon I was on my way. However, just before leaving, I got three pennies of my own money. I didn't like to be away from home without money—a trait that has stayed with me through the years.

On leaving, I told Dad it might take me all day. He informed me that if I got a ride either going or coming back, I should be back by noon. That was his way of saying, "Don't fool around. Get out there and get back."

Once underway, I could hear crows in the woods west of the road. A woodpecker made the countryside ring with the vibration of its beak as he pecked with the speed of lightning on a distant hollow tree. The red clover along the roadside came alive as the bumblebees made their friendly visits. Through my thin blue shirt, the sun shone hot on my back as I traveled by the most primitive method—that of putting one foot in front of the other. So, for the first couple of miles, I stepped along just like I knew where I was going, only breaking my step now and then to kick a tin can.

On reaching the larger of the two bridges beyond Lockwood Hill, I decided to check it out. Leaving the plowpoint at the end of the bridge buttress, I went down the steep bank. But I stopped suddenly when I saw a large bullfrog near the water's edge. Sitting down quickly, I watched him for a while. Being so much bigger than the toads around home, he fascinated me.

I couldn't keep from wondering how far he would jump if I were to take a long weed and prod him lightly as I had done the toads. I slipped away to look for a stick or a weed to poke the bullfrog. Nearby, I found a thin pipe-cane about six feet long. But in the meantime, I found some large ripe dewberries. They took my mind off the frog until after I had eaten a few handfuls of them.

When I got back, the frog was still in the same place. I sat down about six feet from him. I partially held my breath while slipping the cane inch by inch toward him. After a long time the cane touched his rear end. I felt well repaid for my effort, for he let out an offbeat half-bellow, completely cleared the little creek, and went hopping off through the weeds.

This frog incident never crossed my mind again for thirty years, but it was stored away in a far corner of my mind. A statement made by Mr. Brown, an elderly employee and good friend of Lloyd L. Parker's, brought the story back. My wife, Evelyn, and I had gone in to Lloyd L. Parker's furniture store to buy a piano for our five-year-old daughter, LeAnn. Mr. Parker showed us one that we liked. He made a modest sales pitch and quoted the price. Then he was called to the telephone. Before going to the phone, Mr. Parker introduced us to Mr. Brown and commented that he knew everything about pianos and could answer our questions.

We liked Mr. Brown. He seemed like a fellow with whom we could joke. He asked, "Is there anything you would like to know?"

My reply was, "Yes, I would like to know whether Mr. Parker would knock a hundred dollars off his quoted price and make a nice round figure."

Mr. Brown asked, "Why don't you ask him? You can never tell how far a frog will jump until you prod him."

I don't remember the prodding or the jumping with Mr. Parker. The computer of my mind must have been turned off at the time. However, we did buy the piano and still have it today.

After checking out a bird's nest, made of a mud mixture sticking to the inside wall of the bridge, I took up the plowpoint and hurriedly continued on toward the blacksmith shop.

On nearing the store at Rudement, I began to ponder what business-like way I would spend my three cents. Recently my dad had told the merchant, Hosa Parks, that he was "in the market" for two rolls of barbed wire and a half-mile of woven wire. That sounded good to me.

In response to Mr. Parks' offer to help me, I replied in a deep voice, "I'm in the market for some candy and rifle shells."

It was rather unusual for Mr. Parks to smile, but a smile flickered across his face as he asked, "How much candy and how many rifle shells are you in the market for?"

I rubbed my chin as if I had a couple of days' growth of beard on it and asked, "What are rifle shells selling for now?"

Mr. Parks replied, "Twenty cents for a box of fifty or two shells for a penny in amounts less than fifty."

I had had it all figured out before I left home. I just wanted a little conversation with a clever businessman. So I up and said, "Make it four rifle shells and a penny bar of candy." To show Mr. Parks I could handle the math involved and that money wasn't any problem, I hauled out all eighteen cents, quickly counted out three cents, and handed it to him.

I got over to the blacksmith shop about 11:30 a.m. Mr. Turner was just coming in for dinner after plowing corn with a walking plow. He appeared to be rather old. I learned later that almost everyone called him "Uncle George Turner." He shuffled his feet a little when he walked, either because he was old or because he was tired. Our meeting was the beginning of a warm four-generation friendship with the Turner family, even though we started out a little rough.

I introduced myself to Mr. Turner and told him that I needed to get a plowpoint sharpened so that my dad could plow that afternoon. Mr. Turner said, "Son, you will have to leave it because I'm 'dog-tired,' the fire is out in the forge, and it is almost dinner time."

Momentarily disappointed, I quickly responded, "Mr. Turner, I'll just have to wait until you rest. My dad told me to wait until you sharpened the plowpoint and to bring it back as I come. I'm tired, too. If I walk home and walk out here and back home again, that will add up to sixteen miles. By then the seat of my pants will be dragging out my tracks."

I was about to continue when Mr. Turner broke in with disgust in his voice. "All right, all right! I'll sharpen that plowpoint if I fall dead doing it."

His statement jolted me into silence. I followed him meekly into the shop and tried my best to stay out of his way. I thought how dreadful it would be if he did keel over because of my insistence that he sharpen the plowpoint.

As Mr. Turner poked in the forge, I saw a spark from the last time he had used it. He put a piece of soft wood in a vise and with a plane shaved off a handful of thin shavings and placed them on the spark. With his left hand, he began to slowly turn a crank that seemed to funnel air into the fireplace from underneath. Soon there was a red glow that burst into a flame. Mr. Turner slowly pulled some coal over the fire. In a short time he had a hot fire going.

I couldn't keep from wishing that Mom had such an air contraption on her stove. On those times when the fire was contrary and the bread wouldn't rise, or the gravy wouldn't thicken, I could grab that crank and make the gravy bubble and the biscuits brown.

In a short time, Mr. Turner took the plowpoint, placed it in the fire, and continued to turn the crank that blew the air. I could see the fire was getting hotter and hotter. The plowpoint began to get red hot. Mr. Turner took a long pair of tongs, lifted the plowpoint from the fire, looked at it carefully, and put it back into the fire.

When Mr. Turner was satisfied with the redness of the plowpoint, he took the tongs in his left hand and placed the plowpoint on the anvil. Then with his right hand, he picked up a heavy hammer. He bounced it two or three times on the anvil as if getting loosened up and in the swing of it. Then raising the hammer higher than his head, he began to beat on the plowpoint along the cutting edge. After several licks, he placed it back in the fire. He repeated this process three or four times.

I relaxed a little and began to realize that Mr. Turner had more life in him than I had thought at first. My attention turned to a 1909 Model T Ford that was kept on one side of the shop. It was 12 years older than our 1921 model. Standing higher and looking more expensive, it fascinated me because of some of its unusual features, such as carbide lights. When Mr. Turner saw my interest, he seemed to take pleasure in telling me about it.

Mr. Turner's final touch on the hot plowpoint was to dip it into a barrel of water to retemper the steel. He replaced the carrying handle and dropped it at my feet. With a smile he said, "There you are, Son. Your dad can plow now."

I gave him the 15 cents and thanked him. Taking the money, he thanked me and invited me to eat dinner with him. I turned down his offer because I was anxious to get home.

Being happy that all was going well, I approached the highway singing "The Battle Hymn of the Republic," while stomping out the beat with my feet like a country boy at a barn dance. Given my musical abilities, the singing had to have been horrible. And given my lack of dancing experience, an onlooker would have thought I had ants in my pants. But it did get results.

A fellow coming along there in a 1926 Model T Ford saw me. He turned his head as he passed and even looked back after he passed. I stuck up my thumb. He began to stop and motioned for me to come on. He was smiling broadly as he invited me to get into the car. In my opinion, he had had enough to drink to make everything funny to him.

He said, "You know, I have a Tennessee walking horse at home that can't walk as fancy as you were walking there. Maybe I can get you to teach him how to walk."

I explained that I was singing the "Battle Hymn of the Republic" and was stamping out the beat with my feet. He said, "Suppose you and I sing that song together. It is one of my favorites. But first I'm going to 'pull her ears down' a little, because I'm in a hurry."

That was his way of saying, "I want to step on the gas." The gas and the spark were controlled by levers just below the steering wheel, on opposite sides of the steering column. These levers were often referred to as "ears."

His jubilant mood must have affected me because I said, "Yeah, pull her ears down. Kick her in the rear end. Make her tear out a bone. I'm in a hurry to get home, too."

My response caused him to burst out in loud laughter. It was a little while before he could sing. But all of a sudden he surged forth on "Mine Eyes Have Seen the Glory of the Coming of the Lord." His tone and melody amazed me. The quality of his voice made me wonder whether he was a minister. That made me think that perhaps what I smelled was a tonic to ward off a summer cold.

He drove with his left hand and kept time as though he were leading a choir with his right hand. He indicated that he wanted me to sing with him. So I joined in with enthusiasm. I wanted to do something with my right hand, too, so I began to loudly pat the outside of the open car with the palm of my hand. Thinking that was funny, he took the steering wheel in his right hand and began to bang his side of the car with his left hand.

When we went through Rudement, we must have been going forty miles per hour, which was five miles above the Illinois speed limit. He barely missed a goose that was crossing the road. Three or four dogs were barking and chasing after the car. When we passed a team of mules hitched to a wagon, the mules became so unnerved, it was all the farmer could do to keep them from running away.

By the time we got up Lockwood and Buzzard Roost Hills, the Model T was going only about twenty miles per hour. We had been over "Glory, Glory, Hallelujah" two or three times. So we left off singing and talked the rest of the way.

When we reached our drive, which was on the left, he pulled off the road on the right and stopped. He said, "Good buddy, I can't bid you farewell until I explain something to you." So for the next few minutes he explained why his behavior had been almost like that of a drunken sailor. It made sense to me. I took his explanation at face value, and I thanked him for the ride. We expressed heartfelt goodbyes to each other, and I saw him no more.

My dad was sitting on the porch in the porch swing. His shirt was wet with perspiration. I set the plowpoint on the edge of the porch and said, "There it is all nice and sharp."

He looked at it and replied, "That is a good job. George is a good blacksmith."

Dad's curiosity got the better of him because of the extended time that I had spent in the car instead of getting out and coming on to the house. He liked to learn what he wanted to know by judicious questioning. Perhaps he felt that he had missed his calling in not becoming a lawyer. He started by saying, "Tell me about your trip out there and back."

"I walked all the way out there. On the way there, I stopped at the store and bought four rifle shells for two cents."

"Rifle shells! What do you need with rifle shells?"

"I plan to trap the groundhogs that are eating our green tomatoes. As I catch them, I'll shoot them."

"All right. Go on. Who did you ride home with?"

"I don't know. He didn't ask me my name, so I didn't ask him his."

"How fast did he drive?"

"He drove fast because he said he was in a hurry."

"Do you think he was drinking?"

"No."

"Did you smell any whiskey?"

"Yes, I thought I did, but I wasn't sure."

"Now that strikes me as being odd. You thought you smelled whiskey, but you didn't think he was drinking. Did he come close to having an accident?"

"No, not really."

"What do you mean by 'not really'? He either did or he didn't."

"What I meant was he almost ran over a goose."

"A goose! He should have been able to see something

as big as a goose! Was the goose hurt?"

"No, but it scared the gizzard out of it."

"What did you two talk about?"

"We didn't talk very much. We mostly sang."

"What were you singing?"

"Battle Hymn of the Republic."

"How did he act while he was singing?"

"He acted like he was happy. He laughed and sang at the same time. We both patted the side of the car to keep time with our singing."

"Don't tell me you were a party to such carrying on!" Then he got to the question he really wanted to ask from the beginning. "One more question before we go to dinner. What were you talking about after he stopped out there?"

"He was worried I would think he had been drinking and driving when he wasn't. He explained why he smelled like whiskey. Last night he had taken his wife to her parents' home to have their first baby. The doctor had spent the night and had twice thought his wife was dead. But as it turned out, she had only fainted. His father-in-law had drunk almost a pint of whiskey while trying to hold up under the pressure.

"At about eight o'clock this morning, a baby girl was born. Everyone was overjoyed. The father-in-law, who was a little drunk by this time, tried to force a drink on him in fun and accidentally spilled it on him.

"But he seemed like a good man—concerned about his wife and baby and willing to give me a ride even though he was in a hurry to go take care of his stock."

Satisfied, Dad had no more questions. A broad smile came across his face. He said, "I have plowing to do this afternoon and you have groundhogs to shoot, so we had better 'Glory, Glory, Hallelujah' in and eat dinner."

Shocking Behavior

T he extracurricular activities at Sadler School, located near the Womble Mountain in Southern Illinois, were varied and sometimes shocking. Before getting into just a few happenings of long ago, allow me to assure you that a worthwhile measure of learning did take place. In my opinion, the "Illinois State Course of Study" required by law was followed with the same seriousness as it was in other schools.

From the year 1916 to 1934, teachers who left their fingerprints, a touch of their personality, and their brand of "one-room school" teaching are as follows: Verba Wallace, Guy DeNeal, Roy Reynolds, Robert Blackman, Margaret Buchanan, Ethel Estes, Elmo Williams, Ruth Arndt, Otto Williams, Mary Irvin, Eva Millikan, John Owens, and Mary Harper.

The teachers named above varied in personality traits, but they were all honest, friendly, intelligent, God-fearing, and hard working. The teachers taught and the students learned. Often times the teacher and students learned together.

At Sadler School, children learned very quickly how to trade a wide range of articles—sling shots, spool tractors propelled by rubber bands, marbles, apples, turnips, knives, and just about anything that a boy could get in his pocket.

By their own choosing, boys and girls ate their lunches separately—outside weather permitting. Lunch trading was a relished part of the noon break. Two brothers often ate from the same lunch bucket, which was true for my brother Victor, four years my junior, and me.

I fell in love with Victor as a toddler. He was the third son and the fourth child in a family of six children. In his preschool years he delighted me with his keen brown eyes, red curly hair, and a sprinkling of freckles on his face. Even his baby teeth held a special attraction for me.

I gave expression to my warm feeling for Victor by fastening an empty spice box, with a slot cut in it, on the wall. Into this box I dropped coins, as I earned them, toward the purchase price of something Victor really wanted.

This "big brother-little brother" relationship went super until Victor reached the age of six and entered school, and I reached the advanced age of ten and had taken over what I felt was my rightful, God-given position as top dog in the peck system.

The friction between us began when I suggested to Mom that my brother, Byrum, who had already mastered the art of trading lunch bucket items, take his lunch in a bucket by himself, and that Victor and I eat from the same bucket. To this suggestion Victor objected on the grounds that it would interfere with his trading.

After about a month, Mom gave in to Victor's asking to be allowed to take his lunch separately. She promised to fix his lunch in a half-gallon syrup bucket.

On the first morning that he was to have his very own lunch bucket, some neighbor children came by on their way to school before Mom had our lunches fixed. Victor wanted to go ahead with them the one mile to school. I promised him I would bring his lunch bucket.

Five minutes later, I was following alone in their footsteps. The path took me through the woods, up and down little hills, and across small streams.

Half-way to school was a branch or creek we called Rocky Branch. It was dry other than after a big rain, at which time a foot log upstream came into use.

I left the path to explore up the dry creek bed, which was well blessed with grayish-black, coconut-sized rocks. The hazel bushes and the hickory trees well laden with nuts caused me to think of what General McArthur had not yet said, "I shall return."

Near a little pool of water, a huge, yellowish-green bullfrog loomed in sight and grasped my interest. I saw fun and excitement written all over him. I set down the two lunch buckets, took off my overall jacket, and from a distance of about eight feet threw it spread out into the air. The frog jumped, but not in time to escape being captured by the falling jacket.

I quickly transferred Victor's lunch from his half-gallon syrup bucket to my seven pound lard bucket. Very little time passed before I was back on the well-beaten path. The frog was in the smaller bucket well blessed with tiny air holes made in the lid with the point of my knife.

On arriving at school, I saw two almost grown eighth graders, Donald Wallace and Orval Edwards, really tying into each other. Playing rough was a favorite pastime, but I said to myself: "This is a fight if ever I saw one."

I set the lunch buckets down and rushed up to see if I could be of any help to my cousin, Donald. The old saying "Blood is thicker than water" had come into play. Or was it: "Fools dash in where angels fear to tread."

My work seemed cut out for me. It was all I could do to stay out of their way and to keep from getting trampled down or fallen on. They were repeating a pattern of stumbling around on foot, mixing it up, and floundering around on the ground.

Donald got the edge on Orval at one point and got his shoulders to the ground. I rushed in and slapped the ground three times as I counted "one, two, three." Neither of them paid any attention to me. So to make my presence known, I got down on my hands and knees, with my face close to Orval's, and said, "Donald, pour it on him. Churn his head up and down a few times."

Those words were conceived in confusion and were completely void of wisdom and foresight. In other words, I should have kept my mouth shut. I wasn't prepared for what happened next. Very quietly Orval said, "Donald, let me up."

The next instant Orval and I were on our feet. I was looking up at him, too smart to fight and too scared to run. He took me by the bib of my snug-fitting overalls and dealt with me in what I considered an unkind manner. To be more exact, he rudely pushed me backwards about four steps and shoved me on my butt. I came to my feet like a jumping-jack, and the same stunt was repeated. This time I came up more like I had lead in my pants, humiliated, cast down, but not conquered.

When Orval was about to give me a third dose of "tend to your own business medicine," Donald raised his voice and with a touch of authority said, "That's enough."

Orval stopped to consider what Donald had said, but do you think I knew when to pull in my horns? No, I didn't. I still had "face to save" and "pride to avenge."

I threw out my chest like "Popeye" and said, "That is what I say. That's enough."

Orval lunged at me. My hands shot up as if he had a gun on me. I said, "I take that back."

Donald and Orval burst out laughing. I joined them. They were probably laughing because of the "mule eating saw-briars" look on my face. I was happy I didn't get my tail tamped. The bell rang and the three of us walked into the school as friends.

The morning went by quickly. At noon, the teacher dismissed us for an hour lunch and play break. The boys grabbed their lunch buckets and headed for a sagegrass-covered spot on the south side of the playground that joined the woods. Rocks, logs, sagegrass, and the moss-covered ground served as seats.

I sat a little distance away from Victor and watched him closely. He and the little boy next to him promptly exchanged lunch buckets. They just up and traded lunches sight unseen.

Victor pulled the lid from his newly acquired bucket and beamed with pride and satisfaction. When his friend removed the lid from the syrup bucket, the look on his face showed utter shock and disappointment. It was both sad and humorous. Victor sensed that something was wrong and took a look in the bucket at the bullfrog. His amazement exceeded that of his friend. He fastened his eyes on me, while displaying anger and wounded pride. It caused me to want to use the familiar words of many present day men: "It's not what it seems. Let me explain."

The little friend was on the verge of tears when I told Victor that his lunch was in my bucket and explained that I had to use his bucket to bring the frog to school so that he could trade it to someone. Victor responded to my suggestion that he give his friend's lunch back.

They both understood that they could still do some trading if they wanted to.

Immediately Victor had some offers for his frog—a slingshot, some marbles, and a spool tractor. Orval Edwards, addressing both of us said, "I'll even up and give you this sweet, purple-top turnip for that frog." I thought it might be fun for that frog to be in Orval's hands, so I gave Victor a sly little nod. Victor's response surprised all of us. He said, "I'll let you have that frog for that turnip and a doodle bug." He went ahead to say that he had promised his little sister, Hazel, a doodle bug. Orval took him up on his offer and passed the turnip down to Victor and took possession of the frog. The frog trade made Victor's day. He and his friend had a good time sharing their lunches.

Some other trading went on also. The trade that amused me most was between Donald and Orval: Donald offered to trade Orval a piece of pie that he was holding for a meat sandwich Orval was about to eat. Each reached out to make the exchange. Donald then snatched his pie back and took a big bite—about half of it. Orval likewise jerked his sandwich back and took an equally big bite. Then they offered to trade a second time and repeated the same stunt. Their mouths were too full to take another bite so they finally traded. Orval got a pie crust and Donald got just a rim of a sandwich. Both of them almost got choked laughing at their ridiculous behavior.

After lunch, Orval asked if anyone wanted to help him call up a doodle bug, which is a larva-type insect, grayish in color, and no more than a quarter of an inch in length. They live in little funnel holes in the dry dusty ground. All of the boys wanted to help.

The ideal place to call up doodle bugs was under the high side of the schoolhouse, which was about three feet off the ground. The famous one-and-only call that I have ever heard of was and is, "Dooooodle bug, Dooooodle bug, Dooooodle bug, come get a grain of corn," repeated over and over. Each caller has his or her own personal preference, based on past success, as to how loudly or gently they call and how close their mouth is to the ground.

I have called up doodle bugs just to prove to non-believers that it could be done, but I didn't take part that day. The scene made a lasting impression on me. There were at least fifteen boys, ages six to sixteen, on their hands and knees, with their rears in the air, and their mouths close to the ground calling "Dooooodle bug, come get a grain of corn" loudly enough to call in the wild hogs from the woods.

There were two or three shouts of success at the same time. Soon Victor had two doodle bugs in a little matchbox to take to his sister, Hazel.

Back in the classroom the students became as serious about their studies as they were about calling doodle bugs. My attention soon turned to an assignment—that of memorizing the poem "Hiawatha" by Longfellow. My breathing had become shallow and my heart was beating fast as I read about Hiawatha's drawing his bow to kill the red deer, while "hidden in the alder-bushes." There was the flying arrow that was "tipped with flint, and winged with feathers." There was the line that said, "Like a wasp it buzzed and stung him!"

At this exact point in the poem, when I was keyed up like the strings on a banjo, the woman teacher let out a scream that would have caused the hair to stand up on a cat's back. I'm ashamed to admit it, but under the circumstances, I let out a shriek also and looked up just in time to see the bullfrog leap off the teacher's bosom—his second leap after leaving the middle drawer of the teacher's desk.

After the first shock there was an outburst of laughter. It was less embarrassing for the teacher because part of the laughter was directed at me. When it dawned on me that I might be implicated in the incident, I sat with my elbows on my desk and my head in my hands. I recovered from my shock along with the teacher.

She asked if someone would like to take the frog out and let it go. After a slight pause, Orval stood and said that he wasn't all that crazy about frogs, and that he would probably get a wart on his nose as big as the one on his granny's hand, but he reckoned if no one else wanted to, he would.

Orval walked up to the front of the room, where the frog was sitting tall about halfway between the teacher's desk, which was in the middle of the room, and the north wall, a little way out from the blackboard, and not far from the corner.

The first thing Orval did was to get down on his hands and feet and kick back, scraping the floor with first one foot and then the other like a dog. In this position he ventured up about two feet and then shied off three. He next took a crouched position and frog-hopped about a foot at a time, and in this manner caused the frog to hop to the corner where Orval nabbed him. The children were roaring with laughter. The teacher was smiling, and I recovered enough to smile too.

Orval held the frog high in his left hand as he started for the door on the other side of the room. With his back to the chalk dust tray, he moved along the blackboard behind the teacher. She was sitting at her desk again. Orval couldn't resist the temptation of giving the children one more laugh. He lolled out his tongue almost to the end of his chin, and then he grabbed the skin on his throat and pretended to pull his tongue back in. It was a good clown act and laughter broke out again. It was just as funny to see the innocent look that came over Orval's face when the teacher looked around. He raised his shoulders and his eyebrows a little, while he looked puzzled and shook the frog a little so much as to say, "Maybe it was this." The kids laughed again, giving the impression that they just had their tickle box turned over.

At recess, Victor tore himself away from his friends long enough to run by where I was and said, "Aren't we having fun?" He also asked if I could get him another frog for the next day. I told him to forget about the frog. I warned him that if he so much as mentioned the word "frog," the teacher might become angry and start screaming and throwing things.

Before the teacher dismissed us to go home, she had this to say: "Children, we have had some good laughs today. If I could work magic, I wouldn't change a thing. However, what happened today did disturb school for awhile. I hope it won't happen again. Next time I will try harder to find out who did it."

Following these words of wisdom, Victor raised his hand and said, "Teacher about that frog." At that point I cleared my throat ever so slightly.

The teacher asked, "What about the frog, Victor?" There was a long pause before Victor said, "Teacher, I plum forgetted what I was going to say."

Amos, of the Womble Mountain Country

Amos Bixler was born on March 13, 1892, in Ledford, a small coal-mining community between Harrisburg and Carrier Mills, in Saline County, Illinois. He was reared by his grandmother, or Grannie, as he always called her.

Amos couldn't read or write. His excuse for not going to school was that Grannie was sickly, and he had to look after her. Despite his lack of formal education, Amos had a keen mind and could easily remember names, faces, and various statistics.

Ledford was his home until World War I came along, prompting him to join the army. For the rest of his life he delighted in recalling, even exaggerating, his wartime adventures in various countries.

On returning home from the service, Amos married Mina, a young woman from a large, poor family near Herod. Theirs was a marriage made not in Heaven but on the sunny side of Womble Mountain; some of that early radiance clung to the couple through the years. He always called her "Hon."

But don't get the idea that all was roses for the pair, for each had a grave flaw. Amos would go on drinking sprees, during which he would squander much of their worldly possessions. Naturally, this grieved Mina to no end. For a few days following one of Amos's drinking bouts, she would lash out at him. While no one condoned the man's uncontrolled drinking, those who knew the length and intensity of Mina's tirades could not help but be in sympathy with poor Amos. Resilient fellow that he was, Amos took his losses and Mina's reaction as unavoidable facts of life, stayed sober for a time, and then went on another spree.

My friendship with Amos began when I was ten. I had been breaking ground behind a team of horses with a walking plow near the highway. When my nose started bleeding, I sat down on the last slab of plowed ground with my bare feet in the furrow and applied pressure, something that usually stopped the bleeding in a short time.

About that time Amos came walking along the road. Soon he was standing over me asking if I had been hurt. I was impressed by his concern; however, I shook my head "no" when he suggested that I sit in the shade of a tree while he plowed a few rounds.

Later I was to learn that he was well known as a teller of tall tales, as well as a shrewd trader of anything from pocket knives to livestock. Little by little over the next few years, Amos and I established an unwritten, unstated, code-of-the-hills pact that embraced the idea of mutual friendship and respect.

We both profited by the friendship. The sly trader got a mess of fresh meat when we butchered hogs, while the Wallace family rarely saw a spring go by without receiving from Amos a shoebox full of large morels. Later in the year he would provide us with enough big, juicy dewberries to make a cobbler.

When I was fourteen Amos gave me a little insight on trading. One day he invited me over to look at a hog he wanted to sell, but after I arrived, he was slow about showing off the animal, which I thought was strange. Equally strange was his asking me if I knew it was going to be a cold, bad winter. He went on to assure me that old-timers had told him when hogs grow long, thick hair, people could look for a hard winter.

Well, when Amos opened the stall door, I got a real shock. There stood a long-legged, long-nosed, long-haired, razor-back hog that looked more like a wild varmint than anything found in a farmyard. Its hair was no less than four or five inches long! When Amos saw the surprised look on my face, he burst out in a loud horse laugh. As he closed the stall door, he commented, "Kestner, I knew you wouldn't want to buy a hog that looks like that, but I wanted you to see it. Who knows, maybe I can sell it to a circus or a side show so city people can see what a wild hog looks like."

Seldom did Amos and I call at each other's home, but we often met at the country store, public sales, or other public gatherings. The words we exchanged ranged from casual to serious. A character, and considered as such by his neighbors, Amos definitely had a serious side, too, and probably spoke the truth more with me than with most people.

One day I stopped by his place and found him trimming an ax handle with a pocket knife. "I'll give you my knife and fifty cents for that knife," I said.

Slipping the knife into his pocket, he laughed and replied, "You don't want that old knife. I'm just about ready to give up on it. If you want a better knife, you need 'Old Cornbread.'" After saying that, he pulled out a rough looker. "When this knife was made, good steel was really being used. I don't need it. I can get by with that old frog-sticker I just stuck in my pocket. I'll let you have 'Old Cornbread' for forty cents and your knife. Now what do you say?"

"Not being much of a trader, I make it a point not to trade with a trader."

"Kestner, that's where you are wrong. If you never trade with a good trader, how will you ever learn? When someone gets the best of me, I just can't wait to trade with him again in order to figure out how he did it."

He put "Old Cornbread" back in his pocket, took a swipe across his forehead with a red bandana and rubbed a week's growth of beard with his left hand.

"Kestner, I recollect that time I had a pretty good old plug horse named Jarbus. He had an unorganized, gawky appearance, but was better than he looked and, to tell you the truth, I was anxious to trade him after having him only a couple of weeks.

"One day one really sharp horse trader jumped me for a trade at the store at the Gap. He wanted to know how I would trade my horse for his. I told him I would make an offer and only give him thirty seconds to take me up on it. I told him I would trade him my horse, bridle, and saddle for ten dollars and his horse, bridle, and saddle. Out of his shirt pocket he pulled a ten-dollar bill and handed it to me.

"It didn't take me long to find out that the horse was wind-broken. By that I mean he couldn't exert himself very much without breathing hard and heaving.

He started in after I trotted him for about half a quarter of a mile.

"Well, I got off, and for the first time, gave him a good looking over. He was a well-made horse, although his mane was too long and shaggy and his tail touched the ground. I walked and led the horse about two miles to the home of my brother-in-law.

"After I brushed enough loose hair off of that horse to stuff a small cushion, he was slick and shiny. I taper-trimmed enough hair from the tail to give it a short look and trimmed the mane to match the tail. Last of all I took some white paint and with an almost dry brush, I painted three white stocking feet and a white streak from between his ears to the end of his nose. I made him what is called a blaze-faced horse."

"But how did you keep the hair from looking like a paint job?"

"By combing it with a fine comb as it dried to keep the hair from sticking together."

"Okay, so that improved the looks of the horse," I said, "but it didn't make his wind any better, did it?"

"No, but I managed to put some spirit in that horse without affecting his wind."

Gifted storyteller that he was, Amos paused meaning-fully to indicate that the best part was yet to come.

"I got a hickory switch big around as my little fin-ger and about thirty inches long. Grabbing hold of the bridle rein and standing pretty far around to one side, I cleared my throat and busted the horse's rear end with the switch. After letting him have some hickory tea from first one side and then the other, he got so he would act spirited every time I cleared my throat, even if I didn't use the switch. That was what I wanted.

"Just around the bend from the man I had traded

horses with that morning, I waited in the bushes for the sun to go down. When it was not quite plumb dark I was about fifty yards from the house. Of course, his dogs let the man know I was coming.

"Well, I cleared my throat and busted the horse's rear before throwing the switch away and went bounding up in the yard with plenty of style and spirit while the man took it all in."

"I guess he hit you up for a trade right off, didn't he, Amos?"

"No, I didn't give him a chance. Getting off, I told him that I was hungry and thirsty, but only had time for a drink of water because I wanted to cover the next two miles by a little after dark. Also, I told him I had watered the horse back at the creek. Naturally, I didn't say anything about watering him some on the outside too, to make him look, you know, like he had run a long piece."

By this time I was listening with both ears.

"A kid brought me a big tin cup of water, and I forced it down. As my rear came to rest in the saddle, I cleared my throat. Well, the horse reared a little and cantered around which made my heart leap with joy. While I was pretending to get under way the man wanted to know how I liked the horse. I told him that I didn't like the horse because he had three white feet instead of four, and that he was too high-spirited. But I made it clear I wouldn't trade him until Hon got to see him."

"Weren't you afraid to make out like you didn't want to trade when you really did?"

"No, it just makes some traders more anxious to do business. The man wanted to trade Old Jarbus back to me. I told him that Hon would kill me if I traded for him again after trading him off.

"Then the man up and said as he yanked a twenty-dollar bill out of his pocket, 'Amos, I'll give you this twenty and Old Jarbus for that horse.'"

"Did you take him up on it real quick?"

"No, I got off the horse so I could get my clutches on that twenty. I told the fellow he had my attention but he didn't have a trade. I asked him what he would be willing to put along with it. He told me that was all, but he did put the twenty under my nose so I could smell of it. Pretending not to have an ounce of will power, I took the twenty and said, 'I know I'm making a mistake, but I'm going to call it a trade.'"

"Did you get away before the man found out that you had traded him back the same horse he had traded you that morning?"

"Yes, just as I was leaving he asked me to tell him what I knew about the horse."

"How did you handle that question?"

"With a big smile on my face, that's how. I told him that he could find out about the horse the same way I found out about the one I got from him that morning."

When the place where Amos and Mina lived for several years finally sold, to keep from leaving the community, they moved into a house on the Pope and Saline County line on a high ridge about three miles west of Route 34, just north of the Williams Hill Lookout Tower. This place was known as the Old Uncle Joe Travelstead Place. It is said that Mr. Travelstead homesteaded the land from the government.

In the mid-'30s, I had ridden my mule, Sampson, past the place a few times. It appeared that no one had lived in it for many years or would ever live in it again. The closest house was two or three miles away.

I was a little surprised therefore to learn that Amos and Mina had moved into the house. But when I talked to Amos, he bragged on the beautiful view he had, the good picking for the cow, closeness of firewood, and nuts and acorns in abundance to fatten his hogs.

Mina's report to Mom wasn't quite as glowing. She said that the house was cold in winter and kept poor Amos busy cutting firewood for the fireplace. She also said that it was too far to carry cream and eggs to the store and carry supplies home.

Mina was gifted in working Mom and getting certain favors. In the spring of '37, Mina told Mom that she and Amos would give anything for a good garden. But Amos wasn't able to spade up a piece of ground, and out of his little veteran's pension, he couldn't afford to pay what someone would ask to come up and put their garden in shape to plant. Mom told Mina that she would see if I would break and harrow the garden the following Sunday. Just call it an "ox in the ditch" deal.

When Mom mentioned the Sunday garden plowing to me, I griped and bickered a little but promised her I would. Then she commented, "If you don't charge them anything since they are poor, it would be like giving unto the Lord."

I bickered a little more and agreed to make it for free, as I added that I'd never let the Lord forget what I did for two of his little ones. Mom looked pleased at me for being agreeable, but wrinkled up her nose and shook her head at me for doing my good deed for the wrong motive. She quoted to me about "giving, expecting nothing in return."

Sunday morning with a harrow and a breaking plow loaded on the farm wagon pulled by my riding mule, Sampson, and a western mare, I wound my way through the wooded area to where Amos lived. He had a good-sized plot cleared and staked off. I wasted no time in getting the plowing under way.

Amos told me that his mother-in-law and brother-in-law were having Sunday dinner with them, and he and Mina wanted me to eat with them. I told him that I'd try to get done before noon, but if I didn't, I would be happy to eat with them. When he told me that they were having fried chicken and smoked ham, I replied with a grin that I didn't think I'd wind up the job before dinner.

My morning's work was on the northwest side of the spacious log house. The only entrance to the house was on the east side, and what an entrance that was! Almost all of the east side of the house was open. The huge logs on that side must have been stolen. The floor and the sills were missing from the south half of the large existing room. Originally that unusually large room was very likely divided into three or four rooms. Based on the size of the logs, the house was probably among the most outstanding of its day.

The floored north half of the spacious log structure was furnished with two double beds, two rocking chairs, a wood-burning cook stove, an oak dining table, and some straight-backed chairs.

The northwest corner was boarded off to form a pantry to accommodate the kitchen area. Since the crude homemade door was open, I could see three or four wooden barrels that I was almost sure held flour, meal, salt pork, and other staples. On some rough-looking shelves was a good supply of canned fruit and vegetables.

In the middle of the north end was a large, attention-getting fireplace. Pot hooks and a make-shift grill indicated that cooking was done there, also.

Even before taking it all in, I was thrilled with the pioneer look of the scene. After speaking to Mina, her mother, and brother, I took a chair facing the southeast. My mouth flew open. I faked a slight cough and put my hand over my mouth. The large, yellowish-brown milch cow lying in the center of the unfloored part surprised me. Hen's nests lined the south and west wall.

Since there was too much for me to see and mind my manners at the same time, I forgot my manners and tried to see everything. No one seemed to mind. When birds fussed in the tree beyond the open side, Amos observed that a squirrel was probably disturbing them.

Amos explained that he had bought the young cow from a man who had raised her as a pet. She was so unhappy that he had brought her inside to keep her from bawling her head off. Then they all had become attached to each other, and she became one of the family. He said that he only had had to whack her a few times with a leather strap to train her to go out always to do her business.

Amos further explained that he controlled flies and mosquitoes by burning a weed known as "life everlasting" in an old washtub. By sprinkling a little water on the burning weed, it smoked more than it burned. I've been told that the weed got its name from its ability to smoke, smolder, and hold fire.

At the dinner table I was seated with my back toward the stable area. Please believe me, a good meal was prepared. They did have ham and fried chicken. Surprised as I was at the size of the platter of golden brown cornbread, I was even more surprised to see family members take three or four bites off a big piece of cornbread and toss the rest out in the stable.

When I could wait no longer to see what was happening to the cornbread, I looked around. In the stable there were two Rhode Island Red hens, each with about fifteen ten-day old chickens. It was fun to see them compete for the bread. I pitched them a piece, too. But I agreed with Mina that it was time for them to be eating cracked corn.

On seeing that I was in a good mood and while I was still at the table, Amos wanted to know what he owed me for my work. He would have enjoyed his dinner better had he asked sooner.

I replied, "Amos, I've done about a dollar's worth of work, and I've eaten about two dollars worth of good food. Suppose we call it even."

Insisting that he didn't expect the work for nothing, he promised to bring Mom a big fat coon to bake with sweet potatoes and dressing.

Had I not made myself available for that garden-breaking job, I would have been the loser. Mom was made happy, and I still have fond memories.

Before another winter Amos moved to and lived the rest of his life on a large farm that belonged to Earl Wilson, a cattle farmer who lived in Harrisburg. Amos and Mina were happy living on the farm beside Route 34, which was partly in Saline County and partly in Pope County. Amos got free rent and free cow pasture in exchange for checking fences and being watchful in general. Also, getting his veteran's pension increased helped him to walk with his head up.

I had to leave Southern Illinois to get employment, first working in Michigan and then serving in the Navy during World War II. On returning home after being away for six years, Amos and I had a handshaking, backslapping big time. He told me with tears in his eyes that even though he wasn't what he considered a religious man, he had prayed daily for all of us boys in the service from around Rudement, Herod, and up the Eagle Creek Road. Then he confidentially confided that he had prayed more for me than any other.

I thanked Amos for his prayers. We didn't stay very serious too long. We jokingly agreed that which ever of us called on St. Peter first would say a good word for the other. Our mentioning St. Peter in a lighthearted way came back to me more than twenty years later.

Early one August morning in 1967, Jesse Gibbons, from the Gibbons Funeral Home, called and told me that my neighbor, Amos Bixler, had died in his sleep. He asked if I would help his driver carry Amos out to the hearse that he was sending for him. I assured Mr. Gibbons that I would.

I observed that Amos's eyes and mouth were closed. There was a trace of a smile on his face. Mina saw it, also, and it served as a source of comfort to her.

Amos had to be carried down a little steep rocky hill to where the hearse and my car were parked. When the hearse pulled away, I continued to stand there and meditate. Recalling what Amos and I had said about St. Peter caused me to do a little thought communication with St. Peter.

In my thoughts, I said, "St. Peter, Amos is on his way up there. He probably hasn't made it yet, because he had a strong desire to see a few places here on earth first. Then, too, he could want to check the fence, put out some salt, count the cattle, and drop in at the lower barn long enough to feed the old yellow cat and see if she has kittens yet. He shows more concern for a stray cat or a neighbor's sick cow than some people do for their children.

"St. Peter, should you hear a little tap at the Pearly Gates, it will probably be Amos. He isn't very pushy and won't stick around if he doesn't think he is wanted."

Then I thought to myself, why am I worrying? Amos has already shaken hands with St. Peter, slapped him on the back, and said, "St. Peter, Sir, if you will excuse me long enough for me to let Grannie know I made it, I'll let her go ahead singing the Song of the Redeemed under the Tree of Life and I'll come back and wait around for Hon. She is never more than a few steps behind me.

"While I'm waiting, let me tell you about the time I traded a dozen old hens and three shoats for a bully good milch cow."

Fruit of the Vine

A scene that has disappeared with the passing of time is that of our entire family, consisting of my dad and mom and six children, sitting on our porch that faced Route 34.

The day's work was complete that fall evening at the beginning of Indian summer. The hour was early twilight. Our chickens and ducks were drifting to and entering our chicken house. With much ceremony and chatter, a large crop of sparrows was going to roost in a wild cherry tree nearby. The day's activities of work and play had left us children willing to relax for a few minutes before our final expenditure of energy in advance of retiring for the day.

Suddenly a shiny new car slowed abruptly, turned into our driveway, and stopped on the circle drive in front of our house. The driver, a tall, well-built man who appeared to be in his early sixties, stepped out of the car and walked briskly to the porch. He immediately had our attention. We wondered who he was and what he wanted.

With a beaming smile, he told us his name, which I have long since forgotten, and added that he operated the Palace Clothing House in Harrisburg. He told us that he was out trying to engage a bushel of wild grapes.

Dad made some comment to the effect, "You surely like grape jelly."

He seemed apologetic when he explained that he wanted them to make wine. He assured us that he wasn't a man given to strong drink. He said that he had never tasted whiskey or beer—he had promised his mother before she died, while he was quite young, that he would never drink whiskey or beer. Then flashing a broad smile, he said, "I didn't promise her I wouldn't drink wild grape wine."

He told us that each year for many years, he had made a bushel of wild grapes into wine. With a sly knowing lift of his eyebrows, he added that he used it for a stomach tonic. Dad caught his humor and quoted St. Luke as saying: "Drink a little wine for your stomach's sake."

It was agreed that for the price of one dollar, we would have him a bushel of wild grapes if he would call for them the following Sunday afternoon.

My brother, Byrum, and I, ages 9 and 11 respectively, accepted the job with the understanding that we would get the money to divide equally between us.

On Saturday morning, we went to a little hollow where grapes had grown in abundance the previous year. To our disappointment, there were no grapes. Instead of grapes, we found our neighbor, Amos Bixler, sitting on the ground leaning back against a scaly-bark hickory nut tree. He had a two-weeks' growth of beard on his face and a floppy old hat on his head. He held a .22 rifle between his knees.

We exchanged greetings pleasantly. Amos said that he had been watching two squirrels play for thirty minutes. He didn't try to kill them because he already had his limit of two. He looked very sad on our behalf when we told him that we had expected to find some wild grapes on the low-hanging vines all around us.

However, Amos' face became all aglow when he recalled where he had seen bushels of wild grapes while looking for ginseng not too far from our home. We thanked him and were ready to take off in a run, when Amos wanted to know if we knew how to make grape wine. He knew we didn't, but he wanted to put his knowledge on display. So we settled down on the ground and for the next thirty minutes, he detailed every step of wine making. He wound up by saying, "That is the way you make it, by the gallon jug or by the keg."

As we went on our way, neither Byrum nor I said anything for awhile, but we were thinking the same thing. We already knew that we would be making us a gallon of wild grape wine.

That afternoon we found the grapes and carefully selected a rounded-up bushel basket of the best. On Sunday afternoon, this lover of grape wine called and was delighted with the grapes. We supplied him with grapes for the next two years.

Byrum and I asked Mom if she would like to have some wild grapes to make jelly. On learning that she would like very much to have grapes, we proceeded to pick some for ourselves too.

We took our grapes to the spring and washed them. Then we picked the grapes from the bunches and put them in a two-gallon crock jar for smashing and fermentation.

After several days, we used an old milk strainer to separate the juice from the seed and rind. To the juice we added a pint of sugar. After stirring well, we very carefully put it in a gallon jug—cup by cup. We added a little spring water to make the jug almost full.

We managed to get a piece of hose about twice the size of a lead pencil. We put one end of the hose in the mouth of the jug of sweetened, fermented juice, packed cotton around the hose, and sealed it with sealing wax. Then we put this jug in our smokehouse on the meat counter and placed another jug filled with clear fresh spring water beside it. We put the other end of the hose in this second jug—well down into the water.

Almost immediately, the jug with the clear water began to give off a continuous flow of bubbles. We were fascinated at what was taking place. We had a feeling that we had created something for the first time. We covered the jugs with some cloth so that they would go unnoticed.

Byrum and I agreed that we would never look at our wine alone, but would go together to check on it. So at least twice a day, we looked in on it. It always pleased us to see the bubbling action in process. After several days, it slowed to an occasional bubble and then stopped altogether.

We took the plug and the hose out of the wine jug and carefully poured the wine into two half-gallon fruit jars, being careful to leave the settlings in the jug. Then we did away with all evidence that we had been engaged in wine making.

The jars of wine were sealed by using old-fashioned rubber rings and the screw-on type lid. We then hid the jars among the half-gallon cans of blackberries in our fruit cellar.

Making our wine had held a greater fascination for Byrum and me than the thoughts of drinking it. But after a few weeks, we could wait no longer to sample it.

Again we promised each other that we wouldn't sample our wine unless we were together. Since this was a solemn pledge to each other, we shook hands and may have crossed our hearts before proceeding to the cellar.

We hauled out a half-gallon of wine. I removed the lid and smelled of it—breathing deeply as I did so. I held it over for Byrum to smell. He did pretty much the same way as I did. Then I took about a teaspoonful and tasted it carefully. I didn't know what to expect, but it seemed pretty good, so I drank about two ounces and handed it to Byrum. By this time, Byrum was anxious to get his nose in that jar. He didn't bother to further smell or taste. He up and downed about four ounces, snorted, shook his head a little, and exclaimed, "That's good!"

We went together every day or so and had a little drink until the first half-gallon was gone. Then I suggested that we take only one swallow at a trip to make the second half-gallon last longer. That was all right with Byrum. But every now and then, I would sneak in alone and take a swallow or two. However, on seeing that the wine was disappearing too fast from the jar, I decided that Byrum was up to the same trick, so I became Byrum's shadow.

Byrum and I became so involved in our various activities that we forgot our wine for several days. Then one Saturday afternoon, we were working in our woodyard, when I realized it had been quite awhile since I had seen Byrum. I took off to see if he was in the cellar.

There I found him sitting on the top step with the empty jar by his side.

I asked, "Byrum, are you all right?"

He answered, "Yes, I'm fine, or I will be as soon as things stop going around and around."

And that was the first and last time that Byrum and I ever made wild grape wine.

A Dollar the Hard Way
(Well, Almost a Dollar)

The 1932-33 school year had only been in session two or three days when I realized that keeping my mind on my lessons was going to be a difficult task. For health reasons my father could do only a limited amount of light work. Since I was the eldest boy of a family of four boys and two girls, at an early age it fell my lot to assume responsibilities not usually placed on a boy not even in his teens. However, the challenge was gladly accepted on my part, and I searched for still others.

Sitting in Sadler School, our one-room school near the Womble Mountain in southeastern Saline County, my mind was dwelling mostly on how I could earn some money, since needs were many and money was scarce.

The fact that the very capable and likable young man, Mr. Williams, who was teaching our school, was getting the staggering sum of $70 per month was a matter that I turned over in my mind. Things like salary were common knowledge in rural communities. Having noticed that Mr. Williams was doing his own janitor work, I decided to make him an offer of doing the sweeping and firing the coal stove for ten cents a day.

At the next recess I approached Mr. Williams on the matter and immediately learned a lesson that has stayed with me to the present time. The lesson being: "Everybody's business is nobody's business." The offer was barely out of my mouth when another boy spoke up and said, "I was about to ask you the same thing, Mr. Williams." Mr. Williams in his wisdom said that he would give us the job jointly and we could work out the details. We could work together, or we could take turns and work every other week. We chose to work together and learned cooperation and developed a life-long friendship that was more valuable than the other five cents per day.

However, much like people today, not being satisfied with my salary of five cents per day, I began to wonder how additional money could be earned. It occurred to me that later in the fall, kindling would be needed to build fires in the old potbelly stove. Immediately I decided to approach the Board of Education, which was made up of three men called "Directors." Quite often one was a lame duck because the other two worked together forming a majority, and the odd man didn't have much to say in school matters unless there was a falling out between the two cronies.

Feeling that Director Zeak Blake might be most receptive, I went to him first and laid out in great detail the need for a wagonload of kindling for the school, explaining that it would be seasoned tie juggles, which were the large chips or hewings from railroad ties that were being hewed out in the community. I further explained to Mr. Blake, that inasmuch as the juggles would probably be donated for the school, I would deliver a wagonload for three dollars.

Mr. Blake gave the offer deep and thoughtful consideration. After a long silence, Mr. Blake replied, "If it were entirely up to me, I would say go ahead, but it takes two to make a majority. You go and see Rosco Gallager. Whatever you work out with him will be alright with me." With a wise old look, Mr. Blake added, "You know how Rosco is." Not willing to admit that I was uninformed on the matter, I replied, "Yes, I know."

The very next evening after school I decided to call on Mr. Gallager and find out for myself "how Rosco is." Hoping to add dignity to my call, I strapped an old saddle, which had been colored up a bit with walnut stain, on our long-legged and naturally long-eared, three-year-old mule, Sampson. This really didn't prove to be too good an idea because of the time it took to hem up the mule and catch him, and still worse because of his impatient braying while I was trying to convince Mr. Gallager that the school needed a three-dollar load of kindling.

Mr. Gallager listened very attentively as I explained the need for the kindling, the kind, and amount, as well as the price for which it would be delivered. Being forewarned by Mr. Blake, I did my very best selling job.

Mr. Gallager's first comment, which was distracted by the loud braying of Sampson, was as follows: "I'm just one of the directors; have you seen the other two?" Mr. Gallager took on a more serious look when I explained that after talking to Mr. Blake, I had been advised to see him as Clerk of the Board, and further quoted Mr. Blake as saying that whatever the two of us could agree upon would be fine with him. That put a serious look on Mr. Gallager's face. He took his time in deciding how to respond.

Finally Mr. Gallager took a deep breath and commented that in the first place the price seemed a bit too high. He went on to say that in the second place, according to the law, kindling hauling should be put up for bids.

Then in the third place . . . . Mr. Gallager was about to go on when he was interrupted by Sampson's loud braying. Taking advantage of this interruption, I commented that it surely wouldn't be necessary to advertise for bids on an amount so small.

Mr. Gallager agreed that I might have a point and seemed to show a softer side to his personality. In fact, he began to take on the look of a wise old owl, or maybe it was the look of Solomon in all his wisdom. Believing that I was on the threshold of success, a feeling of humble pride came over me, which lasted for a very short time. Mr. Gallager went on to state, "Inasmuch as it isn't my money that we are talking about spending for kindling, but everybody's, in good conscience I can offer you only one dollar." Knowing full well that one dollar was too little, I agreed to accept the offer anyway. After a few brief remarks in general, I stated to Mr. Gallager that I must go, and, in going, assured him a good, big wagonload of kindling would be delivered.

Quickly untying Sampson and leading him toward a wooded area, I picked up an old trail that served as a shortcut home. Before getting on Sampson, I got a reasonably good-sized hickory switch. Do you have any idea for what purpose I got the switch? Yes, I did what most people do at one time or another, which is to take out their frustrations on someone or something.

Immediately after mounting Sampson, I began to talk to him. I started by saying, "You haven't behaved too well. First you played HARD TO CATCH. Then you tried to bray your fool head off. Now if you want to complain and bellyache, I'll give you something to complain about. You long-legged, big-reared, yellow-bellied, no-good-jackass, get yourself moving!" With those words of admonition, I warmed Sampson's backend with the hickory switch.

Before realizing what was taking place, I was traveling at a reckless, breakneck speed. Suddenly, I was possessed with the horrible feeling that at any moment I might go crashing out through the brush on a runaway mule. As it turned out, Sampson used better mule sense than I had used horse sense and reined in beautifully.

A feeling of remorsefulness came over me because of my rudeness to Sampson. To this day I still have pleasant memories of him. Dismounting, I was happy to feel the good earth under my feet and to rub Sampson's nose and offer him a drink at a nearby brook. Furthermore, when we got to the barn, he got an ear of corn.

With a feeling that I had already earned a dollar without even starting yet, the next evening found me over to George Hooker's place. Mr. Hooker lived a little more than a mile from school. Crossties were being made on his place. When asked if he would donate a load of the tie juggles for kindling to the school, Mr. Hooker said that for a small fee he would furnish the juggles and haul them to the school house. This forced me to tell him that the job of hauling had already been given to me and that all I needed were the juggles. Then Mr. Hooker agreed to let me have a load of juggles for the school if I would first haul him a load and make them handy for his "old lady" to use in the cookstove. Again knowing that I was hooked, I agreed to accept his offer. This time my disappointment was not taken out on Sampson.

Saturday morning I hitched Sampson and a western mare to our old farm wagon and went over to Mr. Hooker's to move two loads of juggles. The team wouldn't stand still for me to load the juggles. They had to be unhitched and tied to trees. The juggles were in piles, but they were matted together and packed down so that loading was slow. By the time I got Mr. Hooker's load delivered and got the school's load on the wagon, it was too near dark to deliver. This load was taken home and left on the wagon and delivered on Sunday afternoon. Some of the neighbors probably condemned me for working on Sunday.

On the way home from delivering the juggles, I stopped at Mr. Blake's house to ask about collecting the dollar. He informed me that Mr. Gallager was the Clerk of the Board and that he would take care of me.

Again I was surprised and, naturally, disgusted to learn that Mr. Gallager wasn't the one to dole out the cash, but instead he wrote an order for one dollar and told me to take it to John Thomas, the district treasurer, who lived at Somerset. Mr. Thomas would write me a check, and I could take it to the bank in Harrisburg and cash it.

The next Friday afternoon when the usual "Change of Exercise" began at school, which consisted of adding and spelling matches and other games, I asked Mr. Williams for permission to leave school and trade the order to Mr. Thomas for a check for the kindling.

Sampson was tied in the woods far enough from the school that his occasional bray wouldn't disturb the school children. Being a mile on the way at school, I had nine miles to cover to be home by dark. To avoid the danger of the highway, I took short cuts and back roads. In record time I had the check in my pocket and was on my way home.

On the return trip a rattlesnake coiled in the bridle path caused Sampson to rear up to the point that I chose to slide off over his tail for fear that he would fall back on me. Very shortly the snake was tossed to one side with his head beaten in, and I was back on Sampson cat-loping along with the snake's rattles in my shirt pocket.

When I stopped at the school to get my lunch bucket, it was almost dark. Without the benefit of electric lights, it was quite dark in the cloak room where the lunch buckets were kept. The mouse that ran over my foot frightened me as badly as the snake had frightened Sampson. At first I thought it had run up my pant leg. However, I got back on the path shortly and arrived home without further incident.

On Saturday morning I dressed in my best trousers which, to my surprise, were a little too tight in the waist and a little too short in the legs. I put on a new blue work shirt that was bought a little too big so it would fit when it drew up after being washed. I was planning to hitchhike to Harrisburg to get my check cashed.

While waiting for a ride, I gave some thought as to what I'd buy with the dollar. My tentative list was as follows: one 24-lb. sack of Big M. flour for 35 cents, one 5-lb. sack of oats for 10 cents, 3 lbs. of breakfast bacon for 30 cents, 2 lbs. of mixed, broken stick candy for 10 cents, and 3 lbs. of sugar for 15 cents.

Going to the bank was a new experience for me. I had earned money before and had always been paid in cash, but none of my other earnings, then or since, has stood out in my memory like this one. Walking into the bank and straight to the cashier's window about midway on the right side, I stood as if I owned at least half interest in the institution. Finally, overwhelmed by the grandeur of the bank, I lost my cool demeanor and decided to give the place a good looking over. I looked at the floor and the walls, and was gazing at the ceiling when the man at the window cleared his throat. The sound was well known to me. It was intended to get my attention.

Slapping my check down, like a cowboy slapping his hand on the counter and calling for a beer, I called out, "Cash, please." The cashier was an older, good-natured man, but his businesslike nature verged on sternness. His keen eye read me like a book. However, I didn't realize then how well he had me pegged.

Picking up the check and looking at it closely, the banker asked, "Are you Kestner Wallace?" Even though I was as tall as some men, I tiptoed a little and said in my deepest voice, "Yes, sir." I thought I saw a little twinkle in the banker's eye. Then he commented, "You don't have your signature on this check." Since I didn't know the difference between my name and my signature, thinking it was a term used interchangeably, I said, "I beg your pardon, Sir, my name is on that check in black and white." At this point the banker breathed a slight sigh and said, "Will you please write your NAME, your signature, on the back." Then it came back to me, the difference between my name and my signature, and I came on strong again. "Oh, yes, oh yes, you want my signature." At that same instant taking the pen and turning the check the long way, I wrote my full name from one end to the other. "That is more like it," the gentleman said, slightly amused.

With a feeling at this point that my last hurdle had finally been crossed, I could almost feel the dollar in my hand. However, that wasn't exactly the case. The banker inquired, "Do you have an account here?" I searched his face closely to see if he was serious or kidding. Being unable to tell I answered, "You might check and see if I do." I knew immediately by the look on his face that "no" would have been a better answer.

With a certain softness in his voice, the banker informed me, "If you don't have an account here, it will cost you ten cents to get the check cashed." The whole pop-eyed deal had dragged on so long from start to finish that all of a sudden it struck me as being funny. With a smile on my face and laughter in my voice I replied, "That's fine. Go ahead and take the dime out of the dollar. That will be better than breaking a twenty." Then we laughed together. However, I laughed louder than he did. My jokes have always seemed funnier to me than to anyone else.

The banker gave me 90 cents and good-naturedly added, "Come back again sometime." Still smiling and with country courtesy, I quipped, "If you are ever out our way, stop in and see us."

A Taste of New Molasses

The summer of 1932 was the first and only time our family grew molasses cane and made molasses on our farm. In the spring of that year Dad broke about an acre of ground with a walking plow behind a team of horses. After making a good seed bed with a harrow, he took one horse and a much smaller plow, called a diamond plow, and laid off the ground in rows about thirty inches apart.

The cane seed was given to us by our friend and neighbor, Hardy Younger, who had gathered several clusters of seed from his neighbor's cane patch the previous fall.

As Mr. Younger placed the tow sack of seed on the mule's back in front of me, he said, "some good old sorghum molasses next winter will sure beat sopping the dry side of your plate."

After shelling the seed from the bunches, two of my brothers, Byrum and Victor, and I carefully dropped them close together in the rows so the cane would grow tall and succulent. Dad then covered the seed lightly with the small plow. The improved clay soil along with careful plowing and weeding did cause the cane to grow tall—some said the tallest that they had ever seen.

For the promise of five gallons of molasses, we bargained for an old cane crusher, which hadn't been in use for years and was in need of repair. However, after cleaning, sanding, and replacing some bolts and the sweep, it was said to be as good as new.

We chose a site at the edge of the cane patch, about two hundred yards south of our house and about a hundred and fifty yards east of Route 34. There we set three posts firmly in the ground on which to secure the sturdy cane crusher.

The crusher consisted of two heavy steel rollers, set vertically when in use. These rollers operated on the same principle as the old-fashioned clothes wringer. The rollers crushed the cane as it was carefully fed into the mill. The person feeding the crusher or mill was to use caution and only feed at most two or three stalks at a time, top end first. The mill was geared so that the cane was pulled through quickly.

The rollers were turned by a sweep, which was made from a sapling tree with a natural bow in it. The bow allowed head room for the person feeding the cane into the mill, and also allowed the end, a few feet from the crusher, to be near enough to the ground to hitch a horse or a mule to furnish the power by turning the sweep.

Milo Lambert, Sr., who had previous molasses-making experience, offered to buy a new copper cooking pan and make the molasses. He would take his pay in molasses, providing two other neighbors would bring their cane to our site so that he could run a good many gallons at one setting. That was agreeable with all concerned.

While waiting for stripping time to come along the latter part of September, we cut the cooking wood and stacked it at the site to season.

Removing all the leaves from the cane, called stripping, was a tiresome job. We did it using long, thin, wooden knives, with notches cut along the cutting edges. These wooden knives, as a downward stroke was applied, tore off the leaves without spoilage or loss of sap or juice.

The process of removing the clusters of seed from the top of each cane was called topping. Since our cane was tall, we had to pull the cane stalk over with one hand and with a sharp corn knife or butter knife whack off the top. We put the tops in piles to be used later for chicken and cow feed.

Mr. Lambert and Dad took great care to set the pan level on a stone foundation. They set it a foot or more off the ground, making it airtight by using mud for mortar, although openings were left for draft and firing.

Then a pit was dug around the cooking pan so that Mr. Lambert and a helper could stand in a comfortable position and skim off the scum and impurities as the cane juice cooked in the process of molasses making.

As the operation began early the first morning, my job became that of a flunky and water boy—important, but not too flattering. Neighbors, grateful to use our mill and site, pitched in and finished cutting and hauling the cane to the mill.

I can still see the plodding mule as he orbited the mill, pulling the sweep that turned the rollers. I can see the wooden barrel that held the juice. This juice was produced faster than it could be cooked. The fire was contained and controlled so that it allowed the liquid to boil and cook evenly and lightly, even more so as the liquid passed through certain channels in the pan to reach the end where the finished product was drawn off.

The weather cooperated—hot but dry. All went well, with the number of gallons exceeding our expectations. The quality was excellent. Some of it was sold on the spot for 70 cents per gallon. Generous samples were given to our neighbors and friends, with Hardy Younger getting a full gallon. A great deal of it we consumed over the next two years with fresh butter and hot biscuits, but more of it went into the making of cakes, cookies, candy, and popcorn balls. I will never forget that delicious taste of new molasses.

A Trip to the Gap

On a warm August morning in 1934, Mom asked me if I would go down to Thacker's Gap and get her some can lids. She had been canning pole beans and had run out of lids. She said there wasn't any hurry since she wouldn't be using them until the next day, but she reminded me that I had promised Mr. Guy DeNeal that I would help him bale hay on the following day.

Not being one to put things off, I wasted no time in saddling my mule, Sampson, to run the errand. Sampson was a good-looking four-year-old that tried harder to please than most mules.

About a mile south of our house near the Saline and Pope County line, Amos Bixler was grazing his milch cow along the state road. Amos was not too well blessed with worldly possessions. He was a World War I veteran and got a government pension of $15 a month. He never worked at any regular job. He did, however, do a good job adding to his income by trading. Cow trading was his specialty. Amos and his wife, Mina, fattened a hog or two and kept a few hens. They sold some eggs and cream. Most years they had a little garden.

I was pretty sure Amos wanted to talk, so I slowed Sampson to a walk. Sure enough Amos threw up his hand and wanted to know how I would trade my mule for his cow. I didn't answer his question. I knew that was his way of saying hold up and let us have a little chat. I got off Sampson and complimented him on having such a fine cow. That was the only remark I got to make. For the next ten minutes I listened to him brag on his cow.

When Amos paused, I congratulated him on being a successful cow trader. Then I asked, "Amos, since you and I have always been good friends, will you tell me the secret of cow trading, horse trading, or any kind of trading? You just do too well at it not to have some secret."

Amos laughed a little and took off his hat and scratched his head. He took a red bandana and mopped his forehead. With his other hand he rubbed his week-old whiskers.

Then he said, "Kestner, this is my secret. The only reason I'm telling you is because I like you. First of all, I feed my cow all she can eat even if the cost of the feed is more than the worth of the milk she produces. That makes her look good and give more milk too. Then someone will want to buy or trade for her. The most important thing to remember when you go to trade is: 'You know what you have, but you don't know what you are getting.'"

I thanked Amos for his secret and as I went on my way, mused to myself that Mina helped in some cases by whining, "Now Amos, don't you go selling that cow. You know that is the best cow we ever owned."

About a quarter of a mile farther down the road, Luther Edwards was standing near his mailbox. He raised his hand to let me know that he wanted me to stop. He showed me a huge rattlesnake that he had just killed with his walking stick. Mr. Edwards asked me to take it down to the Gap and show it off.

I couldn't turn Mr. Edwards down because he had given me a ride many times when I had been hitchhiking home from Harrisburg. One time he asked me to come down and spend the night with him and his family. He said that they would do like the old farmer who killed a snowbird. The farmer's wife wanted to know if she should cook half of it or all of it. He said, "Cook all of it. Let us live while we do live."

Sampson didn't like the looks of the snake or the way it smelled. It took a little sweet talk and persuasion to get him to allow me to get in the saddle and drape the snake across his back. Once underway, however, he didn't seem to mind.

When I rounded the curve near Rocky Branch just a short distance north of Ferry Cliff, I saw a new 1934 Chevrolet pulled off on the shoulder. A man was standing beside the car holding a small dog. The look on the man's face told me that he had a big problem of some kind.

I stopped and asked him if anything was wrong. He told me that his little dog got to acting nervous and he had stopped for him to get out for a little while. The little dog had gone under the guardrail and was out of sight for a short time. When the man had reached over the guardrail to pick up the dog to put him back in the car, his false teeth had fallen out of his shirt pocket and rolled down the steep embankment out of reach. He explained that because of a heart condition, he was afraid to get off down there for fear he wouldn't be able to get back. He went ahead to say that he was from Chicago and was down visiting his relatives. He told me that if I would get his teeth for him, he would pay me well.

Jokingly I said, "Mister, if you will admit that you are afraid to go down there and get your teeth for fear of getting snakebitten, I'll go down there and get them for you, and it won't cost you anything."

"Well now, son, in a roundabout sort of way you are right. If I were to see any kind of snake, it would cause me to have a heart attack, and I'd die on the spot."

"In that case I'll gladly go down and get your teeth for you."

I didn't learn this fellow's name, so I'll just go on calling him "this man." I asked this man if he would hold my mule for me. I told him not to get too close to his head or Sampson would bite him and not get too close to his heels or my mule would kick his socks off. I told him to hold to the rein and without looking, in a sort of unconcerned way, to stroke him on the side.

I climbed over the guardrail and slid down the embankment. I grabbed the teeth and put them in my shirt pocket and started scrambling up the bank. Going up was harder than going down. I got back up far enough to peer out under the guardrail. This man was faithfully stroking Sampson. I paused and held my breath. I was afraid I might have a dead man on my hands. With each stroke his hand was coming closer to the snake across Sampson's back.

In the beginning I was setting him up to get his hand on the snake, but in the meantime I lost my nerve. Maybe I had a change of heart. I began to feel it would be too cruel. I called out for him not to worry, I had his teeth in my shirt pocket.

My words pleased and excited the man so much that he changed his petting pattern and brought his hand down on the snake. He snapped his head around and let out a squall that caused the hair on my arms to stand up like cat bristles for a few seconds. Had his words been much, much milder, I might have quoted them for effects. But since his oaths were so vile and harsh, I'll not repeat them.

Sampson didn't get too excited. He pulled away and stood unattended as though nothing had happened.

I had seen it all under the guardrail, but I scrambled out and asked what had happened. I asked him if a bumblebee had stung him. That started him all over again with his cursing. He accused me of setting him up to put his hand on the snake.

I was afraid of the man at first. But when he continued his swearing, I was happy when I felt my spunk begin to rise within me.

I said, "Mister, you have said enough. If I had known putting your hand on a dead snake would upset you that much I wouldn't have done it. I'm sorry. One more unkind remark and I'll throw your teeth back down there where they were."

He changed his tune in a hurry and apologized. We shook hands. I gave him his teeth and refused his offer to pay me.

Taking his teeth with a grin, he said, "I better put these teeth in my mouth so I won't lose them again. Besides I can cuss twice as good with them in my mouth."

He took out his handkerchief and gave the upper plate that had been lost a dry cleaning. He slipped them into his mouth and gave me a smile before walking to his car.

I continued on my way to the Gap. It must have been the day the merchant bought cream, because there were several people around. I got off Sampson and tied him to the tailgate of a wagon that had a good-looking team of bay horses hitched to it. I was almost sure that the team and wagon belonged to Henry Hicks.

I stretched the rattlesnake out on the ground. People gathered around to see it. I made it clear that Luther Edwards had killed it with his walking stick and wanted me to show it for him. One man wanted to know if he could have it to show to his wife and kids, who had never seen a rattlesnake. I was glad to get rid of it.

I left Sampson tied to the back of the wagon and went into the store. I looked around for Henry Hicks to tell him that if he got ready to leave before I did, not to run off with my mule. I didn't see him, but I knew he wouldn't anyway. What I didn't know was that Mr. Hicks's young hired hand had delivered a double bed load of corn nearby and had stopped there on the way back to the farm.

Amos Bixler's mother-in-law, whom everyone called Aunt Becky, and her son, Johnny, were being carried high in a teasing, good-natured way. Johnny had bought a Model T Ford, his first, for $15. He and his mother, Aunt Becky, were really proud of it.

One fellow told Aunt Becky that he would bet five dollars that the Model T would take out on them before they got home. That really turned Aunt Becky on. She began to express how much confidence she had in that car. It sounded like a preacher expressing his confidence in God. At the height of her bragging, which reminded me of Amos bragging on his cow, she said that she wouldn't be afraid to take off to Chicago in that Ford.

Johnny didn't drive himself. He had an ailment that made it painful to sit and drive over the rough, gravel road to their home. A neighbor boy did his driving for him. Johnny rode on the running-board of the topless Model T at the elbow of his driver and gave very exacting orders.

We all looked on with a great deal of interest as Johnny and his driver and Aunt Becky loaded up to leave. Aunt Becky got in the back seat. The driver got under the wheel. Johnny spun the crank around a few times. It started with a great deal of noise and vibration. Johnny took his place on the running board and they moved out.

Just then to my surprise, I saw the wagon to which Sampson was tied pull out onto the road. The driver was about fifteen or sixteen years old. He was really urging the horses on. He may have wanted to see how long he could stay ahead of the Model T.

I took off as fast as I could after the wagon, but I made no gain at all. The team was in a gallop soon after they got on the road.

While the Model T was spitting and sputtering, trying to make up its mind if it was going to run, I got a head start on it. When it came along beside me, I hopped on the running-board across from Johnny. It was a wild ride. It was easy to see why Johnny chose to ride the running board instead of the seat. There must have been a boot in the right front tire and in the left rear.

I asked Johnny to have his driver to pull alongside the wagon so that I could cross over into the wagon. Johnny passed the request on to the driver. He gave the appearance of trying to comply, but he was more in sympathy with the driver of the wagon than he was with me. They may have been brothers. He stayed even with the wagon, but he wouldn't move in close enough for me to make the transfer.

I began to get my nerve up by recalling how we boys at school would spend our recesses by climbing tall, slim, hickory saplings and swinging back and forth and jumping from one to the other. It helped. This didn't seem too bad in comparison. The car edged in about a foot and the wagon moved in a little at the same time. I made the leap. It was a good one. My hands grasped the top of the sideboard. My feet came to rest on the side step. With very little further effort, I was in the wagon holding on the back of the spring seat where the young driver was riding.

I was glad to see the Model T get on around and safe on its side of the road. I waved a thank you to Johnny. All three of them waved back. I glanced back toward the store. Some people who were standing in the middle of the road waved at me. I was pleased to know that they were concerned.

When I got my breath I asked, "Buddy, are you going to run these horses until they fall dead? What is Mr. Hicks going to think when you come in with that team dripping with sweat? My advice to you is to stop under the shade of the next tree and let them rest and cool off before it is too late."

He took my advice and brought the team and wagon to a standstill under a tree. This young guy and I stared at each other for the longest time. Then we gave each other a little grin and laughed it off as a joke.

Back at the store, I stopped Sampson directly in front. I got off and left the reins hanging loosely over the saddle horn. I gave Sampson a few pats on the neck, which was my way of saying, "Be a good mule and don't run off."

When I got near the door, I saw several people standing around outside. Uncle Tom and Uncle Charlie were sitting on blocks of salt stacked two high. I nodded to them and to some other people.

All at once a loud harsh voice called out, "Young man, if that mule kicks my dog, I'll kill him."

I looked around. A black and white cur was standing within reach of Sampson's heels. Sampson had his ears laid back against his neck like they were glued there. He didn't look like the same mule. With all the authority I could put in my voice, I called out Sampson's name. He brought his ears to a half-cocked position. To me that was satisfactory. He was saying, "I don't like the dog, but I won't kick him."

Then I walked over to the man who feared his dog would get kicked. I put my mouth within six inches of his ear and in a voice no one else could hear, I said, "Why don't you call your dog away so he won't get kicked?"

I turned and went to the door, where I paused and took another look at Sampson's behavior. I heard Uncle Charlie ask Uncle Tom, "What did he say?"

I heard Uncle Tom wrongly quote me as saying: "Kill my mule and there will be Hell to pay."

I squared my shoulders and tried to stand a little taller. I didn't make the statement, but I didn't plan to deny it either. For fear I would miss something, I paused a little longer. Uncle Tom said, "That boy is going to be just like his daddy. No one ever gave him any lip and got by with it."

I stood there frozen in my tracks feeling like a "cool cat." My eyes were on Sampson, but my ears were tuned in on Uncle Charlie and Uncle Tom.

Uncle Charlie responded, "You are right, Tom. He is the spitting image of his dad, but he is like his mother too. She is a peacemaker."

With that statement I came back to my normal size. I wilted like a morning glory in the summer's sun. I went into the store and got the can lids. Without looking to my right or left, I went out and got on Sampson and took off for home.

I was surprised to see that Amos was grazing a different cow. I didn't want to be late for dinner, so I short-loped on by him. I knew already—he had traded for the "boot" and got a younger and better cow in the deal. At least that is the way he would have explained it.

I just made it home in time for noon-day dinner. After Mom asked a blessing on the food, my sister Mabel wanted to know what all had happened while I was gone. Somehow more things seemed to happen to me than to most people.

I told Mabel that Mom didn't like for me to talk with my mouth full. I assured her for the next little while I planned to keep my mouth full. By the time dinner was over, Mabel had lost interest in my trip to the store.

Unless she reads this story, Mabel may never know what happened on that trip to the store on a warm August morning long ago.

Rabbit Soup and Salvation

One frosty November morning in the mid-nineteen-thirties, I was preparing to go rabbit hunting. Our farm mule, Sampson, was saddled to furnish transportation the two-and-a-half or three miles to where the rabbits were plentiful.

Sampson was an outstanding four-year-old that got his fancy gait and his good manners, for a mule, from his mother, a gaited, western mare. I taught Sampson a few things and in turn learned from him. I learned that firmness and kindness bring out the best in a mule.

I had a sawed-off, 12-gauge shotgun, which was ideal for quick, close shots in the brush. It was neatly fastened to the saddle in a homemade, sheepskin sheath.

My foot was in the stirrup to mount when I looked up and was surprised to see a neighbor, Rosco Gallager, from over the way. It was easy to see that something was wrong. He seemed to have aged years since I'd seen him a few days before. I greeted him in a friendly manner, hoping that nothing was amiss.

Mr. Gallager grunted and nodded in reply to my greeting, but with all the feeling a man could put in four words went on to say, "Something terrible has happened."

Trying to enter into the spirit of Mr. Gallager's sorrow, I lamented, "I'm so sorry. What can I do?"

Instead of answering my question he asked, "Are you fixing to go somewhere?"

I told him I planned to rabbit hunt west on the county line, but went on to say the rabbit hunt could be put off until another day if I could be of help. By now I could hardly wait to learn what terrible thing had happened.

He didn't seem to be in any hurry to tell me. Next, he wanted to know how many rabbits I planned to kill if I had a chance. He seemed pleased when I told him that I only killed two rabbits per hunt.

The painful cloud shadowed his face again, and he blurted out the cause of his grief, "Poor old Billy died last night."

He and his wife were the only members of his household to my knowledge. That left me at a loss as how to respond. So I stalled for time by exclaiming, "You don't say!"

He didn't help when he went on to say, "He died in his sleep."

Instead of asking, "Who is Billy?" I continued to fish for clues, "Had Billy been in poor health?"

Mr. Gallager continued, "Well, yes, and no. His age was against him. I could tell he had slowed down in the past year."

By now I had run out of questions. So my reply was, "I'm at your service."

Mr. Gallager's face brightened and he said, "I knew I could depend on you. I would like for you to dig Billy's grave. I don't want just anyone digging the grave. I feel I owe that much to Billy, having a nice fellow like you digging his grave. We had him since he was a pup. He saved my life one time by killing a big rattlesnake I would have stepped on."

This new revelation shocked, surprised, and amused me. We had never become that attached to our dogs. It was only later that it fully dawned on me the extent of Mr. Gallager's sadness.

"Mr. Gallager, you ride Sampson. I'll come along on foot. Sampson will be there to take me on hunting when Billy is laid to rest."

Mr. Gallager seemed pleased with the ring of "laying Billy to rest," but he snapped, "Why can't we both ride Sampson? He is as strong as an ox."

"Mr. Gallager, Sampson's mother never would allow two people to ride her at one time. We have never tried to ride Sampson double. At your age, I don't think it's a good idea."

"At my age, my foot! I've been riding horses and mules since I was eight years old. That's sixty years. I've never been thrown. I can hang in the saddle if you can hang on behind me."

"You get in the saddle. I'll load on behind you. If Sampson doesn't like two on his back at once, I'll bail off running. Then perhaps he will calm down."

The challenge of riding Sampson took Billy off Mr. Gallager's mind. He walked up to Sampson and patted him on the neck. He ran his hand up and down from the tip of his nose to the top of his head a few times. Then he took the rein in his left hand and grasped it to the saddle horn with all the slack removed. He put his left foot in the stirrup. With a graceful spring he was in the saddle. He gave Sampson a little pat on the neck.

Mr. Gallager removed his left foot from the stirrup and held it toward me with his toe. At the same time he talked mule talk to Sampson, such as "hoe-boy, good-boy," etc., I popped my foot in the stirrup and in no time I was seated behind Mr. Gallager, with a firm grip on the back of the saddle and possessed with a determination that if the saddle stayed on, so would Mr. Gallager and I.

To my surprise nothing happened. Sampson would have liked to have taken us across the way in a slow lazy gallop called a short-lope, but Mr. Gallager only allowed him to go in a fast, lively walk.

As soon as we got under way, Mr. Gallager dropped back into his unhappy mood. After two or three attempts at conversation, I gave up and indulged in a little gloom of my own.

I recalled the day when I was six years old that the Saline County Superintendent of Schools, A. A. Moore, visited the one-room school that I attended. He had given each student a celluloid book marker. On it was a quote from Abraham Lincoln that read: "I will study and get ready, and some day my chance will come." I kept it for a keepsake. My feeling was that if it had worked for Abe Lincoln, it would work for me. However, after ten years, I was beginning to have second thoughts.

Just a few days prior to this particular morning, without really being serious, I had made the statement that I would probably spend my life hunting, fishing, and piddling around. I knew how Mom's lecture would end, so I had my rebuttal in mind. Mom started out by saying, "Son, you must set higher goals for yourself. Remember there is more room at the top."

Then she quoted from the Psalm of Life:
"Lives of great men all remind us
We can make our lives sublime,
And departing, leave behind us
Footprints on the sands of time."

After a rather lengthy and inspirational lecture that impressed all of us, she was about to conclude, as I thought perhaps she would, by saying, "Set your sights high. Hitch your wagon to a star."

At that point I butted in and said, "Hold up, Ma, hold everything. I can go along with most of what you have said, but when you go to talking about hitching our wagon to a star, that is more than I can swallow. You know what happened when I hitched Old Beck to the sled the other day. She ran away and tore it all to pieces. Now you want me to hitch our old wagon to a star. Then we don't have any sled or wagon, either." That amused my brothers and sisters. Mom was used to my turning something serious into a joke.

Running this incident through my mind and dwelling on the serious rather than the silly part that I had injected, my face probably became as long and sad as Mr. Gallager's.

My meditation was interrupted when we met a young fellow who was well known to both of us. He was nosy and as bad to gossip as anyone you ever heard about. He didn't happen to be one of my favorite friends. He threw up both hands and exclaimed, "Where in the Sam Hill are you two going on that mule all long-faced and toting a shotgun?"

Mr. Gallager pulled back on the rein and Sampson stopped. He looked back over his shoulder and said, "You tell him."

Since I didn't like this fellow too well, I would have resented giving him the time of day. So on the spur of the moment, I up and said, "Mr. Gallager says I've got to marry his granddaughter."

This fellow's mouth flew open. Mr. Gallager nudged Sampson to move on. I looked back over my shoulder to see how he was taking this latest news. He had his hat in one hand and was scratching his head with the other. I read these words on his lips, "I'll be damned."

On reaching the Gallager place, I was taken to the garage. An old touring car was on one side with the hood up. It probably had failed to start, causing him to come to our place on foot. Billy was on the other side, lying on a pile of straw.

We stood for a good while with bowed heads looking down at Billy. Finally, Mr. Gallager said, "We will take the body to the grave site in the wheelbarrow." He pointed to the nearby wheelbarrow about half full of straw.

I had Billy sized up. He was about the same in weight as the blocks of wood that I'd been recently tossing in the wagon. So without much thought, I stooped, grabbed Billy by the ear and tail, and tossed him in the wheelbarrow.

Both of Mr. Gallager's hands shot up. Out came a bitter wail, "Oh, Lord have mercy."

I was suddenly ashamed of what must have been rudeness on my part and doubled my effort to please. Ever so tenderly, I brushed away small particles that were clinging to Billy. I elevated his head by slipping a little straw under it. I gently pulled one leg out a little and pushed the other one in some. Everything that I did seemed to please. Mr. Gallager kept nodding his approval. The tail was given a little artistic curve before a cloth was spread completely over Billy. Again the nod of approval was given.

The trip to the grave site was marked by its slow, solemn, measured pace. Mr. Gallager's instructions were, "Please don't hurry. This will be the last time Billy will make this trip out here."

The grave was made wide and deep. The cloth that covered Billy was put on the ground beside the grave. Billy was placed on it ever so gently. The straw that was in the wheelbarrow was carefully spread in the bottom of the grave.

I stood up from placing the straw in the grave and stepped back. At this point Mr. Gallager broke down and cried like a baby. It was a touching scene. I could have wept in sympathy with him had I not used considerable restraint.

Then came the shocker. Mr. Gallager asked in a tearful voice, "Kestner, will you say a word of prayer? I'm too choked up."

We both removed our hats. This was my attempt:

"Thank you, Lord, for the sunshine. It brightens this sad day. We thank you for the sunshine of your love that can take away Mr. Gallager's sadness and fill his heart with joy and happiness. May the sorrow caused by Billy's passing soon disappear and pleasant memories of Billy remain always. Amen."

Billy was placed in the grave. He was covered with the cloth. The soil was placed over him in a caring manner.

At this point Mr. Gallager took out his billfold and stated with firmness, "I intend to pay you for this, Kestner."

My reply was just as emphatic, "Never in a thousand years. This has been a neighborly act for which I'll accept no pay."

Mr. Gallager took out two one-dollar bills and pleaded, "Let me explain it this way. I'll feel better if I'm out some money putting Billy away."

My response was, "If you put it that way, I'll take one. You keep the other. You have lost a dear friend. I've only been out a little time."

"Kestner, you don't know how much I appreciate what you have done. Now I'll tell you what I want you to do. I want you to go out along the garden fence and get two big fat rabbits as an extra bonus. You and everyone else know that I don't allow hunting on my place, but for this one time I sincerely want you to step out there and get a couple."

"Mr. Gallager, that is mighty generous of you. I'll accept your offer most kindly."

"By the way, Kestner, how does your mother cook rabbit?"

"She cooks them the way they go the farthest."

"How is that?"

"She makes rabbit soup out of them. It is really rabbit stew, but we call it rabbit soup."

"Is it good?"

"Served with cornbread for supper, it is out of this world."

"I'll have to have the 'Old Lady' to fix me some some-time."

"When you smell the aroma of the rabbit, potatoes, onions, and other spices and vegetables cooking, this is what I predict will happen. Your wife will want to know why you are wearing a red necktie. Then you will have to admit that it isn't a red necktie, but that it is your tongue hanging out for some of the rabbit soup." That amused Mr. Gallager. It was a thrill to see him laugh after all the gloom.

I will report the rabbit hunt briefly to conserve time and space. I went out—boom—boom—and came back with two rabbits.

Mr. Gallager was happy for me. They were extra fine. He watched me put them in a canvas pouch and fasten them behind the saddle.

It was quite noticeable that Mr. Gallager had a rather serious matter that he wanted to talk about. He started out rather bluntly by asking three questions which were: "How about your soul's salvation? Have you made peace with God? Are you a Christian? You have me buffaloed. Sometimes I think you are. At other times I have second thoughts."

I lowered my head and gave my reply, "As yet I have made no profession of faith."

His face became still more serious as he admonished, "Son, Son, Son, don't put it off too long. Life is uncertain and death is sure."

With bowed head, I replied, "Thank you for your concern."

I pulled myself slowly into the saddle, nodded a farewell to Mr. Gallager, and moved out.

Mr. Gallager called after me, "I'll be praying for your salvation."

I moved out about thirty paces and turned Sampson around to show him off and say my final goodbye. I spread my arms up and out as in a presidential greeting or farewell. That was Sampson's cue to rear up on his hind legs. He performed perfectly. Mr. Gallager was impressed and returned the gesture.

As Sampson took me away in a graceful short-lope, my mind went gradually from salvation to rabbit soup.

Bringing Home the Bacon

On a summer evening of 1934, Mom and I lingered at the supper table after the other members of our large family had finished and excused themselves. We often discussed matters that concerned the well-being of all. We both agreed that we would need an additional two or three hogs for our next year's meat supply. Mom loved using pork in the various ways she prepared meals. I always enjoyed spooning a piece of side pork out of beans or white soup beans.

As a result of our discussion, it was decided that I would saddle my mule, Sampson, the following morning and go looking for some shoats, which are young pigs ranging from forty to eighty pounds, or perhaps a full-grown hog or two.

I had decided to go south of Herod a few miles to the community of Sodom, since we knew of no hogs for sale near home. There I hoped to get a bargain.

The following morning I planned to leave home between four and five o'clock on Sampson, a prize mule that could move a load or give a racehorse a workout. It was an unusual scene because besides being saddled, Sampson was in a full set of harness. Extra rope was tied to the saddle along with a sharp hand saw. In the saddle bag was a claw hammer, a small crowbar, and about three pounds of nails.

Right before I left, I went back into the house to get the few dollars laid aside for such an occasion and to get Mom's blessings for a successful trip. I told Mom that if I traded work for hogs, I'd be gone for a few days.

A few minutes before seven o'clock, I was at the sawmill run by Reasor Belford three or more miles south of Herod. It was only a short distance from the dirt road leading to Sodom. Mr. Belford's sawmill was run by an old-fashioned steam engine that had a whistle on it that could be heard for miles around. The boiler had a safety valve on it that would pop off now and then and frighten man and beast until they got used to it.

I told Mr. Belford that I wanted to buy enough lumber to build a sled four feet wide and eight feet long. I wanted the runners out of seasoned oak 1 x 8's and the rest out of poplar. I showed him a rough drawing, which included sides that amounted to a built-on hog coop. I told him that I would put it together on the spot. I offered to pay him cash for the material or work it out at the mill.

He didn't give me an answer at first. Instead he wanted to know whose boy I was. When I told him, he remembered that he had set my Dad's arm after he had fallen from a horse at age seven. He also knew that my grandfather was Jonathan Wallace, who had fought in the Civil War with a friend of their family. Mr. Belford bragged about his ability to set bones and to build or make anything with his hands.

After telling me a number of interesting things about my grandparents on both sides of the house, he told me that for 75 cents, I could help myself to enough lumber to build the sled. He made some helpful suggestions concerning the lightness and toughness of some of the material that I could use.

Between nine and ten o'clock, the sled was complete. Pieces to close in the back and top were cut to size and ready to nail in place when my hog or hogs were bought and loaded. I placed a twelve-inch board through the slats on either side about eighteen inches high to make a seat and nailed it temporarily in place. For a cushion, I added a gunny sack of sawdust on top of the board.

Mr. Belford could see that I was proud of the sled when it was finished. He seemed pleased for me. I had seen Mr. Belford a time or two before that morning and a few times afterward. But the only time that I ever saw him laugh was when I pulled away from the mill on the sled. It was probably because I looked like I had the world by the tail.

The mill had been running while I was working on the sled. The steam build-up and the amount being used had been in balance. The boiler hadn't popped off, but just as I got Sampson turned around and headed toward the road, the safety valve on the steam engine popped off. The sudden release of steam frightened Sampson and caused him to rear up and lunge forward a time or two. Both my weight and the fact that the sled runners were not yet worn smooth kept Sampson from jerking the sled into his heels and causing him injury. That incident was solemn warning to me that smooth sledding would be a result of extreme care. This was a drag-type sled without shafts, which would have given greater control.

Once on the road Sampson went in a brisk walk for a few hundred yards. The sled swayed more to the right and left than I would have liked. The swaying was no worse with Sampson trotting, so we took time about walking and trotting.

Before going very far we came upon a bundle of loose, newly mown hay. It had probably fallen off some farmer's hay wagon. I stopped long enough to pile it in the sled coop for Sampson's dinner, in case he wouldn't be able to pick grass.

I had never been to Sodom; therefore, I wasn't sure when I got there. I passed a few houses. Most of them were fifty to seventy-five yards off the road more or less. These modest homes had porches on which were porch swings, benches, wooden boxes, and cane-bottom chairs. Often the whole family appeared to be on the porch in a happy, contented manner. I enjoyed the attention that I got mid-stage.

I saw a big man and two half-grown boys building a fence near the road. My first impulse was to stop and tell them my name and business and see if they could be of any help to me. When they stopped working and all three stood there dying to know who I was and what I was doing, I couldn't resist the urge to keep them wondering. I gave them a reserved nod and slid on past.

My conscience afterwards bothered me a little for fear that I might be punished for sledding by with my nose in the air, when I might have to come slithering back later for help. However, it didn't turn out that way.

As I came to the next house, I decided to become more serious and let my business be known. Two men about thirty years of age were talking in the yard. Before I had a chance to introduce myself, one of the men, who turned out to be named Ralph, said, "You are just the man I'm looking for. I would like to hire you to haul five bushels of potatoes over to my place a quarter of a mile down the road. What would you charge me to move them over there?"

"I'm Kestner Wallace. I'm looking for some hogs to buy for winter's meat. I won't charge you anything—I'm going that way. Maybe you can help me in suggesting where I can find a large hog or three or four shoats for sale that would make good meat hogs by early winter."

"I'm Ralph. I'm a preacher. The Lord is smiling on me today. Brother Joe here has just given me a six-months supply of potatoes because he loves me and because he loves the Lord. You have already expressed your love for your fellow man by offering to move my potatoes. Do you love the Lord, also?"

"I would like to say, 'Yes,' but my faults are many and my virtues are few. If I were weighed in the balances today, I would probably be found wanting."

"You sound to me like a young man who is being far too hard on himself. I would like to further discuss this subject with you. Perhaps we could discuss it over a dinner of fried chicken. We have some young roosters just right for frying. My wife said one might not be quite enough for the two of us, so I dressed two this morning. There will be plenty. Will you eat with us?"

"Talk about the Lord smiling on you—He is laughing out loud all around me. You make it easy to say 'Yes.' I'm glad I didn't have to hint for something to eat. I might have sounded like a tramp that came to my grandpa's place one time and said, 'Mister, could I have a drink because I'm so hungry I don't know where I'm going to sleep tonight.'"

We all three laughed and loaded the potatoes on the sled. When we got to Ralph's, he went in the house and got a key to the fruit cellar, where we unloaded the potatoes. The cellar was well-blessed with canned fruit and vegetables.

Ralph took me into his neat, comfortable home and introduced me to his wife, Grace. She was a good mate for Ralph. She had blondish, brown hair and blue eyes. She and Ralph had the same gift of being able to put a stranger at ease. The friendly way that they treated me couldn't have been better had I been one of their favorite in-laws, a minister, or the governor of the state.

Grace said that she had a feeling in her bones that Ralph would invite someone for dinner and had cooked some extra. She explained that they had bought one hundred baby chickens, and it seemed that more than half of them had turned out to be roosters, which were now frying size. She said that if today's fried chicken sampling turned out well, she and Ralph would be butchering and canning the others over the next week. She explained that she would trade some of the canned fried chicken to her mother for canned pork sausage. She was convinced that no one could make sausage like her mother.

The food was all delicious—the mashed potatoes, green beans, cooked cabbage, etc.—but the part one would never forget was the mouth-watering fried chicken, biscuits, and gravy. Those young roosters must have been about three and a half pounders on foot. They were old enough to be flavorful and young enough to be tender. They had been fried in bacon grease. Enough fat fried out of the chicken and mixed with the bacon grease to make a chicken gravy that was packed with flavor. At first I thought it was the best that I had ever tasted. Then I decided it was mostly because I'd had an early breakfast, and I was hungry. Actually, it reminded me of my mother's and grandmother's fried chicken and gravy.

I was glad that Ralph was a big eater. He took somewhat bigger helpings than I, but I was full and satisfied before he was. It also pleased me that he didn't talk about religion.

Ralph asked Grace if her dad didn't have some hogs for sale. She was pretty sure that he wanted to sell a big bacon-type Hampshire sow that weighed more than three hundred pounds and perhaps a couple of shoats.

Ralph kidded, "You are in luck. George lives the next house down the road. He likes to trade, talk tough, and joke. He is a wicked man in a way and in another way he is as good as gold. He has a daughter, June, about your age. You may want to look at her out of the corner of your eye."

My mind clung to each comment, but perhaps least of all concerning the daughter. Getting home with a sow and two shoats on a homemade sled behind Sampson, who didn't like hogs, was about all I wanted on my mind at one time. I thought, however, that it would be a good opportunity to compliment Grace. I inquired of her, "Does your little sister look like you? Will she become the outstanding cook that you are?"

Like most good women who receive too few compliments, she flashed a smile and gave her modest reply.

"Junie had me beat for looks from day one. People say I'm like my mother and Junie is like Daddy in personal traits. Mom insists that Junie help with the cooking, and she does quite well."

"Grace, Junie would be pleased to hear what you have just said. For now, however, I'm going to set the pleasant thought of Junie to one side and ask Ralph about his father-in-law and just about what he would ask for his sow and two shoats."

At this point Ralph picked up on George. He described him as being "one of a kind." He explained that until one got to know George, it was almost impossible to tell when he was serious and when he was joking. Ralph continued, "Kestner, you will be safe in guessing he is kidding more than half the time. He will pretend he doesn't like mules. He will refer to Sampson at least once as a 'damned jackass.' He will pressure you for a quick offer on whatever he has for sale. Just don't let him cause you to get in a hurry. You can slow him down by asking him if the sow has any bad traits. When he explains that away, ask him if she has big litters of pigs. Before he gets over answering that question—if you think they are worth it—offer him four dollars for the sow and two dollars each for the two shoats. He will jump about two feet off the ground and declare he won't take less than six dollars for the sow. Then you will have to jaw it out from there. I'm pretty sure he will take two dollars each for the shoats. They are really worth all of two dollars each. They may look small beside that big sow, but they will weigh seventy-five or eighty pounds each."

All of this time Grace listened with an amused look on her face. She added, "We are not plotting against Daddy. We love him and know the more jawing and bickering that goes on during the trade, the better he likes it. We don't want him to scare you off when he might have the best buy you will find."

I thanked Ralph and Grace for dinner, their kindness, and the information that they had given me. On leaving, they told me that they would keep their fingers crossed that I'd find what I was looking for.

Sampson appeared rested after the noon break. He had eaten about half the hay from the back of the sled where he was tied and was nipping the grass within reach.

...

George must have heard me coming bouncing over the rocks and clods in the road. He walked part way out to the road to make it easy to pass the time of day.

I pulled up to where he was standing and introduced myself. I told him I was breaking my mule to work to a sled. His first comment was as follows:

"Son, you better watch that 'damned jackass'—he will run off with you and get you killed."

"His name is Sampson. He isn't for sale. So you don't need to run him down. He has more brains in his tail than most mules have in their heads."

"Well, son, I'm glad to learn where mules keep their brains. I haven't seen one yet that had any brains in their head."

George looked pleased because of his quick reply. He stuck out his hand and said, "I'm George. People around here call me George, the trader."

"I'm pleased to meet you, George. What do you have for sale or trade today?"

"Would you be interested in a sow and two shoats?"

"I might be if you would deliver them."

"Where do you live?"

"About two miles north of Thacker's Gap in Saline County."

"That's too far. I'm afraid to put my team and wagon on the state road. People drive too wild with that thirty-five mile per hour speed limit. But let me show you that sow and shoats. It won't cost you anything to look at them. With all the brains that mule has in his head and tail, you could probably get home with them."

George took me to a building about twelve feet by sixteen feet and made of rough lumber. It had high windows and was probably used at times for a chicken house.

I was amazed when George opened the door and showed me the longest and tallest hog that I had ever seen. Hampshire hogs have long legs. That makes them appear bigger than they really are. That sow looked as big as a good-sized calf. The shoats were of a different breed.

George wasted no time in trying to make a sale. He came to the point.

"What will you offer me for all three of them?"

I barely heard George's question, because at that moment Junie appeared at his elbow. Her showing up caught me off guard. My mouth probably flew open, and my eyes may have gotten wider. I was trying to decide whether she would have Grace's disposition or whether she would be cantankerous like her daddy.

I felt George's hand on my shoulder. In a soft tone he asked, "Son, did you come down to Sodom to look for a gal, to brag on your jackass, or to buy hogs? It would help me to know."

When I got control of myself, I replied.

"George, I like all three. Now that I'm over the shock of a fellow like you having such an attractive daughter, we can go on with our hog talk. Does that sow have any bad characteristics?"

There was a long silence that was finally broken by Junie, who said, "Daddy, you'd just as well tell him that she eats chickens."

"Yes, Honey, I was getting ready to tell him. If he plans to keep her penned up to fatten, it wouldn't make any difference."

"The big difference is a chicken-eating sow wouldn't be worth as much if I were to decide to sell her. Does she have a big litter of pigs at pigging time?"

Again there was a long silence. For the second time, Junie broke the silence.

"Daddy, do you want me to tell him?"

As he lowered his eyes, he replied, "Yes, Honey, you are my old trading partner—you tell him."

"The first time she had two pigs and mashed one of them. The next time she had one pig."

George coughed and cleared his throat and said, "Again, that doesn't make any difference if you are thinking of a smokehouse full of smoked ham and bacon. Do you have any more questions?"

"Yes, just one more. I want to know why you allow this beautiful daughter around while you are trading. She hasn't helped you very much today, has she?"

"I'll have to answer this way. She likes to be around and listen to the jawboning. For me that is reason enough."

Junie stiffened a little in resentment. I thought that she was on the verge of unkindly telling me and my mule to get out. So in haste I replied, "I'm satisfied with that answer. In fact I was only joking. I'm ready to make you an offer. If you will help me fasten that sow and two shoats in the coop on that sled, I'll give you four dollars for the sow and two dollars for each of the two shoats."

"Lord have mercy, Son. I can't take four dollars for a big piece of meat like that sow. I'll let you have the shoats for two dollars each, but I would have to have six dollars for the sow."

"I'm going to make you my best and last offer for that smokehouse full of tough sow meat. I'll give you a new crisp five-dollar bill for her."

"Well, what do you think, Junie?"

"Daddy, I'm going to say, 'Sell her,' because Mom said a few minutes ago if you get a chance to sell that sow and don't, she would kill you with the churn dasher."

"Well, Son, with two against one, a man doesn't have a chance. I'm going to let you have her."

George and I shook hands to put the final touch on the deal. Of course the nine dollars was the real clincher.

Then after taking Sampson loose from the sled, we slid it by hand up to the door of the building. We removed the board that was used for a seat and left the uneaten hay in the sled to cushion the ride. To entice the hogs, we put a little shelled corn on the ground behind the sled and some more in the sled. Soon all three hogs were nailed securely in the coop.

After allowing Sampson to smell of the hogs through the slats of the coop and listen to their grunts and squeals, I hooked him back to the sled. I didn't like the way he kept his ears laid back, so I petted him on the neck and let him eat some shelled corn out of my hand. When I called on him, he pulled out the same way that he had done with the potatoes.

I left George and Junie smiling. To me it was an ideal trade, because we were both happy and satisfied. Unlike Lot's wife in the Bible, after bidding George and Junie farewell, I left Sodom without looking back. Even though I've always had pleasant memories of Sodom, I've never been back.

Ralph and Grace came out to the road to see if all had gone well. I told Ralph that if it had not been for his good suggestions, things might not have worked out as well as they did. They asked me to come back and see them. I thanked them and continued on my way. I walked all the way home to make the load lighter on Sampson. I watched the sun and let Sampson rest as often as I could and still get home by dark.

The family had already eaten supper, but as I ate, they gathered around. I told them the entire story, including a detailed account of the return trip, bringing home the bacon.

My Friend Ed

His statement—"I spent eleven long years in the Menard State Prison at Chester, Illinois"—caught my attention as two fellows sat down near me on makeshift seats in the general store. The speaker was less than medium build—perhaps five feet six inches tall and a weight of 150 pounds. His keen blue eyes that took in everything and his spryness made him look young, but a wrinkled face brought his age into question. However, there was no question about his having young ideas and a desire to be seen, heard, and accepted.

The man looked at me and asked his friend, with whom he was renewing acquaintance, whether I was his son. The friend's eyes got big and his mouth flew open and out rolled these words, "Hell, no! I don't even know him." Then he looked a little embarrassed and said that his boys all turned out to be girls—the oldest about my age—15. I made no comment concerning his guess. To relieve his embarrassment, I told them that I was Kestner Wallace and extended my hand in a friendly gesture.

The man shook my hand and said that everyone at the "Big House" called him "Cap," since he had been captain of both a baseball team and a boxing team while in prison. However, his friend called him "Ed," and so did I.

Ed was most emphatic in explaining to his friend that he "did time" for another fellow. "This blankety-blank, no good, son-of-a-blankety-blank got this 15-year-old girl in trouble and I got blamed for it."

For an instant, he appeared angry enough to kill. He patted what appeared to be a concealed handgun and stated, "I'll kill him if it is the last thing I ever do."

Then, practicing my hobby—that of a close scrutiny of human nature—I picked up a mannerism of Ed's that told me a great deal about him. After making a statement just a wee bit louder than necessary, he would look straight ahead like a bird dog on point, take a little extra air into his lungs, which would make his chest stand out, and without moving his head, he would turn his eyes to the right and left until he exhaled, at which time he looked pleased with himself.

Ed kept me spellbound for almost an hour as he gave his friend a detailed sketch of prison life. He seemed quite pleased to have me listen. Perhaps my keen interest fed his ego. He really put the best possible face on a notorious experience.

After Ed's friend went home, I asked Ed if I could buy him a bottle of pop in appreciation for his allowing me to listen to a very private part of his life. I went on to tell him that he told his experiences in a most interesting way.

He beamed with pleasure and replied, "I won't let you buy me a drink, but I'll buy you one."

I countered, "Ed, suppose we stack three of these blocks of salt on top of each other and have that good-looking clerk cut each of us a nickel's worth of bologna and a nickel's worth of cheese and give us some crackers to go with them."

Ed must have talked up an appetite. He was pleased with the idea. I placed the order for the food while he got us each a tall bottle of strawberry pop.

Ed and I eyed the clerk as we waited for her to catch up enough to fill our order. Since it was Saturday, the three or four clerks were really busy. Actually Ed watched her, and I studied him. My desire to know what made him tick was of greater interest to me. I already had her figured out. She was attractive in a wholesome way, with a personality that demanded attention and respect. However, even if she were single (neither of us knew), she was too old for me and too young for Ed.

After a time, she brought our food, and with the grace and poise of a professional, placed it on a piece of white paper on the block of salt. She smiled and thanked us as she picked up 15 cents from each of our separate assortment of coins.

Ed surprised me by saying, "Thou preparest a table before me. Good cheese, good crackers, good meat. Amen, let's eat." However, with a pleased look on his face, he threw out his chest and looked to his right and left to see whether anyone saw any humor in what he had said.

When Ed got a chance, he asked our waitress if she was married. She told him that she wasn't, but hadn't yet lost hope. With a broad smile, Ed told her that he was two-thirds married. When she looked a little puzzled, he quipped, "I'm willing and the preacher is willing."

I shamefully regret ribbing Ed by asking, "Ed, did you notice how she looked at you? She gave me a little grin because she thinks we are good friends, but the smile she gave you was warm and friendly."

Ed beamed with happiness as he said, "We are good friends. Two can't eat cheese and crackers and bologna off the same block of salt without being friends forever."

We spontaneously grasped each other's hand. A bond of true friendship blossomed and never wavered thereafter. Our lunch took on a special flavor.

Early in our friendship, I heard Ed mention that he was working for a moonshiner. His statement both intrigued and disturbed me. It disturbed me because I didn't want him to run afoul of the law again. But I was intrigued because I had always wanted to see a still in operation. I recalled my dad's showing me a rock beside a spring of soft, cold water, a short distance from our log barn. He said, "This is one of the four rocks that my pa's whiskey still sat on." Dad had hastened on to say that his pa wasn't a moonshiner or a bootlegger, but that in the 1870s, he had had a federal liquor license out of Paducah, Kentucky, to make corn whiskey and peach brandy to sell wholesale by the keg.

I never got to see Ed's still. Several weeks later, when I saw Ed again, he looked younger and happier. He said it was because he was making an honest living working in the spar mines. He grinned and commented that he would much rather be on the lookout for falling rock than for revenue men.

The pleased look on my face spoke for itself, but I added, "Congratulations. I'm glad to hear it."

With his moonshining days over, Ed took more pleasure in being a part of community activities. At hog killings he prided himself in his ability to shoot, scald, and gut hogs to perfection. He performed many tasks well and enjoyed having his ability recognized and appreciated.

Having a good team of horses and mules was a top priority of Ed's. He was skilled at buying and selling horses at a profit. However, his preference for his own use was a team of large, well-matched mules. On a number of occasions, Ed displayed a heart of gold by breaking gardens free of charge for the poor and elderly.

The friendship between Ed and me was mutual and sincere. On meeting after not seeing each other for awhile, we would shake hands. He would call me, "Ole Pal" and on occasion I would call him "Brother Ed." We both seemed flattered by the handles.

Pie suppers, held as fund-raisers at one-room schools, were a special delight to Ed. He justified the sizable amount he spent each time by saying, "It is going for a good cause." Auctioneers were always glad to see Ed show up because he had a knack of running up the bids and knowing when to stop bidding. He made many men pay dearly for the privilege of eating with the lady of their choice. Sooner or later, Ed paid a handsome sum for the pie or pies he bid on one time too many.

One time, when I had limited funds, I wanted very much to buy a pie brought by a certain young lady. Ed told the auctioneer, who was trying to egg him on, that he wasn't going to bid against his "Ole Pal." No one else did either. I got a bargain.

In the summer of the late 1930s, Ed put forth a special effort to invite me to attend a baptizing the following Sunday afternoon, in the creek across from the Cliff Cafe at Herod. When he added that he was one of the ten or twelve being baptized, I assured him that I would be there.

It was a baptizing that stands out vividly in my mind. Conditions were ideal. The sun was shining and there was a slight breeze. The water was pleasantly cool. The trees served as an umbrella for the water and the creek bank. The colorful clothes of the one hundred or more people in attendance complemented the beauty of nature.

The people formed a group at the water's edge and sang, "Shall We Gather at the River." I was pleased to be a part of a religious ritual that has continued for over two thousand years.

The candidates for baptism lined up and joined hands. The minister led the way out into the water, with Ed immediately behind. They pioneered the way for those who followed. The group formed a semi-circle, and the last one to enter the water was the first one to be baptized.

Following each person's immersion, he or she waded out and was given hugs and kisses and pats on the back by friends and family as the group sang. I could see that Ed was lined up so that he was going to be last. For fear that he might be slighted in some small way, I stepped out of my shoes and was standing with my toes in the water waiting for him to come out. I handed him a towel and was the first of many to shake his hand and embrace him.

A few months after the baptism, Ed performed a favor for our family that I've never forgotten. I had been working in Michigan from November 1940 to April 1941, when I got a telegram telling me that my father had had a stroke and wasn't expected to live. He was dead when I got home.

Dad lay in state in our home where the funeral was held. Neighbors assured us that they would dig the grave and told us not to worry.

Ed came to our home around 9:30 a.m. the morning the funeral was to be held that afternoon. He told us that he wouldn't be able to attend the funeral, but he wanted to come by and say "Hello" to me and express his sympathy to the family.

About that time, the neighbors who were digging the grave came from the nearby family cemetery in a state of panic. They were down about three feet and had struck sandstone rock too solid to pick. Naturally that was alarming to all of us because of the limited time.

Ed's face lit up as he said, "Don't any of you worry. With the help of these fellows, we will have that grave finished in time for the burying."

He went home and got some dynamite, blasting caps, and some fuses for removing stumps. By using light shots that loosened the rock, the grave was completed in ample time. I was almost as pleased as Ed to hear people compliment him.

During the advanced years of Ed's life, Coe Wallace and his wife, Ora, operated the general store and post office at Herod, which made an ideal place for Ed to pass pleasant hours with Coe and his friends. He expressed his fondness of Coe by saying that Coe treated him like a brother. He also said that when his clock ran down, Coe would be in charge of his funeral arrangements. That clock of time for Ed stopped in the fall of 1964.

On arriving at the Aly Funeral Home in Eddyville, I was surprised that callers made up of neighbors and friends filled the entire seating area.

At first, I stood alone at the casket and felt no emotion. However scenes from the past with Ed flashed through my mind—our first meal together on a block of salt, the friendship and fellowship we shared at various social and community events, and his taking over the digging of my father's grave.

What touched the most tender spot in my heart was recalling the way the sunlight had flickered through the leaves on the people at Ed's baptizing. A parting of the leaves by the breeze had caused a ray of sunlight to illuminate Ed's bald head, giving a halo effect.

My reminiscing caught me off guard. A lump formed in my throat. Before I could get my handkerchief out, tears were dripping off my chin.

Suddenly, I felt the strong arm of Coe Wallace around my shoulders. He said, "Kestner, we are going to miss Uncle Ed, aren't we?"

Coe's presence and words were magic. The lump left my throat. And there were no more tears.

I answered, "Yes, Coe, you are right. There will never be another Ed."

Sampson Goes to Church

Mr. Alfred Baker, our neighbor, gave me a ride as I was thumbing my way home from Harrisburg High School in late September of 1936. Mr. Baker was well known for his loud musical laughter.

I can still see him as we chugged along in his old black touring car. He kept his eyes riveted to the road about 95% of the time. That suited me fine since he had rather piercing eyes. I felt more comfortable with them on the road than on me.

On that Friday afternoon Mr. Baker was joyous in a serious sort of way about a revival that was in progress at the Big Saline Baptist Church. He wasn't a member there, but was a big hand to go to different churches and make himself at home.

Mr. Baker told me that he would like very much to take me to the revival that night, but he had a carload already promised. He went on to say that I could hop on my mule, Sampson, cut through near Sadler School and on past Blue Springs Church, and could get there almost as quickly as he could go around on the gravel road.

I thanked Mr. Baker for the invitation, but told him if I could make it over at all, it wouldn't be before Saturday night. He was pleased with the prospects of my attending Saturday night and promised to be looking for me.

When Mr. Baker got me to our driveway, he pulled off on the shoulder of the highway and proceeded to tell me of his deep concern for my soul's well-being. He exclaimed, "Kestner, I firmly believe if you attend that revival tomorrow night, you will come away a different boy."

"Mr. Baker, I'm not sure I want to be any different. I'm pretty well pleased with myself. I'm not as mean as I was a couple of years ago when I used to drive your horses off in the lake and get a free ride across to the other side holding to the tail of one of them. I will also give you my word of honor that I'll never tie a tin can to your dog's tail again and scare him off home. However, I did get mighty tickled when I saw your dog pass two cars and a motorcycle on the way home."

That slowed Mr. Baker down a little. For a few seconds after hearing my true confession for the first time, I wasn't sure if he wanted the good folks at Big Saline Church to help pray my sins away or if he wanted to beat the Devil out of me himself.

After some delay, to my great relief, Mr. Baker burst out in his usual musical laughter and exclaimed, "I wish I had time to tell you some of the things I did when I was a kid. You come over to Big Saline tomorrow night if you can. Even if you don't feel impressed to make any move or commitment, you will never forget being there."

Mr. Baker never knew with what accuracy he prophesied. I thanked him most sincerely for the ride. He assured me that I was welcome and gave me a departing smile.

That night, after the evening chores and supper were over, I did the unusual for most high school students on a Friday night. I did my assignments for Monday while they were still fresh in my mind. As I worked on my lessons on the dining table by an old-fashioned kerosene lamp, I told Mom about riding home with Mr. Baker and of his telling me about the revival at Big Saline Church. She thought it would be a refreshing change for me to attend Saturday evening services.

By the middle of Saturday afternoon, I had Sampson brushed and saddled for what would be a most leisurely trip to Big Saline. On the way I wanted to locate a bushel of wild grapes for a man who worked at the Palace Clothing House in Harrisburg. I was planning on keeping a lookout for a bee tree. I also wanted to locate some raccoon den trees to make coon hunting a little easier in the season.

To attend the rural church, I felt reasonably well dressed in a four-button pair of overalls, a white shirt, and a fairly new pair of work shoes. As I was leaving, Mom put a paper bag in my hand and remarked that the food would taste good about six o'clock. I thanked her and was on my way.

Sadler School was a woodland mile northeast of our home, which was near the Saline and Pope County line in Saline County. This was a trip that I had made daily on school days as I progressed from grade one through eight.

About halfway to Sadler School was a rocky branch. It was dry the year round except after a big rain. I went down the branch about two hundred yards. To my delight, wild grapes were hanging on vines that were clinging to low undergrowth bushes. There would be plenty for the bushel that was engaged and some for Mom to make jelly.

Up the branch on the other side of the trail, I found a bee tree, but the hollow branch that the bees were using was too small to yield much honey. However, nearby were some den trees that were very likely used by raccoons.

Next I swung by a couple of old pear trees, which were all that was left of an old homeplace. These trees never failed to have pears that in the fall were sweet and somewhat mellow. They fell short of canning quality, but they had been fine to eat evenings on the way home from school through the years. They were of a yellowish gold and as sweet and delicious as ever, even though they were only the size of a hen's egg. I ate all that I wanted, fed Sampson several, put a dozen or more in the saddle bag, and took off again.

The next stop was Sadler School. It stood on an acre of land in the middle of the woods. The students who attended came in from all directions.

After tying Sampson to the well curb, I stepped into the schoolhouse. In the two years since I had been a student there, the building had somehow grown small and humble, yet in other ways remained the same. The chalkboards and the teacher's desk were still in the east end of the building, while most of the north side was still made of windows.

I took a seat in the back of the room near the windows. About thirty feet away stood a big hickory nut tree surrounded by smaller trees. It had nuts on it almost every year. Squirrels came to it in numbers. Some of us boys spent more time than we should have watching the squirrels. We would usually wait until we saw two or three, and then in a whisper, we would sound off to those around us, "pow, pow, pow," as if we were using an automatic shotgun. I doubt whether any of us had ever seen an automatic shotgun.

I didn't have to wait too long until I spied a red fox squirrel perched on a limb near the trunk, cutting away on a nut. Immediately the search began for two more. Before long I saw leaves bob up and down as cuttings struck them. Looking up, up, up near the top of the tree, I saw another squirrel. Still another was located on the other side of the tree in the same manner. I came up with my imaginary automatic shotgun and went "pow, pow, pow." The squirrels didn't move and I didn't give them a second thought.

Then my mind turned to a good buddy, Quay. I would probably be more correct to say a partner in crime, because it really was a crime the way that we had carried on now and then. He was a little smaller than I, but, pound for pound, was meaner, too.

One day Quay and I were sitting side by side on the recitation seat in a geography class. Topics from the textbook had been assigned. Each of us was to stand and tell his or her topic when called upon.

Quay whispered to me that he would preach his topic if I would preach mine. I had no doubt as to what he meant when he said "preach." He was an orphan kid in a way. He was being reared by his grandparents. His grandpa couldn't read or write, but he could preach up a storm. He could hear some preacher preach and six months later he could preach the sermon over himself almost word for word, with a great deal of arm-waving and enthusiasm. I nodded to Quay that if he wanted to preach, I would too.

The lesson that day was on lumbering in the Northwest. The time that had been allotted for us to study our geography, Quay and I spent shooting squirrels. I only went "pow, pow" two or three times, but Quay went "pow, pow, pow" over and over.

He caused me to recall a tall tale that my dad had told

about an old shaggy-eyebrowed mountaineer who shot a box of shotgun shells at a squirrel at close range. To his amazement he didn't kill the squirrel. As it turned out, he wasn't even shooting at a squirrel. He was looking at a louse in his eyebrow.

Two or three students told their topics before getting to Quay. When he was called on, he got up and said:

"Fellow classmates, I'm going to tell you about the most important thing in the whole wide world. That thing is lumbering. When you think of lumbering, you might think of a big black grizzly bear lumbering through the forest. That isn't the lumbering I'm talking about. You might think of a big lumbering ox stumbling around like a pig with the blind staggers. That's not the kind of lumbering I'm talking about. I'm going to make it so simple that anybody can understand what I'm talking about."

By now Quay was holding his book in his left hand and was waving his right hand a great deal. I would have been rather amused, but I was racking my mind about what I was going to say. It didn't help much when I chanced a glance at the teacher, Miss Rachel Raye. She looked like a thundercloud.

Quay continued, "I'm talking about trees. I'm not talking about persimmon sprouts and sassafras bushes. I'm talking about big, big trees. I bet one of these big trees could have a tow sack full of squirrels in it."

All of a sudden the outline of my talk popped into my mind. I relaxed and gave my brother, so to speak, comfort and support by nodding my agreement and understanding to what he was saying. This stopped suddenly when I realized that I was provoking the teacher's wrath against me. She was rapidly and wrongfully coming to the conclusion that I had put poor little Quay, as she thought of him, up to clowning around.

Quay had the attention of the whole school. He said some things that were rather appropriate and reasonable. About every third statement was something funny or ridiculous. He concluded as follows:

"In my mind's eye, I can see two men cutting down a big hickory nut tree. The tree reels around this way and that and can't make up its mind which way it wants to fall. This drives the two woodcutters nuts. They don't know which way to run, so they start running around the tree looking up so they would already have up speed to take off as soon as they find out what way the tree is going to fall. That works alright until one of them gets tired of stepping on the other's heels. He turns to run in the other direction. A great collision takes place. After the tree is down and they come to their senses, they want to know if there has been an earthquake."

The same moment Quay sat down, I was on my feet. In keeping with my word of honor and the code of the hills, I had no other choice. Even though I knew that I was on a collision course, it was full steam ahead in the manner that follows:

"Before going on with my topic, 'Forest to the Mill,' I want to tell an important part that Quay left out. This was always called out just before a tree was about to fall."

Then I threw back my head like a lonely hound dog howling at the moon and at the top of my voice, I yelled, "TIMBER—TIMBER!"

Before I got the second "timber" out, Miss Raye let me have three or four whacks across the shoulder with a great long hickory switch. That pretty well took the talk out of me. The previous amused look on my face changed. Old-timers would have likened my changed facial appearance to that of "a mule eating sawbriars."

Still wishing to add a little more comedy toward carrying out my promise to Quay, I made one more futile effort. In response to the licks with the switch, I wailed, "Lord have mercy on one of your little ones."

That was the straw that broke the camel's back. Miss Raye cut loose on me with that switch and wore it out over me.

When Quay and I had a chance to talk it over, he told me that since I had gotten the worst end of that deal, the first time that he caught Miss Raye in a good mood, he would tell her that it was all his idea. I told him that he had better leave well enough alone. He either took my advice or never caught Miss Raye in a good mood. She never reformed us; she drove us underground.

We had a big Christmas play that year. A stage was made of wooden blocks and boards of rough lumber. Bed sheets were fastened on a smooth wire for curtains.

One day when play practice was about to get under way, I knew Quay was the only one behind the curtain. I was on the opposite side with my shoulder touching the curtain. All at once I got a blow on my shoulder that shook me in my flimsy rubber boots. About that time, Quay opened the curtains from the center and gave me a most pleasant and innocent smile. I returned the smile as though nothing had happened.

A good while later after some practicing had been done, I was again sure Quay was the only one on the rather low stage. The curtains were closed. I saw a bulge in the curtain that had to be Quay's back end. I drew my right knee hard against my stomach. Ever so carefully I brought my foot within a fraction of an inch of the bulge. Then I let go with a thrust that gave the same effect of an earthquake. I heard Quay slam into the chalk board and stagger back, making tremendous noise on the old loose board stage.

Miss Raye rushed up there and threw open the curtains and demanded, "What in the world is going on up here?"

I put on my pleasant innocent look and added, "That is what I want to know. What is going on up here?"

Quay quickly got control of himself and answered, "I caught my toe in the curtain and stumbled all over myself."

I knew he wouldn't turn state's evidence.

In the present once again and realizing that it was time to be on my way to Big Saline, I slowly walked to the door. On passing the wastepaper basket, I saw a faded, red bandana with a big hole in the middle. I took it and on the steps, brushed the dust off my shoes. Thinking that they might need another brush before going into the church house, I hung it on the saddle horn. Before leaving I gave Sampson three or four more pears for waiting patiently.

About a quarter of a mile east of Sadler School, I passed a one-room log cabin that had fallen to ruin. When I was about six years old, I had gone there with my mother to visit a woman who lived there. She was past ninety years old. Mom called her Miss Reader.

Miss Reader told us that one cold night she had let the fire in the fireplace go out. The next morning she didn't have any dry kindling to build a fire. So she went up on the north end of Womble Mountain, which was behind her house, and from the sheltered side of the bluff got an arm load of dry limbs and branches for kindling.

It wasn't long until she had a good fire going. She said that all at once one of the limbs on the hearth started moving. It turned out to be a snake that she had carried in frozen. I asked her if she had killed it. She said that she didn't think it was a bad snake, and it had crawled out through a hole near the fireplace.

A half-mile farther east was Blue Springs Church. Church was no longer being held there. The spring was about three hundred yards south of the church-house. I lay on my stomach and drank from the spring. Sampson drank from the brook that flowed from the spring. Sampson ate of the lush green grass along the brook while I ate the food that Mom had fixed.

The next stop was Big Saline Church, which was three or four miles north of Blue Springs. I had it timed right and arrived about dusk dark. I tied Sampson in a grove in the northeast corner of the churchyard.

People were entering the church just ahead of me. I followed them and was glad not to draw attention to myself. The church was almost full and more people were arriving. It was a warm evening. The windows were open. I chose a seat on the left side about midway of the building, over next to the wall.

Several people sat up front in pews that ran at a right angle to the other pews. This was sometimes referred to as the "Amen corner." This was where Mr. Alfred Baker was seated. There were other familiar faces, but at first glance I didn't see anyone else that I knew.

The song leader called the meeting to order and led the congregation in two lively songs. Then the pastor asked as many as would to please kneel and join in a united prayer. A good many people got down on their knees. Others, including myself, placed their elbows on the back of the pew in front of them and put their head in their hand, which gave an appearance of reverence and cooperation. In my mind I was thankful for the love, mercy, and goodness of God, for a good afternoon, etc.

The praying went on for a long time. I decided to take a little peek out between my fingers and get some idea how the good folks were acting.

I checked on Mr. Baker first. He had completed his praying and had located me. He kept his eyes on me. Since I knew that he was watching, I thought I'd hold my position until a little after the conclusion of the praying to make the best impression possible on him.

About thirty seconds before the praying was over, Mr. Baker lost interest in me, only to become amused at something that was taking place on the other side of the building. Someone else saw it too—I could tell by his smile. When Mr. Baker nodded at whatever it was that was so interesting, then pointed at me, I was bewildered because this time I hadn't done any mischief at all. Even so, I thought it best to show no emotion.

The prayer ended. After about three seconds, I raised my head, and, sure enough, several people were staring straight at Kestner Wallace. Then they looked across the room.

No longer able to stand the suspense, I turned my head. Across the way and about two pews behind me, Sampson had his head and neck through the window up to his shoulders and was chomping on a pear. Over his head was the faded bandana where some prankster had tied it under his throat. His ears were sticking out of the big hole in the middle.

Shocked amazement must have shown on my face. People began laughing the moment that I looked.

The pastor came to the rostrum and raised his hands for silence. I was surprised how well the group responded. By then I was over the initial shock.

The pastor requested, "Will the owner of that animal please take charge of him."

The request was barely out of the preacher's mouth before I was on my feet. I raised my hand to indicate that I would speak if recognized. The preacher gave me the nod.

In a clear pleasant voice I responded, "Reverend Roberts, I will volunteer to hitch that animal out in the grove near where my horse is tied."

He responded, "Thank you, young man."

Before I reached the end of the pew, a light wave of laughter went up. It was led by Mr. Baker. I knew that there were two more waves to come, because Mr. Baker did his musical laughter in series of three. I also knew that my hypocrisy would soon be known by all. By the time that I was halfway to the door, the second wave came forth, joined by others. The laughter reached its climax as I reached the door.

My feeling was that whoever untied Sampson, fastened the bandana around his head, and enticed him with the pears did it in the spirit of a good-natured joke. However, I felt that my showing up had caused enough disturbance for one night. So I quickly led Sampson out to the road and made sure that there was no burr under the saddle. Then I mounted and turned my face homeward.

Sampson wanted to gallop. I didn't want to get home that quickly. After a little negotiating, he settled down to a smooth, easy pace.

Mom had stayed up to read. She wanted a report of the evening's service.

I said, "Mom, what I forget to tell, Mr. Baker will tell you when you see him. He seemed to enjoy the service more than I did. He laughed a great deal. I didn't laugh very much.

"Let me start at the beginning and tell you what happened and then tell you what didn't happen.

"First I went over to Rocky Branch and located some wild grapes. Then I went by the pear trees and ate some pears. Next I stopped at Sadler School and relived some bygone days. As I passed Miss Reader's old house place, I waved in case she was there in spirit. At Blue Springs I ate the good food you gave me to take along.

"Now, for the things that didn't happen.

"They didn't invite me to sit up in the Amen corner. I wasn't asked to lead the singing. They didn't call on me to lead in prayer. I wasn't asked to preach. In fact, taking everything into consideration, I came away a little disappointed."

Mom smiled and replied, "Son, you have had a long day. You had better go to bed. Perhaps in the morning you can recall who preached and what he preached about."

After relaxing in bed a short time, I came to the conclusion that I didn't fare too badly. Some people get excommunicated. Some get kicked out of church. I only got laughed out.

On the Wings of the Morning

Will that Model T Ford ever run again? That was the question I asked myself scores of times between the years of 1928 and 1938. It was bought new by Dad in 1921 from a Ford dealer in Golconda for $540.

I was too young to remember to what extent Dad used the car for the first five years. But judging from the number of times he drove from 1926 to 1928, it was driven very little. Dad was in his mid-fifties when he bought the Model T. He was rather mechanically minded and had a good understanding of how the car operated. However, he had spent too many years using good saddle and buggy horses for transportation to want to get out on the bad country roads and risk car trouble.

Dad kept his Model T in a lean-to he built on the chicken house. It was never called a garage. It was called "the car shed." In 1928, Dad drove the Model T into the car shed and put the key in his secret hiding place, and there the car sat for the next decade. Even though a license cost only eight dollars per year, Dad's comment was that he could put the eight dollars to a better use. For him the Great Depression had already begun.

The car was driven so seldom that it really didn't make very much difference in our life style. In the imagination of my two younger brothers and me, we never stopped driving it.

We would go into the car shed separately or collectively from time to time and grab the crank and spin it a few times and with our mouth we would make a buzzing noise to indicate that the car had started. The car had a different sound depending on which one of us was driving.

Dad referred to his Model T as running like a sewing machine. He commented that some people's cars sounded like a threshing machine compared to his. Depending on our mood, we boys would make the car sound like a sewing machine or a threshing machine or somewhere in between.

Dad put the car on blocks to keep the tires and wheels off the ground. In time the tires dry-rotted anyway. However, having the rear wheels off the ground made it easier to turn the crankshaft with the crank and keep the engine from freezing up.

As we boys grew older, the car served as an avenue by which we could escape reality and enter into a world of fantasy. Now and then I would crank up the Model T and look moon-eyed as I drove with my left hand while my right arm lay on the back of the seat. However, when we boys wanted some real action, we would ride a bull calf, a young mule, or we would all three attempt to ride a western mare, who even refused to be ridden double.

In 1932 I broke my favorite mule, Sampson, to ride. He was an offspring of the above-mentioned mare, who was a combination saddle and work mare. Sampson was sired by a jack owned by Sam DeNeal. Sampson was not just a mule; he was a mule among mules. For the next six years, I lost interest in the Model T Ford and spent my spare time riding the back roads.

I hitchhiked the first two years I went to Harrisburg High School. The distance was twelve miles one way. I will always be grateful to neighbors and friends who gave me rides. As in fishing, I found hitchhiking much better some days than others.

The family very much wanted my two younger brothers to enter high school as freshmen as I started my junior year. Three of us hitching to and from school at the same time was out of the question. Therefore, when school was out in the spring, I hitchhiked to Ypsilanti, Michigan, to get a job and earn enough money to buy a Model A Ford to drive to school that fall.

There was much unemployment in Michigan. I worked two months and saved $80. With a feeling of pride mingled with fear I offered to buy a 1930 Model A Ford for $50 subject to approval. The car looked good and appeared to be well worth the money. But when it failed to start I withdrew my offer. The owner seemed honestly amazed that it didn't start. I was relieved because I just barely knew how to drive and didn't have a driver's license. I got home with $75 of the $80 that I had saved.

Within two or three days, I ordered four new tires and tubes, a battery, and a set of side curtains for the old Model T in the car shed. The order amounted to about $36.

While we waited for the order to come from Montgomery Ward's, my brothers and I got busy with sandpaper and took the rust and old paint off and made the metal shine. We got some fast-drying black paint that was almost as thin as water. When applied with a brush, it spread and left no brush marks. A second coat gave the car a new look.

We had plenty of advice from neighbor boys as to how it should be painted. Some thought it should be painted red. Others thought it should have been painted red, white, and blue.

The dressing had weathered from the car top so that light could be seen through it. I couldn't afford a new top. The advice of the neighbor boys was to take the top off, but I chose to go a different route.

I went to a canebrake and got a number of long slender pipe-cane. We used them to reinforce the top by placing them between the top and the wooden ribs or framework that held the top. This kept the top from sagging when I put a top-dressing on it.

Next we took a lump of road tar about the size of a large head of cabbage and melted it in an old lard can over an open fire. When it was really thin, I painted it on the car top. It went on smoothly, but it didn't dry very well and had a messy appearance.

We took care of that problem by taking some red clay dust and sifting it evenly over the tarred surface. The tar turned the clay dust black and took away the sticky look and feel. After a few days baking and bonding in the sun, I gave it a coat of the same black paint that was used on the car body. Sun nor rain nor snow penetrated that top.

I know that you are wondering how it looked. Well, this might give you some idea. When I wanted to make a good impression, I was at a loss as to whether to drive the Model T or ride Sampson.

The tires, battery, and side curtains came about a week before school was to start. The tires were described as high pressure tires—33 by 3 on the front and 33 by 4 on the rear. They were to carry fifty or more pounds of air pressure. We pumped them up with a hand tire pump. Since we didn't have an air gauge, we gave them the kick test. By the time all three of us boys got through kicking them, they knew that they had been kicked. That was one thing we had down pat.

We installed the curtains. They were neatly strapped up or back until needed. We didn't mind getting wet in the summertime, but we preferred to choose our time and place. So the curtains were along in case of a sudden thunder storm.

We almost dreaded to find out whether or not the Model T would start for fear it wouldn't. The battery didn't come with a charge in it. However, the Model T's didn't have to have a battery to run. They could be started by cranking. Earlier models didn't have starters on them. A magneto produced an electrical current that was created by passing through a set of four coils. In our case the battery was to build up to a full charge from the generator as we drove the car.

Since Model T's had a reputation for breaking arms while being cranked, we brothers decided the best way to start our car was to hitch Sampson to it and trot him around the willow grove in the barn lot. We hoped it would start easily and run quietly so as not to frighten Sampson.

With a long rope we hitched Sampson some distance from the Model T. One of my brothers was to lead Sampson around the circle in a trot. The other brother was to run along with a corn knife, and if things got out of control, he was to cut the rope. My job was to sit behind the wheel, turn on the key, and manipulate starting. My little sister and still smaller brother had their strict orders to perch on the top rail of the lot corral.

The Model T was light and Sampson took it around the circle a couple of times in a lively trot with the key off and the car in neutral. We stopped and took council. Our decision was to make a couple more rounds with our car in gear, but with the key still off. However, this time we decided to sing "She'll Be Coming Around the Mountain When She Comes." That went off as planned. Sampson didn't seem to mind. He probably would have rather heard a donkey braying than listen to our singing, but he was too polite to say so.

Not being able to think of any way to further procrastinate, we decided to go for real. We chose to sing again so that Sampson couldn't hear when the car started. I had the spark level advanced a little too much, and the first thing the Model T did was to backfire loudly. That frightened Sampson and caused him to make a few wild lunges. My brother sprang forth with corn knife drawn and was ready for action when Sampson calmed down. It scared us boys as badly as it did Sampson and put an end to our singing. Almost immediately the Model T started and sounded more like a sewing machine than a threshing machine. The battery soon built up, and we never had to call on Sampson again to help start the car. We got brave and cranked it when we needed to.

The day after Labor Day, we three brothers were up early. In addition to doing the chores, we all three in turn kicked the tires, checked the oil, stuck our fingers in the radiator, pushed down on the spark plug wires, examined the wire running from the magneto, and even checked to see if there was any grease or lint on the armature of the generator.

While we were eating breakfast, my younger sister glued to the top of the windshield a narrow strip of paper on which was professionally printed, "ON THE WINGS OF THE MORNING." I don't know where she got it, but it stayed there until the sun and the rain took it off.

After breakfast, Mom gave each of us boys a lunch in a paper bag. All family members followed us to the Model T. I saw a tear in my mother's eye. To this day, I'm not sure why it was there. She revealed her emotions by a tear or a quiver in her voice. It was either a tear of gratitude that her three sons would have transportation to and from school and wouldn't have to stand three deep with their thumbs up and praying for a ride, or it could have been caused by a fear that the Model T might backfire and roll over and play dead before we got out of the driveway. I'm inclined to believe that it was the former. We left the driveway in as graceful a manner as one could hope for in a car that was made for a former generation.

In those days there were no school buses in use to transport students to school. We had five other students, who fortunately were small, who paid us 10 cents per day to ride with us. That more than paid for the gas at 15 cents per gallon. We rode four in a seat. Crowded? Yes. Complaints? None. We all saw a better day ahead. We had all been examples of the importance of perseverance. Had we not been a rugged breed, we would have died of self-pity and of some kind of complex we couldn't have pronounced, much less spelled.

Preventive maintenance resulted in almost no on-the-road trouble. To increase the speed and gas mileage, which was already excellent, I put a three-in-one ring gear and pinion in the rear end of the Model T. That gave it a top speed of more than fifty miles per hour. However, we did most of our driving just a little over thirty miles per hour.

...

One day on the way home from school, one of my brothers was driving. The curtains were open making for good two-way vision. Two fellows in a 1926 Model T Ford roadster with the top laid back were closing in behind us just south of Pankeyville. They appeared to be tobacco-chewing, cigar-smoking, good-natured hillbillies in their forties. My brother began to increase speed so gradually that they didn't realize a race was about to take place. It wasn't very often that there was another car in our class on the road. I didn't believe in racing, but I wished very much to have been under the wheel. The fellow who was driving the roadster pulled out much sooner than necessary in preparation to go around. I became a little afraid, because we had never opened our car up and held it that way. I knew that that was what my brother had in mind. I had mixed emotions, however.

My brother allowed the roadster to get his front fender even with our rear fender. That seemed to be all the roadster could do. As my brother reached for the gas lever to move on out and leave the roadster behind, I reached under the dash, and out of the coil box, I lifted one of the four coils. That cut our car's efficiency twenty-five percent. Still, with our special gear, about all the roadster could do was to come alongside even with us. That gave our gang a chance to give the men a good razzing for thinking that they could pass us. All they did was hold the roadster wide open and draw their cigars a little farther back in their jaws. The passenger took his cigar out of his mouth long enough to get rid of his chew of tobacco. Then the driver did likewise.

One of our boys yelled, "That will help some but that won't get the job done."

When their rear fender was even with our front fender, I dropped that coil back in place. Our car came alive.

"We showed them our back end," as one of our group expressed it. Almost immediately the race was over and the two Model T operators continued on as though nothing had happened—about thirty miles per hour.

Fortunately for all concerned, our Model T Ford was called on for only two years to make daily trips to high school. The year following my graduation, a school bus was put on the route out our way.

My youngest brother, Gaylord, still remembers his driving the Model T at age seven. He and I had gone to the store. On the way home Gaylord asked if he could drive. He wanted to impress a neighbor who had a large family of children. I told him that he could.

When we were about a quarter of a mile from the neighbor's house, which was on the passenger's side of the car, I climbed over the side and hunkered down out of sight on the running board. I held to the side of the car with one hand only inches from the steering wheel. I watched the front wheel to see that it followed a straight line. The gas lever was set at a lively speed.

The car was open and it appeared obvious that Gaylord was the only one in or near the car. As we passed the house, Gaylord gave the horn a little toot and gave everyone a friendly, exaggerated wave.

When I next saw the neighbor, he remarked with a little barb in his voice, "Don't tell me that you are allowing Gaylord out in that Model T alone."

I laughingly replied, "If you saw him with your own eyes, I don't have to tell you."

Now let me give you my evaluation of the Model T age, as it was thrust upon me out of due season. It more or less falls in line with the time I spent in the Navy during

World War II. It was an experience I wouldn't have wanted to miss—and one I have no desire to repeat.

The needs of the human race are legion. Whether your yearning is for a sincere smile from the right person, or a life or death need for eight million dollars, may the real "WINGS OF THE MORNING" supply that need.

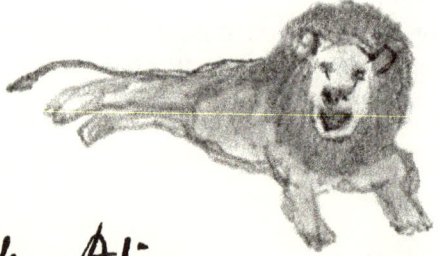

Sakes Alive

Only a day or two following the close of school in 1937, my brother, Byrum, and I—ages 15 and 17 respectively—started hitchhiking to Michigan in the pursuit of summer work. Our first ride took us from in front of our house (twelve miles south of Harrisburg, Illinois) to Carmi, Illinois, a distance of about fifty miles.

No later than 9:00 a.m., we were standing under a roadside shade tree on the north side of Carmi, confident that at any minute, we would be offered another ride. We agreed that we would stand tall, look pleasant and alert, face the traffic, and take turns putting up our thumbs.

To our amazement, we were still waiting under that tree as the sun hung only inches above the western horizon—like a huge golden ball, having no more effect on the eyes than a harvest moon. Before or since that time, thirty minutes would have been a long time to wait for a ride.

Suddenly, and in an almost phantom-like manner, a sleek, black car appeared no more than fifty yards away. In response to our almost robot-like gesture at thumbing, that car came to a tire-squealing stop even with us.

The driver—a middle-aged, medium-sized, well-dressed man—gave us a friendly invitation to "hop in." While making us feel that we were welcome guests, he stated that he was headed to Bellefontaine, Ohio. In turn we told him that we were going to Michigan. Byrum rode in the back seat along with our suitcase, and I rode beside our newly acquired friend. After we had engaged in a little small talk, which set all of us at ease, we buried ourselves in our own thoughts.

By nine o'clock, the sway of the car on the curves, and the gentle vertical motion, like an Indian cradle tied to the bough of a tree, had lulled Byrum to sleep. Aside from an occasional question or comment to appear sociable, I spent most of the ride with thoughts zooming through my mind like the telephone poles fleeting past, keeping sleep far, far away.

It seemed almost impossible to put from my mind how much better it would have been for Byrum and me if our cousins, Kenneth and Donald Wallace, who were a few years older than we were, would have waited two or three days longer to go to Michigan to look for work, so that we could have gone with them.

In our speech of persuasion, we had offered to help out with the gas money for Kenneth's good-running 1930 Chevrolet. With regrets, they felt that they should go on and try to get work ahead of high school and college students who would be seeking employment.

About 2:00 a.m., as that faithful car pressed forward with a pleasant hum and an even speed, the driver announced that the lights in the distance were those of Bellefontaine. The sincere expressions of gratitude from Byrum and me seemed too small for the ride, warmth, and kindness we had received, but it was graciously accepted. We wished each other well and parted ways.

We didn't really see Bellefontaine, but we appeared to be on a by-pass that led on toward Toledo. Floodlights from an all-night station in the distance cast a shadowy light in our direction. The aroma of newly-mowed hay greeted us pleasantly. We raked together a quantity of this freshly cut road grass, carried it to a secluded spot, and bedded down with some under us and some over us. In a short time we were asleep.

Byrum and I aroused from our sleep when only a sliver of the sun could be seen on the eastern horizon, and a cock pheasant was bidding us to rise and shine. We gave each other a good brushing and pulled and jerked at the wrinkles in each other's clothes. A little brook in a cove across a fence in a farmer's field supplied us with water to wash and shave. After dampening and combing our hair, we were pretty well pleased with our appearance.

We crossed the highway to be on the right side for hitchhiking. The driver of the first car, a fancy big convertible, gave us a ride. He was a distinguished-looking man in his late fifties—tall with grayish-black hair. His mind snapped to attention when we told him that we were from Harrisburg, Illinois. Immediately he told us that he was Fred Farcus, and that he had never been in Harrisburg, but he had living there a sister-in-law and a niece, Mary Farcus, whom he hardly knew. His face asked me to tell him more when I told him that Mary Farcus was in my class in high school. I added that she was attractive, tall, and slender with dark brown hair and eyes.

Byrum and I told Mr. Farcus that we were on our way to Michigan in search of summer work. We explained that we had money for eats, but that we were saving bus fare by hitchhiking. In response, he told us that he was on his way to Chicago by way of Toledo, less than a hundred miles away.

We had gone only a short distance when he announced that there was a fine place on our left to get breakfast. We told him that we planned to eat in Toledo and suggested that he go ahead and eat, and if we hadn't gotten a ride with someone with a Michigan license plate, we would be happy to ride on to Toledo with him.

He didn't pay any attention to our suggestion and whipped that big convertible up to a fancy restaurant as he said, "Don't try to fool me. I can still remember when I was in my middle teens and what tasted good for breakfast. That's not all. I'm paying." We went with him into the restaurant and enjoyed a breakfast of country-smoked ham and eggs, toast, orange juice, and milk.

As we continued on our way, the noise of the traffic and the sound of the air as it zoomed past our ears in the open convertible kept us from talking very much. We learned that there was no by-pass at Toledo and that our route led us through the city. Our sojourn with Mr. Farcus ended in the heart of Toledo. We thanked him again for the good breakfast and expressed our appreciation for the delightful ride. Byrum and I were well pleased with ourselves. We had ridden with three different people while traveling more than four hundred miles, and hadn't spent a penny.

We had walked less than a block in the direction of the north edge of Toledo, where we could continue our hitchhiking, when our cousins, Kenneth and Donald, passed going in the opposite direction without seeing us.

I asked Byrum to run and try to catch them at the stoplight. I followed more slowly with our suitcase. He succeeded and got in with them before the light changed. They got a parking place just beyond the light. We were delighted to see each other. Byrum and I sat in the back seat as we compared notes.

Our experience, as we related it to them, was a success story. Their story was one of gloom. There was no work to be found.

I told them that in spite of what they had said, we would go on. Their sympathy seemed to go out to us. They suggested that we go with them to Alton, Illinois, by way of Springfield, and look for work along the way. I hem-hawed as though I didn't know, with a gut feeling that our luck might not hold out if we continued. Byrum gave me a little bump in the ribs with his elbow—his way of saying: "That is too good to turn down."

Kenneth said, "It won't cost you a cent if you want to go with us." I asked, "Byrum, what do you think?" Without hesitation, he said, "Let us go with them."

With that settled, Kenneth and Donald decided we should spend the rest of the day seeing the sights around Toledo and celebrating our most unlikely getting together. That decision made me wonder whether we were looking for work or if we were about to start goofing around. Deciding that it was the latter, I purposed in my heart to make the trip one that we would never forget and to have a rip-snorting good time, too.

After acquiring some feel concerning the size and importance of Toledo, we decided to go to the zoo. There I pulled a boo-boo. A sign said, "Admission ten cents." I said, "Fellows, why should we pay forty cents to go in there when we can go down the side here and scale the fence and see all there is to see and walk out the front gate as if we owned the place?"

Kenneth had two expressions he used often. They were: "Sakes alive!" and "I don't think that is the proper thing to do." He should have been complimented for saying, "Sakes alive!" instead of some curse words. The other statement should have been accepted as intended: "Caution—think before you act." However, over the past few years, people got in the habit of laughing when Kenneth made either of the expressions, regardless of how appropriate they seemed to be. Kenneth didn't seem to mind.

Naturally when Kenneth came out, in response to my proposal, with his "Sakes alive! I don't think that is the proper thing to do," we all laughed—all except him.

All four of us followed the fence until we reached a spot where we didn't see any people inside. Here the metal link fence appeared to be about ten feet high with a top portion made of several strands of barbed wire extending inward. I explained that we could mount the fence, hang down, and drop inside.

After putting our fingers in the fence as high as we could reach, we walked our feet up until they were even with our hands. Then by pulling hand over hand and by clawing and pawing with our feet, we all perched on the barbed wire about the same time, putting on a big front and feeling as guilty as sin. Kenneth broke the silence by saying, "Boys, I don't think this is the proper thing to do."

We laughed at him but our laugh wasn't a belly-shaker. However, it helped relieve the tension. Byrum, Donald, and I hit the ground in rapid succession, with no snags, scratches, or tears. Kenneth, however, had a little more trouble getting turned around in a position to suspend himself for the final drop. He hit the ground only seconds after we did. His descent was less graceful, for a barb caught the leg of his trousers at the crotch and ripped it open all the way to the bottom.

Kenneth came out with a loud "Sakes alive! See what you caused me to do."

Our sympathy for him kept us from laughing. Smiles changed to smirks and froze on our faces when we looked up and saw a full-grown lion, with its attention focused on us. Standing there at a distance of about 30 yards, with nothing between us, it nervously twitched its tail and let out a slight roar.

For a moment, we stood motionless. Kenneth exclaimed, "Sakes alive!" Donald shouted, "Good God Almighty!" I probably whispered, "Lord have mercy." If Byrum said anything, I didn't hear him.

When Kenneth, Donald, and I whipped around and gave that lion a rear view of us, Byrum was already giving us a lesson as to how to negotiate that barbed wire from the inside. His example helped me. At one point, I was ten feet high, with my back parallel to the ground, looking up at the blue, blue sky through those strands of barbed wire. Our only scratches from scrambling out were on our shoes.

With the loose end of his trouser leg stuffed in his hip pocket, Kenneth looked a little far-out until I tied a handkerchief around his trouser leg at the ankle to hold it in place. Fortunately for me, I wasn't blamed for this ill-advised adventure.

Moments later, as we viewed the lion's habitat from a different view, we observed that a few yards inside the fence that we had gone over was the real barrier that held the lion in captivity. It was a deep pit with a wall of steel and concrete too high for the lion to climb. The dirt from the pit had formed an elevation inside that made the lion easily visible.

After we fully realized the reality of our observation, with tongue-in-cheek, I exclaimed, "We really weren't in any danger after all. Suppose we go over that fence again?"

Three pairs of eyes searched my face to see if I was serious. Kenneth must have taken me seriously. He let out an exaggerated "Sakes alive, I wouldn't go over that fence again for all the cattle in Texas!" To assure them that I was joking, I led Byrum and Donald in laughter.

Trying to salve my conscience and to make restitution for what I had put the fellows through, I offered to pay their way to enter the zoo. Their collective response was that they had seen all of the zoo that they wanted to see. So we left Toledo with Donald at the wheel. Byrum and I were in the back seat.

Once out of the city and going toward Springfield, I told Kenneth that I had a needle and a spool of strong, dark thread in the suitcase. I suggested that he take off his trousers and let me sew them up. He passed them back to me to do just that.

The tear was a straight one about a quarter of an inch from the inseam. I turned the trouser leg inside-out and used a running stitch to hold the two raw edges together. Stitched closely and back-stitched, my work passed inspection.

When Kenneth got back in them, he bragged on my work some more. It was then that I told him that if I had known he would like my work that much, I would have ripped the other one open and fixed it the same way.

I had already anticipated his response: "Sakes alive, I wouldn't have wanted you to do that!" By this time, he was in a good mood and laughed with us.

It was agreed that Donald and I would buy food at grocery stores to save money throughout the trip. When we came to a suitable place, Donald and I bought bread, milk, lunchmeat, bananas, and some sweet rolls for our evening meal. As the sun went down, we were eating with pleasure and satisfaction at a roadside table. From things

Kenneth and Donald said, I got the feeling that they had given up on finding work, and if they got back home by the weekend, they would be happy.

As darkness slipped up on us, like a thief in the night, we left the roadside table and got back in the car, with Kenneth behind the wheel and Donald and Byrum riding in the back seat. I stated that my goal would be that of keeping the driver awake. My statement must have set Donald and Byrum's mind at ease, because they were both asleep before we had gone more than fifty miles.

Kenneth suggested that we look for some sleeping rooms. I countered by saying that Donald and Byrum wouldn't sleep any better in a bed, and if he would quietly pull off the road in a good spot, we could sleep the same way. He admitted that he could hardly keep his eyes open and readily went along with my suggestion. Three or four minutes after we had pulled over, Kenneth was asleep. It wasn't until after I had relived and evaluated the happenings of the past two days that I joined them in sleep land.

The early morning sun brought us back to the land of the living. After getting out and stretching our legs and getting the kinks out, we were ready to continue.

For the first several miles, we were too quiet for comfort. I liked it better when we were arguing about something, even if it didn't make too much sense. When Kenneth made two or three attempts at clearing his throat, I knew that things were about to change, and that I would disagree with him regardless of what he said.

When he thought he had our attention, he said, "Fellows, if I were to happen to let any of you drive here in Indiana, and if a state police would happen to stop us for any reason, just say, 'I'm sorry, sir, I'm from out of state.' Then he will probably let us go without saying very much."

I said, "Kenneth, Kenneth, Kenneth. That doesn't make a lick of sense to me. What would being from out of state have to do with doing something wrong?" Then, trying to get some support from the back seat, I asked for their opinions. Byrum said, not too convincingly, that he agreed with Kenneth that we should let it be known that we were from out of state. Donald agreed with me that being from out of state wouldn't make any difference. I commented that there were no winners and no losers—the count was two and two. I said no more. Kenneth gave his rebuttal, mostly repeating what he had already said.

Almost immediately thereafter as we traveled along, we approached some construction work under way. Kenneth was in the process of easing past the workers at a speed of about ten miles per hour when we heard a loud police whistle.

"Sakes alive!" Kenneth exclaimed. "What have I done?" Very calmly, Donald replied, "All you did was run a stop sign." I just barely heard Byrum mischievously say, "I don't think that is the proper thing to do here in Indiana."

As the state police approached, Kenneth's countenance was that of one who was about to receive an award for bravery. He said, "Fellows, just keep quiet. Leave everything to me. I'll take care of this."

The policeman stormed, "Can't you read? Is there something wrong with your eyes?" As he took off his cap and wiped the perspiration from his forehead with the back of his hand, he asked, "Didn't you see that stop sign back there?"

In a clear pleasant voice filled with confidence, Kenneth replied, "Sir, I'm from out of state."

The policeman slapped his forehead a mighty blow with the palm of his hand, turned completely around in a gesture of exasperation, and shouted, "Hell, man, 'STOP' means 'STOP' if it is in England!"

Well, that struck me as hilarious. Still fearing to be seen laughing, I slipped forward out of the seat, sat flat on the floorboard, and held my hand over my mouth while I shook with laughter.

The policeman didn't turn out to be too bad. His act may have been partly for the benefit of the workers nearby. Our being from out of state may have helped. He had us back up past the stop sign, pull up, stop, and then go on. On leaving, we gave him more than he gave us. We gave him a big smile, and he gave us a little grin.

We all agreed that after that close call, we should have a good breakfast at a restaurant. We stopped at exactly the right place.

The lovely, motherly lady who operated the restaurant said that we would probably be her last breakfast customers and that she would give us some extra food at no extra cost. She brought us family-sized bowls of scrambled eggs, fried potatoes, gravy, a pan of biscuits, and a platter of sausage. We had a choice of milk or coffee. We enjoyed this meal to the utmost. It wasn't our only restaurant meal, but it is the only one that stands out.

As we neared Springfield, we decided to visit Lincoln's home. However, the home was closed for repairs. We then decided to say "hello" to Governor Henry Horner. We identified ourselves to his secretary as being from Saline County. The governor was out of town, but we were impressed by the friendliness of the secretary. She showed us the governor's office.

To add one more dimension to my first trip to Springfield, I went to the proper office and made application for a birth certificate, which was mailed to me. We spent the rest of the day and night in the Springfield area—not as guests of the governor—and went on to Alton the next day.

Just before reaching Alton, we decided that we should have all the ice cream that we could eat. We got four quarts for 25 cents per quart. We knew what we wanted, but we didn't know how much. It was more than we could eat.

In Alton we called on an acquaintance, Melton Bramlet, who formerly lived at Herod, Illinois, not far from where we lived. He and his wife were glad to see us and inquired about their friends and relations around Herod. They told us that there was no work. Some of their folks were living with them and looking for work.

Knowing that the Bramlet people were big-hearted, I was sure that they would ask us to stay all night. However, it was plain to see that their home was too small to entertain company. I said, "Fellows, we better be getting along." Melton said, "Don't hurry off. Why don't you stay all night?"

A smile came over Kenneth's face, but before he could accept, I gave Donald a wink and said, "Thanks a lot, Melton, but we already have sleeping rooms for tonight." Kenneth's mouth flew open and his face asked the question, "When did you get sleeping rooms?" I explained to Kenneth that while he was getting gas at the edge of town, Donald and I had spoken for rooms. His response was, "Oh, well, that's okay."

When we got under way, it was moving on toward darkness. Kenneth expressed his surprise that we could have made arrangements for rooms without his knowing it. Donald and Byrum were as much in the dark as Kenneth was, but they kept quiet.

When we got back to the station where we had gotten gas, I had Kenneth drive to the far west edge, just beyond what appeared to be the station property. Here was a good place to park well off the road, with a thicket of bushes just ahead to offer seclusion.

It was then that I confessed to my deception. I explained that with four adults and that many or more children, Melton didn't need any overnight company. When that had time to soak in, I said, "He made us feel good by asking us to stay all night. We did him a favor by declining. Now we are on our own." I went on to explain that across the road from us were many shocks of hay. My plan was for each of us to go across and bring back all we could carry for bedding.

I could tell that Byrum and Donald had bought into my plan; the price was right. Kenneth had reservations. He came out with a healthy "Sakes alive! I don't think this is the proper thing to do."

That was what we needed—a good laugh. Then we all went across the road and soon returned with giant armfuls of soft, fragrant, red-top hay. We all slept well.

On returning home, the sight of Womble Mountain pepped us up. We joyfully expressed to each other what a good time we had had. Byrum thanked Kenneth for a good safe ride. I expressed my thanks by shaking Kenneth's hand and leaving a "five" in it.

Kenneth was surprised. He said, "Sakes alive, you didn't need to do that." I winked at the others and said, "Well, I thought it was the proper thing to do."

My Last Mule Ride

This was a unique Saturday because it marked some first and last experiences for me. It would be the last time in six years that I would see some of my favorite haunts and crannies. It was my first and last time to go courting on a mule.

In the fall of 1940, it became clear to me that if I raised my social status above the poverty level, a term then unknown, I'd have to leave Southern Illinois. My leaving wasn't a first or last for youth of our community. Sad to say, it was the rule rather than the exception. In fact my two previous summers had been spent working in Michigan to provide needed money to complete high school. Now I was leaving for an indefinite time. It would be 1946 before I returned to Southern Illinois after serving in the U.S. Navy during World War II.

Since my younger brothers had no interest in Sampson to ride or to work, I sold him for the handsome sum of $125. I gave the money to my mother. It was understood that the men who bought Sampson wouldn't pick him up until after I was on my way to Michigan early Sunday morning.

I had mixed emotions about leaving family and friends, and I regretted not having a serious girlfriend with whom to correspond while I was gone.

My mind kept going back to Lloyd Marlowe. I didn't know exactly where he lived, but our paths had crossed several times. We knew and held each other in high regard. He was the father of a number of good-looking daughters, most of whom were married.

The word was out from the sons-in-law and others that Mr. Marlowe and his wife, Grace, were truly remarkable people. Mrs. Marlowe was known as an excellent cook. The two of them made young men feel welcome to call at their home, and they were encouraged to eat if it happened to be meal time.

While Mr. Marlowe and I were donating our time for a couple of days helping a poor family rebuild after their home was destroyed by fire, we got to know each other quite well. In my effort to make a good impression on Mr. Marlowe, I really did this poor guy two good day's work.

Along in the afternoon of the second day, I told Mr. Marlowe that I'd seen his daughters around here and there and hadn't been able to understand how a man that looked like him could come up with such good-looking daughters. He wasn't a bad-looking man. I just said it to check his reactions and tolerance. He seemed amused at the comment and told me that his daughters got their good looks from their mother's side of the house.

Since he took that pretty well, I decided to go a step further. I said, "Mr. Marlowe, before you run smack dab out of daughters, I want to speak for one of them."

He shot back, "Young man, my daughters have been much in demand. If you are interested, you better not let any grass grow under your feet. I have only two single girls left. The next to the youngest is engaged."

"Mr. Marlowe, I have two means of transportation. I can call on your daughter on a fine young mule, or I can come rattling along in a 1921 Model T Ford. One is as much out-of-date as the other. Do you have a preference?"

"You are welcome to call regardless of how you get there."

"Mr. Marlowe, I'll call on you sometime, but I'll not embarrass your daughter by showing any interest on my first call. I'll just drop in and inquire about some feeder calves."

"I'll go along with that and show you what cattle I have. Make a point to get there around dinner time."

Early Saturday morning I saddled Sampson and struck out across the country. While never considering myself lost at any time, I was on unfamiliar turf within a couple of hours. Five or six hollows later I crossed the first north-south gravel road and, continuing in the same general direction, crossed other gravel roads.

Along after ten o'clock in the morning, I came across a sparsely wooded area where a new barbed wire fence was being built. Traveling on this ridge was easy, so I followed it for a while before realizing the need to bear to the left. A strong fence prevented me from doing so. I decided to follow the fence which would presumably lead to a farmhouse where I could get further directions to the Marlowe's.

The fence closed in from opposite directions and fastened to the south end of the barn. This left me no other choice except to go through an open hallway of the barn. Being unsure of the head clearance of the hallway, I got off Sampson and led him through. I didn't like the idea of trespassing, but feeling that time was beginning to be precious, I took the chance.

Things didn't look any better on the other side. Where the barn lot gate would be later was fenced across, still leaving me fenced in. Beyond a neat, rather large farmhouse, a lane could be seen that probably led out to the main gravel road. My hope and prayer was that no one would be at home. I could go through the back yard gate, around the house, and out the front yard gate, and on my way unnoticed. However, luck was not with me.

With much nervousness and weakness in the knees, I led Sampson through the gate. I was stepping softly and halfway holding my breath as I weaved my way in and out around the flowers and shrubs. At the front corner of the house, Sampson nearly scared me to death by suddenly letting out a wild bray close to my ear. Had I been on him, he would have cleared the front yard fence, or torn it down trying.

Struggling to control my emotions, I continued as though nothing had happened. Suddenly I was face to face with a surprised and irate woman who was well along in years. She had a garden rake in her hand and appeared angry enough to use it.

She stormed, "Young man, what do you mean tracking through my flowers scaring the living daylights out of me with that long-eared, braying jackass? Do you know you could have caused me to have a heart attack? Who are you and what are you doing here?"

"Ma'am, my sincere apology for trespassing and for Sampson's lack of manners. His dad is a jackass, but his mother is a thoroughbred."

"I'll forgive your mule if you can give me a good reason for being here yourself."

"Suppose we start all over again. Good morning,

Ma'am, I'm Kestner Wallace. I live a little ways north of Thacker's Gap. I'm a good friend of Lloyd Marlowe. I have attempted to cut through the country in order to get to the Marlowe's in time for dinner. Your new fence funneled me into your barn lot. How much farther do I have to go to get to the Marlowe's?"

"Oh, Mr. Wallace, I'm so ashamed of myself. I wish I were more like my brother, Lloyd. You are almost to his house. Follow this lane out to the gravel road and turn right. Brother Lloyd's home is the first house on the left."

"Ma'am, what would you like for me to call you?"

"Lloyd's girls call me 'Aunt Dora.' Most of the young people around here call me 'Aunt Dora,' also."

"I'm not one to be different. I'll call you 'Aunt Dora,' too."

"Kestner, forgive me for being so nosy, but I'd really like to know if you are interested in one of Lloyd's daughters."

"Aunt Dora, I hardly know Mr. Marlowe's family. For all I know, all of his daughters could be married. Would you mind giving me a little update on his daughters?"

"Kestner, if you really do have any interest in Lloyd's youngest daughter, you will have to work fast. She is beginning to get starry-eyed about a fellow who is calling rather often. Between you and me, I'm not too crazy about him."

"Really, Aunt Dora, I'm looking for feeder calves. However, I plan to go into your brother Lloyd's house with both eyes open. In case my eyes and heart zero in on the same target, only the Good Lord knows what will happen. I'll probably forget my name and introduce myself as 'John the Baptist,' the voice of one crying in the wilderness."

Aunt Dora laughed and mischievously confided, "Lloyd told me you might show up over at his house one of these days. I should have known you by his description the minute I laid eyes on you. Now you hurry on up to Lloyd's and start looking at those calves. That will give the womenfolks a chance to start slinging the pots and pans and putting the finishing touches on dinner."

I took Aunt Dora's advice, and in a short time I was at the Marlowe's home. He was in the yard and didn't seem surprised to see me. He gave me a friendly handshake and told me that he would step in the house and get his hat. Then he would take me out and show me his livestock. He was gone long enough to alert the family to set another plate for dinner.

Mr. Marlowe suggested that I remove the saddle from Sampson and put him in a stall where there was plenty of hay in a manger. This I did gladly.

Then I was given a tour of the barn lot. Everything interested me: tractor, cattle, hogs, geese, ducks, etc. It wasn't long until the dinner bell sounded.

Mrs. Marlowe and two daughters were standing in the middle of the living room ready to greet me. Mr. Marlowe made the introduction in a pleasant manner. In turn we all shook hands without my feeling too ill at ease. Both girls were very pleasing to the eye. The younger held the greater attraction for me. I'll call her Kitty.

Kitty had hazel brown hair, blue eyes, and unplucked eyebrows on which no artist could improve. Her perfect teeth accented a lovely smile. Without further belaboring her description, allow me to say, she had a body that went well with the above-described face.

Mrs. Marlowe brought me back to planet Earth by lightly placing her hand on my shoulder and saying, "While you and Lloyd wash, the girls and I will put the finishing touches on dinner. Please excuse us."

To behold the table, it would have been difficult to believe that they weren't expecting company for dinner. Perhaps they were, company that was providentially hindered. There were at least three or four attractively prepared dishes besides a big steaming pan of meat pie in the middle of the table.

Mr. Marlowe asked the blessing on the food and their guest. His prayer was sincere and impressive.

I was glad that Mrs. Marlowe served the meat pie because she gave me a much larger serving than I would have given myself. It was really good, the main ingredient being pork spareribs. Ladies, you should try one sometime.

I was generous with my praise of the dinner, including the pumpkin pie, without overdoing it. Food didn't dominate our table conversation. We touched on various subjects, including my trip the next day to Michigan for an extended time.

Following the meal, Mr. Marlowe, Kitty, and I went into the living room. Mrs. Marlowe and Kitty's sister began to clear the table.

All of a sudden a pick-up truck pulled up out front. Mr. Marlowe said that it was his stock trading buddy and asked to be excused. In a few minutes they drove off together.

Then Kitty and I were all alone. We sat on the davenport somewhat forward, facing each other. We searched each other's face, mind, and soul. I leaned slowly toward her, stopped, and came back to the starting position. She did the same in perfect timing with me. I smiled at her and got a smile in return.

Things were moving in a manner that exceeded my fondest expectations. The most that I had hoped to accomplish was to see if we liked each other and if she would correspond with me when I went to Michigan. I very much hoped that we could put in words the feelings that we apparently felt.

I held out my right hand palm up. She placed her hand in mine. Again we exchanged smiles. I gave her hand a little squeeze. Kitty gave my hand a little squeeze in return. The smiles and the hand caressing put my confidence in good shape.

While still holding Kitty's hand, I took a deep breath. In somewhat of a sigh-like manner I lamented, "Kitty, Kitty, had I known, I would not have stayed away so long."

Kitty showed regret also as she replied, "Kestner, had I known, I might not have become engaged last night."

That remark hit me rather hard. It was so unexpected. I struggled to put on my poker face. Both of our chins twitched ever so slightly. My poker face took over, but my eyes began to burn. Kitty's eyes filled with tears. Our faces expressed nothing, but tears dripped off our chins. Neither of us seemed to be ashamed of them. In a short time we had our tears brushed aside and we were more in control than ever, because the picture was in focus.

"Kitty, do your parents know?"

"Mom and Sister know. We haven't told Dad yet."

"I hope you will tell him when he returns so he will understand why I'm cutting my visit short."

"I will do that. I should have told him before now."

"Kitty, I want to be first among your admirers to wish you happiness. I must go very shortly, because this lucky fellow may come flying in any time. If I'm gone, you won't have to explain my presence."

"Kestner, I heard you tell Dad that you talked to Aunt Dora this morning. She will be watching for you. She is almost dying right now to know how we got along. Are you going back that way?"

"No, I plan to go down the road a ways before cutting across the country."

"Do you have any word for her? She really craves news, gossip, or attention. She is a pain in the neck, but we all love her."

"Kitty, it will be easy for me to remember her as 'Aunt Dora.' I like her, too. You tell her that I jerked my mule around and made him mad, and he took off before I got on him. Tell her that before the mule got up too much speed, I ran up and grabbed him by the tail and that the last time you saw me, I was hitting the ground once in about every thirty feet in a cloud of dust. The third hill over I almost caused a fox hunter to wreck his pick-up truck when I passed him, while hanging on with one hand and with the other high in the air, exclaiming, 'The Lord giveth and the Lord taketh away. Blessed be the name of the Lord.' Kitty, tell Aunt Dora that other fox hunters from the Stonefort Fox Hunter's Association saw me along the first half of the trip home. One saw me leapfrog on Sampson's back when he slowed down near the top of Tom-Dick Hill. Another saw me when I crossed Battle Ford Creek singing 'Back in the Saddle Again.'"

Before I got halfway through the above speech, Kitty was laughing and crying at the same time. My tickle box got turned over, too. An observer would have thought that we were trying to outlaugh the other.

About that time Mrs. Marlowe and Kitty's sister came into the living room. They were happy to see so much merriment in progress and wanted to know what was so funny.

I explained it this way: "If Kitty wishes she can tell you in detail when I'm gone, but for now let us say it is a result of Kitty's announcing to me that she has recently become engaged. I'm sure we are all in agreement that it is better to laugh than cry."

Mrs. Marlowe kidded, "You were laughing too big for me to settle for less than the details."

"Mrs. Marlowe, I have enjoyed the hospitality of your home and the good dinner. Getting to know your daughters has been a delight. But I must go now in order to spend some time with the family before leaving for Michigan early tomorrow morning. It is almost unbelievable that on Monday morning, I'll be reporting for work at the Jig Bushing Company in Pontiac, Michigan."

At the conclusion of the above remarks, I shook hands with Mrs. Marlowe and Sister and would have shaken hands with Kitty, but she took me by the arm and said she would walk with me to the gate. There we said a cheerful goodbye. She continued to stand there while I went and fetched Sampson.

Please understand that I left in the saddle and not holding to Sampson's tail. Kitty and I waved to each other and in so doing we went out of each other's life.

Weaving his way through the countryside, Sampson took us home. It was my last mule ride.

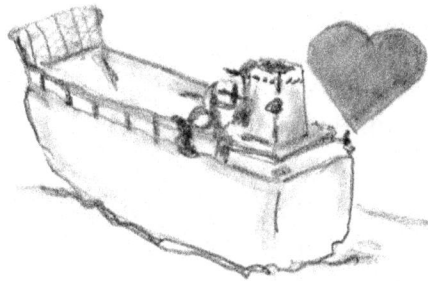

Love, Land, and Sea

While working in a defense plant in Pontiac, Michigan, and after receiving three six-month deferments, I was drafted into the Navy in 1943, along with several others from the Pontiac-Detroit area. Two other groups of about equal size from Chicago and rural Western Kentucky were combined with our group to form a company of about 150 sailors. We were given five weeks of boot camp training at the Great Lakes Naval Base.

Having lived and worked in Michigan for three years, I felt comfortable with the city dudes from Michigan and Chicago. Still, deep inside I was a Southern Illinois hillbilly and felt a kinship with my country cousins from across the Ohio River. I made it known to them that I was a Southern Illinois farm boy. In front of the city guys, from time to time, I would let out a sigh and exclaim, "What I wouldn't give to be back in Detroit!"—in other words saying, "Don't you guys forget that I'm one of you." The best of both worlds fell in my lap.

After five weeks at Great Lakes, our company was sent to Fort Pierce, Florida, for amphibious training,

153

which was explained to us as training for warfare on land and sea. Part of our training was much like that of the Army. It also included firing 50-caliber machine guns at a sleeve or a target pulled by a plane. However, the greatest emphasis was put on the operation of small boats, which included the 50-foot L.C.M. landing craft. The L.C.M.'s cockpit was a steel-plated enclosure on the stern. The entire bow could be lowered with a winch, thus allowing jeeps, half tracks, and servicemen to enter.

Our group of sailors was divided into L.C.M. boat crews of five—two engineers, two deck hands, and a boat operator known as a coxswain. Each member was advised to master each other's operation in case some of the sailors were picked off by sniper fire.

Each boat crew was assigned a floored, screened-in 16-foot by 16-foot tent in which to live. These tents had sides that could be raised or lowered depending on the weather. Our crew was assigned tent C-10. The fifth member of our group went to the hospital, and we lost track of him before we really got acquainted. The four of us decided to be a crew of four. We told those who inquired that the fifth man would be back any day.

Our crew was made up of Arthur Hughes from Chicago, known to us as "Pop"; Vick, a youngster of 17 also from Chicago; Scury, and me, both 22 or 23 years old.

Pop told us that he got carried away with patriotism and insisted that he be allowed to enlist in spite of his age. He was dignified in appearance—tall, slender, balding with graying hair, with a neat moustache and a deep bass voice. He said that he cursed himself for volunteering when he learned shortly thereafter that his request for a commission was denied and that his wife was pregnant.

Vick was short and stocky and as tough as they come. He had bugged his parents until they had signed the papers for him to join the Navy.

Scury was tall, moderately thin, intelligent, and good-looking. His mind was far, far away most of the time. You will learn about me as the tide ebbs and flows.

As a whole, the four of us were light-hearted and happy. However, a great source of discomfort was caused by the mosquitoes and sand gnats attempting to get a meal off of us oftentimes as we were standing barefoot at attention in the burning sand. We also very nearly waged a losing battle at keeping enmity toward officers out of our hearts.

Three or four times per week the entire group would go out in boat crews on L.C.M.'s and make mock invasions, referred to as "hitting the beach." Hitting the beach in the daytime was done under a smoke screen, which was laid down from the air by planes. After a number of these invasions, the C-10 crew began to feel "salty"—you know, downright cocky.

The four of us took pleasure in outwitting the "brass" without getting in trouble. We observed that every third time at sea, those in charge were having us hit the beach just as the tide was going out. They gave reprimands to the boat crews who were left beached by a falling tide and were skeptical of those who almost never had to spend a night on the beach. Their feeling was that the crew had failed to do something that they were required to do. However, improper engine care and lack of alertness were the root causes of most beachings.

We declared it a must that one person devote his attention to the care of the two gray marine diesel engines by changing the sand traps often. The other two were to alternately man a stubborn, hand-operated winch. The coxswain's job was to keep the boat at a right angle with the shore and keep backing it off as the tide dropped. We found that by keeping on our toes with no lost motion, we could fulfill the requirements and get out to sea again and back to spend the rest of the night in our tent.

When it became apparent that we seldom spent a night on the beach eating sea rations, but rather slept in our tent and ate at the chow hall, it was decided that an ensign, a commissioned officer, would go with us on our next round.

He came to our tent. We could tell that he was young and about as arrogant as they come. On his entering our tent, I called out, "Attention." We all stood, but just a shade off of looking sharp. He gave us an evil eye, and we pretended that we were doing the best we knew.

Taking Pop to be the leader or of the highest rank, the officer addressed him while leaving all of us at attention. He said, "Men, I'll be going on your boat on maneuvers tonight. I'll be in charge and as long as you do as you are told, you will get along okay." As he looked up into Pop's face, he asked, "Do you understand?"

Pop's reply shocked me. In a deep and dignified voice that revealed surprise at the question, he replied, "Oh, hell, yes, we understand the chain of command."

That answer shook the officer a little. If I read him correctly, he was thinking: "Five weeks of boot camp wasn't enough for these birds."

The four of us took council and decided not to push our luck any further, but to be on our best behavior. We greeted the officer in a friendly, military manner as he joined us on the dock at the appointed time—about an hour before sundown.

For weeks we had been maneuvering in various formations prior to our hitting the beaches. We would start out in single file. Then we might change to two abreast, four abreast, "V" formation and others. We usually brought up the rear when leaving the jetty to go out to sea.

We decided to impress our officer by having Vick, our youngest and smallest member, take our boat out. Pop climbed up on the bow, which we called the "ramp," to be the flagman. Scury and I cast off bow and stern lines, and as those two powerful diesel engines purred, we positioned ourselves on opposite sides of the cockpit, with the officer directly behind.

He was quick to suggest that we put our boat fourth in the line formation of many boats. By the time we were past the jetty and into the open sea, our officer felt the urge to start giving orders. He asked me to relieve Vick and told Vick to replace Pop on the ramp. It wasn't long until Pop was to replace me in the cockpit. All of this time the entire fleet was gracefully gliding in and out of different formations at a brisk speed. Our officer told Pop that he would take over the control. Pop looked surprised and asked, "Do you think you can manage it?"

The officer sharply asked, "Do you know the meaning of insubordination?"

Pop shot up both hands as if a robber had a gun on him and exclaimed, "Excuse me, Sir." He stepped out of the cockpit and was immediately replaced by the officer. At that time, the entire fleet was abreast, or in one horizontal line.

The first change the officer executed was from abreast to a line formation—one boat behind another. He did well. His aptitude was excellent. The speed kept changing—half speed, below half, and above. Then there was a call for full speed ahead.

When the boats began to slap the water in a wild manner, a call or signal went out for a drastic decrease in speed. Our officer was slow to comprehend the signal and lost precious time. He should have released the throttle, put the engines in neutral for a second, and then shot them in reverse and given them heavy throttle—called "backing her down."

He did manage to release the throttle, but momentum was still rushing us through the water. He looked at Pop, who was in the middle of a "pout," and in a voice that touched me, cried out, "I'm going to hit it! I'm going to hit it! I'm going to hit it!" It was really a desperate call for Pop to take over. Pop's curt answer was: "You're damn right you're going to hit it." And hit it we did. We all hung on. The greatest damage was to our officer's pride.

The boat we had struck was being steered by a young officer, who was beginning to give us a reprimand when he saw his friend and fellow officer in the cockpit of our boat. At that point they "sir"-ed and saluted each other and agreed to share the blame and forget it. The other officer stated that perhaps he had decreased speed too suddenly.

Our officer, now somewhat subdued, said with all the authority in his voice that he could muster, "You men, man this boat in your regular manner, rendezvous at the 12-mile buoy, and hit the beach at the appointed hour." We all responded with a healthy salute and a vibrant "Aye, aye, Sir."

Scury stepped into the cockpit. I relieved Vick on the ramp, and we went single file at a much more pleasant speed to the buoy. Pop appeared to be conversing pleasantly with our officer as we made a few quarter-mile diameter circles around the buoy. Just slightly before dark, we left the rendezvous area to hit the beach with

Pop at the control and Vick back on the ramp. Scury and I stood in the well, or cargo area, ready to dart in the engine room when Pop gave us the word. After a long time, he called out, "Sand trap time," which meant that we were in shallow water, and the sand traps that kept the sand out of the water that cooled the engines would need to be changed. Scury checked the gauges as I began changing the traps. Suddenly we struck shore, scooted a few feet in the sand, and were still.

Scury made a wild dash out to help Vick crank down the ramp and crank it back up again. I was left in the 115° engine room, where I switched the traps back and forth and removed the sand. I knew what was going on topside by the vibration the winch made as the ramp was lowered and the slower grind as it was cranked up. Pop's backing up and pulling forward almost continuously told me that we were still afloat. Finally, the grinding of the winch stopped. As the perspiration dripped off my nose and chin, I wondered whether the winch was jammed.

Pop revved the engines three times lightly. It was his way of telling me that he was about to back away from the shore. I kept changing the traps until clear water was running through them.

When I joined the others around the cockpit, darkness was all around. However, the glow in the heavens on the western horizon guided us until we saw the lights of Fort Pierce. Scury brought the boat in beautifully, and Vick and I made it secure while Pop engaged our officer in small talk.

The officer won us all over by telling us that we had performed admirably. He further stated that if the jam-up was reported, he would take the blame. We gave him our best salute, which he returned and went the extra mile by shaking hands with each of us as he commented that half the crews were spending the night on the beach.

The highlight of returning from an afternoon and half the night at sea was to find mail on the bunk nearest the tent's screen door. My mail was extremely light. I was happy to see the others get letters regularly, even if I didn't get any myself, except for an occasional letter from my mother. My mother was a widow overseeing a scaled-down farm operation, with a son and daughter in high school, and three sons in the service. That didn't leave her much time to write.

One night we returned to our tent after our regular maneuvers. There were three letters on the bunk. Soon three sailors were laughing and sharing quotes from their letters—Pop's from his wife and Vick's and Scury's from their girlfriends.

Then all of a sudden, a giant case of the blues struck me. I felt sad and depressed, wondering, even though I knew better, if anyone cared whether I lived or died.

Yes, I had had far better than average girlfriends in both Illinois and Michigan. However, none of these acquaintances had progressed beyond friendship and all had slipped through my fingers, with no regrets on my part until that hour.

As Pop, Scury, and Vick read their letters and chatted happily, I lay on my bunk flat on my back, with a newspaper over my face as though shading my eyes from a light bulb that hung from the center of the tent. Had I been alone, I probably would have shed a few bitter tears of self-pity.

My valley-of-despair experience subsided enough for me to give this troubling matter some serious thought. As a child I had read and been told that Indians prayed to the

Great White Spirit. Knowledge of a small amount of Indian blood in my veins (from my mother's side) caused me to direct a prayer to the Indian's God once in a while.

The urgency of the case at hand caused me to address the ruling power of the universe as the "Great White Spirit, Lord God of Heaven and earth." My petition was simple and to the point: "Impress on my mind the young lady to whom I should write."

I gave the deity no assistance, such as "What about this one or that one?" I was motionless as time passed. Suddenly, a young lady was very much present. No, not a dream or a vision, but by the miracle of memory and recall, Miss Evelyn Green was in my presence. She held her head high and was both shapely and charming—tall and slender, with dark brown eyes and shoulder-length black hair.

I had seen Evelyn only once, at the home of her Uncle George and Aunt Mertie Green, whom I had met years before in Dudley, Missouri. They were friends and neighbors of my Aunt Rosa Affolder. They invited me to Sunday dinner. While I was there, Evelyn dropped in to say hello. In keeping with the Green's style of Southern hospitality, they insisted that she stay for dinner.

On my part, it was "love at first sight." When I wasn't watching her, I was wanting to. I was impressed with how becoming her clothes were and how striking was her choice of lipstick and nail polish.

During dinner, Evelyn's cousin, who was her own age, made an unkind remark about a fellow worker. Evelyn's response stuck with me. With a smile, she said, "Now I could have talked all day without saying that." I must have thought, "A girl after my own heart—one that doesn't go around blowing her guts." (That was back when my thought process was less refined.)

Evelyn's aunt was a matchmaker and could see a gleam in one's eye from a mile away. No doubt for my benefit, she asked, "Evelyn, do you still work at General Motors and live at 84 Oliver Street?" Evelyn nodded that she did. The street and number stuck in my mind.

At that time, I had already had my three six-month deferments from the draft. Any additional deferments had been denied, but I was allowed to work while a replacement was being trained. My realization that my call to service could come any day caused me to put forth no effort to date Evelyn, even though my call was delayed for weeks.

The day following this pleasant reverie, I wrote Evelyn a letter telling her of the impression that she had made on me—one that would be with me always. The last part of the letter said, "It will make me happy to get an answer to this letter, but if you don't feel so inclined, please accept it as a compliment to your charm and attractiveness."

In less than a week after mailing the letter to Evelyn, our group was transported to Camp Shoemaker in California, the first step of a long journey to serve the war effort in the South Pacific. After spending three weeks in California, it took us ten days by ship to get to Hawaii. We spent another three or four weeks there before shipping on to our final destination, Saipan, an island about five miles wide and twelve miles long, with a mountain-like terrain, intense sunshine, high humidity, frequent rains, and much vegetation.

In addition to being a B-29 bomber base, Saipan was a relay supply station. Supplies were unloaded from large supply ships with booms into the L.C.M.'s and transferred to trucks, then stored on land, often in the hills, and returned as needed to other ships. The L.C.M. crews were kept busy as ants going in and out of the harbor. However, at times we would catch up in our supply shuttling and have some free time. From Fort Pierce to Saipan, I thought of Evelyn often. There was a mail tie-up. Since no one was getting mail, I didn't feel alarmed.

We braved the heat of the sun and the drenching rain that could occur suddenly day or night. People who became overwhelmed in some degree by the rigors of the duty and the climate were said to be "rock happy." My case of "rock happiness" was lighter than that of other people because of my staying extremely busy in my spare time. (It was only after I returned home that I realized I had not escaped unscathed.)

Fortunately, there on Saipan, I found suitable material to make a small bench-type table that could serve as a desk from which to write while sitting on the side of my bunk. It was also strong enough to serve as a bench on which fellows could sit while I cut their hair. Barbering was a hobby that I had taken up in Fort Pierce.

Necklace-making, a second hobby, was taught to me by a sailor who had learned firsthand from a native of Hawaii. He and I dived for shells at low tide in neck-deep water. We chose only live shells, since they were more attractive. Once out of water, life ceased and our find of shells took on a most unpleasant odor.

The first step in the cleaning process was to bury the shells in the ground in a thicket of undergrowth and cover them with sticks and leaves. It took about two weeks for the ants to find them and really clean them out. A final cleaning was made with a toothbrush and paste. The necklaces were linked together with stainless steel wire and made secure with cotton and airplane glue.

One day when I went to retrieve a batch of shells that had been hidden deeper in the wilds than usual,

I picked up an unusual odor. My first impression was that it was a fallen human being. I was relieved to find a dead four- or five-foot crocodile, at least one foot in diameter at its center.

My interest in the crocodile suddenly left me when I looked to my left and saw a human skull, which had been bleaching in the sun for quite some time. I returned to the barracks with my shells and the skull. I placed the skull on my three-foot high plywood locker. The most often-asked question from my buddies and those who came for haircuts was, "What in the hell are you doing with that skull?"

I might have immediately returned the skull to where I found it had it not been for the fact that a letter from Evelyn arrived that same day. Somehow the thought seeped into my mind that the skull had brought me good luck and that I should keep it.

Someone answering mail call in the Harbormaster's office claimed the letter and placed it on my bench-table. The gracefulness of the writing on the envelope caused me to feel that it was from Evelyn even before I saw her name. The feeling that I had experienced in Michigan and in Fort Pierce returned as I read the return address—Evelyn Green, West Main Street, East Prairie, Missouri. The letter had been months in reaching me—Fort Pierce, California, Hawaii, and finally, to Saipan.

I opened the letter with unsteady hands while I wondered whether the contents would justify my continuing desire to idolize her. I was not disappointed. Her greeting pleased me. She explained that my letter had gone to Michigan after she had returned to East Prairie to care for her ailing grandmother, who had raised her. The landlady had been slow in forwarding my letter. She thanked me for my letter and expressed pleasure in receiving it. In fact, she said all the right things, and following her closing, she placed the imprint of her beautiful red lips.

Evelyn's letters were all equally inspiring, but the space between letters was almost unbearably long—even to the point of creating anxiety. My salvation was a busy schedule: doing my share with my boat crew, barbering, making and selling necklaces, and buying Fiji cat's-eye rings from Fijians and selling them at a modest profit.

Finally the war with Japan ended. Servicemen were sent home from the South Pacific on a point system: points for time served, age, dependents, whether or not one volunteered, and others. I was among those with few points who continued on Saipan through 1945.

My last night to spend on Saipan finally arrived. Only a few of us remained. Near midnight, as I pondered my past, present, and future, a moonbeam made the skull on my table very visible. I had thought of taking it home as a conversation piece and then decided against it. My real regret was that whoever it belonged to wasn't taking it home. I even felt sentimental about my writing desk.

I arose, dressed, and eased out the back entrance with a flashlight in one hand and the skull in the other. I went directly to the hole in which my last batch of shells had been buried. I gently placed the skull in the hole. Just before covering it with a flat rock and some leaves, half in jest I addressed both the skull and the Great White Spirit, saying, "Speak unto this numbskull some words of wisdom."

In a strong and impressive manner, three words rushed on the scene. Those words helped me stay the course as the romance between Evelyn and me traveled on sometimes stormy seas over the next few years.

However, the ending couldn't have been better. We were married August 22, 1950, and our marital happiness has increased each year.

And this old sailor commends those three words to all:

"Follow Your Heart."

Life or Death
in a Banana Grove

T he entire year of 1945 I spent on Saipan, an island of forty-seven rough and hilly square miles in the West Pacific. While there I had to decide whether or not to kill a man.

When I arrived with one hundred forty-nine other amphibious sailors, Saipan was considered relatively safe; even so, we were asked to stay out of the hills, which served as hiding places for hundreds of dangerous Japanese. Although our group was sent there to service the ships that continually came and went, each of us, as a matter of policy, was required to do guard duty periodically.

I had been on Saipan about a month when my turn came up. My orders were to go into the hills about a half-mile and report anything that looked like an organized group planning an attack. I was told to keep my eyes open and not to take chances.

I took a carbine, which is a short rifle, and went into a forest-covered area behind our barracks. There was not a cloud to be seen anywhere. Just before I crossed into the area that was thought to be dangerous, I took a last look at the harbor, which was about a mile away. From where I stood, approximately five hundred feet above sea level, the view was unforgettable: cloudless blue sky above, and below, an ocean, equally blue.

After slipping as quietly as possible for fifty yards into an area thickly covered with vegetation, I stopped and stood motionless for several minutes. When my feet began to tingle from standing still so long, I began to look for a place of seclusion, where I could sit and watch. Seventy-five yards ahead, and somewhat to my left, was a wild banana grove covering an area of perhaps one thousand square feet. I approached it slowly and carefully. Once in the grove, I was pleasantly surprised to find a large supply of ripe bananas, which I wasted no time in sampling. Peeled, they were only about the size of a man's thumb, but their flavor was superior to any that I had ever tasted. By the time I had finished three or four, it suddenly occurred to me that, judging from the appearance of the well-beaten ground, others were using that grove also. Somehow I had the feeling that I was not safe.

On the north of the grove a large tree had broken in its fall, leaving a space of five or six inches between the two parts of the trunk. Hiding in the undergrowth just beyond the fallen tree, I snapped off enough twigs to make it possible to see out in all directions. After applying a heavy application of mosquito repellent, I relaxed a little and began to think that maybe guard duty was not too bad after all.

When I had been in my hiding place about an hour, I got a glimpse of a Japanese coming down the hill from the east. He moved along quietly but with more speed and less caution than I had used when approaching from the other side. He wore a marine uniform, carried an American carbine, and appeared to be an experienced, hardened soldier. My first impulse was to shoot him on the spot. Then I decided to wait to see whether or not he was alone. As he entered the grove, I stretched out on my stomach just beyond the fallen tree and took a "bead" on the man through the broken tree trunk.

My heart was beating very, very fast. My breathing was fast and shallow. I thought to myself, this will be the first human being that I have ever killed. I could not help wondering how many of our boys he had killed. Under the same circumstances I felt sure he would have killed me. For fear he would hear me, I held my breath, took the carbine off safety, then closed my left eye for a finer "bead." I took the play out of the trigger. By this time the Japanese was snatching bananas with all his might. I eased my finger off the trigger with a feeling that it would be too bad to kill a fellow while he was so hungry.

For the next twenty minutes while he ate bananas and filled a little satchel to take with him, I wondered what to do. Dozens of thoughts rushed through my mind. Thoughts of self-preservation were high on the list. Among my other thoughts were: What does the line of duty require of me? Will I be breaking the great commandment that says, "Thou shall not kill"? Are those bananas for a hungry child hidden in a cave high in the hills? Does he have a mother, a wife, or a sweetheart back on the mainland yearning for his return?

Just as he got up to leave, I made the decision, and to this day have never regretted it. Watching him walk out of sight, I exclaimed "Thank God!" and burst into tears.

George, Fred, and Fannie

Just home from the Navy in 1946, I met George, who was in his fifties. I was 26. George was living a single life pretty much to himself, but was striving to get back in the mainstream of society. We saw each other here and there and at public gatherings. We were somewhat loners. He was more lonely than I.

Our friendship started out gradually—just a nod at first, later a spoken greeting. By and by, we were pumping each other's hand and joking like long-lost friends.

I learned from others that George had an outstanding reputation as a story teller. I asked a trusted friend if his stories were true. His reply was, "I don't know. You will have to listen to him and decide for yourself."

It became evident that one-on-one talks with George would be most effective. During one such talk, George told me in a low confidential tone that during prohibition, he had had the name of making the best corn whiskey anywhere.

I asked, "George, how did you get rid of it after you made it?"

"I didn't take part in the selling. The guy I worked

for had a man from St. Louis pick up what we had made twice a month."

"I suppose you got well paid for your time and the risk you took?"

"Well, Kess, old buddy, I'll put it this way. It was lighter work and safer than working in the spar mines. My boss paid me a dollar a day and a gallon of whiskey every two weeks. I bootlegged my gallon. I would add a little vanilla and sugar to some and recommend it highly as cough syrup and a heart regulator."

I inquired, "What made your whiskey better than others' whiskey?"

"I was careful what went in it, used good, cold spring water and the best corn money could buy."

"Why did you stop making whiskey?"

"Kess, there were two reasons. I had about a halfway change of heart that caused me to live inside the law, and my back got better so I could go back to work at the mines."

Some time later around Halloween, I asked George if he had ever seen a ghost. He answered, "Yes and no. A time or two I saw something I couldn't explain."

"Like what?"

"One night I went to church in an out-of-the-way location. I was taking a shortcut home following a foot or bridle path. Suddenly a man appeared in the path about 10 feet in front of me. The moonlight made him plainly visible. I asked him to identify himself or step aside so that I could pass. He did neither. I decided to bluff him into action. I took out a .38 automatic, which I never left home without. I said, 'This is a warning shot.' I shot in the air. So help me God, that man vanished—disappeared and was gone before my eyes without a sound!"

"Did that scare you?"

"Yes, more than if he had pulled a gun on me. How did I know he wouldn't slip up from behind and clobber me? I sat down for a few minutes and let my heart slow down. Eventually I was able to get up and make my way home."

I said, "George, let me clear up this mystery for you. You must have drunk a little too much of your famous cough syrup after you left the church."

George assured me that that wasn't the case. He told me that he had sworn off booze in his younger days after the time he had had a snootful and gotten an underage girl in trouble. That roll in the hay had cost him eleven years in prison. Worst of all, it had wrecked his happy marriage. However, his wife had forgiven him and longed for his return. Unfortunately, she had died while he was in prison. He truly loved her dearly.

I asked George about prison life. He talked about it freely. I questioned, "What stands out most in your mind?"

"Kess, it all stands out as if it were yesterday. After I became a trustee, I had freedom others didn't have."

"How was that?"

"I had light work that left me time to roam around and find good things to eat. I organized baseball teams and set up boxing matches."

"Did you take part?"

"You bet your life I took part! I managed a ball team that never lost a game."

"How did you do at boxing?"

"I could whip anyone in my weight range. I nearly got killed by challenging a big ox of a fellow that I knew could whip me, but I thought it would prove that I wasn't afraid of anyone."

"And how did that turn out?"

"It was the biggest mistake I ever made. I made a deal with this big brute that he wouldn't lower the boom on me until the fourth round. I bribed him with a dollar and a pack of cigarettes. I made a ten-dollar bet with another fellow, who always seemed to have money, that I could stand up to this guy for three rounds."

"I wish I could have seen that fight!"

"The first three rounds would have been something to see. I realized if I made a good showing for the large number on onlookers, I'd have to be lightning quick. From the jump start, I dashed out shadow-punching, wheeling, and twisting. Now and then I'd place a pretty good punch that made me look good. Each attempt to make myself look good made murder and 'hell-fire' show in the fellow's face. If the Devil looks that bad, I hope I never see him."

"How did you feel while you waited for the 4th round to begin?"

"I felt it was my last day alive on earth. I prayed that a heart attack would take me to the Great Beyond. I felt too weak to stand."

"Come on, George, before I have a heart attack, tell me what happened."

"The last few seconds before the bell, I began to say, 'Lightning, lightning, lightning.' It helped some, but not much. I dashed out as before. This big brute just stood there. He put me in the mind of a cat that had a mouse in his spell while trying to decide when and how to end the game.

"Without closing his fists, he pecked me on one side of the head and then on the other. Then it seemed that all hell broke loose. If I didn't know better, I'd have thought he had an extra pair of hands landing rapid, repetitive pecks on me like a redheaded woodpecker on a hollow tree. I longed for a good hard punch to my jaw so I could fake a knockout. It came like lightning. That was as near death as I'll be until I witness the real thing. I spent the night in the prison hospital, but I was OK the next morning.

"When that big guy got a chance, he told me that he had heard about my ten-dollar bet. He further said that I should give it to him because he allowed me to stay in the ring for three rounds. I told him if he got that ten dollars, he would have to fight me for it. He told me what he would knock out of me if I didn't give it to him. In prison a lot more talk than knocking goes on. We agreed to split the ten. He became my best friend the rest of my prison stay."

From time to time during our conversations, George dropped the hint that he would like to get married. I told George that we were in the same boat. I was looking, too. I told him that what we needed to do was to open our eyes a little wider, move in larger circles, and stop being so pop-eyed particular. That didn't cheer him up much. He commented that he was already running around like a crazy man.

George told me that he wanted a woman that was a good cook. I asked, "How can you know if a woman is a good cook?"

"That's easy. I go to all of the big dinners and home-comings and take notice what dishes the different women bring."

"That's good, George. But when you spot a good cook, you need to check out their husbands to see if they are on their last leg."

"Don't think for a minute I haven't thought of that."

Interrupting his thoughts, I said, "George, we are on a tangent here about women and our lonely, bleeding hearts. Since it's almost Halloween, what I want out of you is a ghost story."

"Kess, instead of a ghost story, allow me to relate to you a most unusual experience—not exactly a ghost story, but perhaps a cousin to one. This is a story that has never yet been told. If I tell it to you, will you promise not to tell it to anyone until after I'm dead and gone?"

"Yes, George, I promise. Blaze away on your story."

"This story involves a couple in their early sixties down from Chicago. They moved into an old, well-built abandoned house a half-mile off a rough, almost impass-able road. It was likely on government land. I was the first and maybe the only one to call on them. They were well settled in when I learned about them.

"They were making use of a fenced-in chicken lot in which they kept a small flock of fryer-sized chickens and a large, white milk goat. Near the path leading from the chicken pen to the house lay a huge dog. He appeared to be too lazy to scratch if he were full of fleas. He opened one eye, looked at me, and went back to sleep. I went on the north side of the house, passing a window that showed no sign of life. From the porch, I knocked on what appeared to be the front door, which faced nothing except a huge oak tree. An uneasy feeling came over me as I waited for my knock to be answered.

"The door opened and shoulder to shoulder stood a very surprised couple. I tried to put on a disarming smile. It worked. They smiled in return and asked me to come in. Once inside, the two of them got control of themselves and expressed pleasure to see me. But that didn't expel the eerie feeling that something was wrong.

"I told them that my name was George. In turn they told me that they were Fred and Fannie. They were free to tell me how well they liked living in the wilderness.

They said the cawing of the crows and the singing of songbirds by day and the owls, whippoorwills, and other sounds of the night were a healing balm for their minds. I listened with interest as they told me of life in the fast lane in Chicago.

"I called on them about 2:00 p.m. The afternoon zipped by. With a sudden urgency, Fannie exclaimed, 'I must be about preparing an evening meal.'

"I protested, 'Not for me. I must be on my way.' With an excited elevation in her voice, she exclaimed, 'Not on your life, Mr. George—it will do me a pleasure to fix you a quick meal. There are almost enough good leftovers from dinner. In almost no time, I can slay a chicken and have it ready for the skillet.'

"Suddenly she was a changed woman. She expressed wild determination as she jerked open a dresser drawer and whipped out a wicked-looking, long-bladed knife and dashed out the door. I was sitting near the window facing the chicken pen. She made a wild gesture with the knife as she wheeled around several times, jabbing in every direction. It made cold chills run all over me.

"She opened the gate to the chicken pen. All the chickens appeared to be pets. She very gently picked up a young, fat Rhode Island Red rooster. She held it by the feet under her arm and caressed it gently as though it were her favorite of the flock. Then she let out a horrible scream, the kind that would wake up the dead. She threw that young rooster high in the air. Faster than a cowboy could draw and shoot, Fannie seized that wicked knife and lobbed off the chicken's head in mid-air. She then went beside herself with glee.

"I looked over at Fred. He knew by my startled expression what I had seen. Fred said, 'Now that you know, I might as well tell you that she is a crazy woman. These spells come and go. Now she may be fine for awhile. But the doctors can't do anything for her. She has done better down here than anywhere else. She is an attractive woman and made me a good wife until this curse came on her. I love her too much to do anything except take care of her the best I can. I would like to have your promise that you will tell no one what you have seen and heard.'

"I assured him, 'My lips are sealed. And I'm a man of my word.'

"In almost no time, Fannie was in the house with a dressed chicken. She must have skinned it, because she didn't have time to pluck it. It had been washed in the spring and was ready to be cut up and put in the skillet.

"While Fannie fried the chicken, Fred told me what he thought was her trouble. With a look of despair, he said, 'I fear that she is possessed by a demon or devil. That is many times worse than death. Demon possession is mentioned in the Bible, you know.'

"Before we could further discuss demon possession, Fannie eased in and most graciously invited us to the table. She assured me that getting the meal was no trouble. She said that she had had a feeling that morning that they would have company, so she had potatoes, green beans, and cornbread already cooked and in the warming compartment of the wood range. She had each of us a cold glass of goat's milk from the spring.

"I was glad that she seated me with my back to the wall. That long knife was still on my mind. I nearly swallowed my Adam's apple when Fannie spoke with a touch of harshness in her voice, 'Brother George, will you return thanks?'

"I bowed my head and placed my left hand to my forehead with my fingers spread. I remembered that the Bible says, 'Watch as well as pray.'

"With more fervor than I felt, I prayed, 'Thank you, Lord, for this day, for this home, and for this food. Amen.'

"The prayer, feeble as it was, set the tone for an enjoyable meal. Soon thereafter, I made my departure with a warm invitation to come again soon.

"Being on my way home gave me a burst of energy, making me feel years younger. I jogged most of the way home. My dog heard me coming and came to meet me. I was pleased he wasn't like their dog, Bruno.

"Over the next three weeks, Fred and Fannie were on my mind. Early one morning, I went over to check on them. By walking fast and jogging, I got to their home around 10:00 a.m. I knocked and heard a weak voice say, 'Come in.'

"I went in and there sat Fred looking worse than death. I exclaimed, 'Fred, what is wrong with you? Are you sick?'

"He replied, 'This is the saddest day of my life.' He nodded for me to look in the large bedroom. One glance from the door told me that Fannie was dead in bed, lying with her hands folded. She had a peaceful look on her face. Bruno lay on the floor nearby.

"My first reaction was that of relief. The demons couldn't torment her any more. That feeling of relief was short-lived, however. I took a step toward the bed as a matter of respect. That formerly dead-head dog took a 10-foot leap and landed at my feet in a crouched position and showed his wolf-like fangs.

"It crossed my mind that if, in life, Fannie had had an evil spirit, when she died, it may have gone into Bruno, making him more like an angry wolf than a dog.

"I slowly backed up and went over to sit by Fred. I was too weak to stand. He was too deep in thought to notice how the dog's behavior had affected me. We sat for a long time without saying a word.

"Finally, Fred became himself again. He explained that Fannie had complained of a sharp chest pain and in no time she was gone.

"Fred asked me if I would spend the day with him and help him bury Fannie in the morning. I told him I would and weakly asked if it would be legal to bury her without an inquest and the proper legal procedure. He said to do so would open an unnecessary can of worms. I pretended to go along with the idea and hoped that the morrow would make known the right thing to do.

"Fred and I talked away the afternoon in a long-faced manner. We ate some leftovers and drank some goat's milk about dark.

"Later as Fred and I sat in the living room, Bruno came through showing his teeth with a deep growl in his throat. Fred said with concern in his voice, 'George, I'm beginning to be fearful of Bruno. He started acting different right after Fannie died.'

"Not long after dark, Bruno nearly tore down the screen door getting out. Almost immediately he barked 'treed' at the large tree at the outer edge of the yard.

"Fred, with alarm in his voice, asked, 'What could he be barking at? He doesn't pay any attention to coons or squirrels.'

"The moon was beginning to come up in the east. I told Fred that I would sit in one of the big chairs on the porch and watch the crown of the big oak for any movement. In turn, he said that he would sit with Fannie for a while and then join me.

"After more than an hour, I began to fear that something had happened to Fred. Before I could go in to check, Bruno started barking again. Then for a while, he just sat and looked up the tree. I saw on a big limb about fifty feet up the tree an object big enough to be a huge bobcat or a small mountain lion. The color changed from dark to light. I feared it might be something from the spirit world.

"As I sat there, I wondered what durn-fool thing would happen next. In the past, I had been thrown off a barge on the way to New Orleans, and had nearly gotten killed in prison and in the mines. Now I thought, 'Lord, what else could possibly happen?'

"I placed my chair so I could watch the door and the tree, too. I opened the middle button of my shirt and placed my hand firmly on the butt of my pistol. The door opened quietly and Fred stepped out holding that long knife. He stood there for what seemed like a long time, with his eyes on me. Then he said, 'I brought this along in case we need it.' I said, 'Good thinking, Fred.'

"Fred said, 'I got Fannie ready for burial in the morning. I put a perfumed towel around her head and wrapped her in a new sheet and her favorite blanket. Then I tied her firmly in an extra oilcloth tablecloth.'

"I said, 'Fred, that should get the job done.' Fred seemed distracted and puzzled. When I asked him what he was thinking about, he explained, 'Something strange happened while I was preparing Fannie's body. I didn't see anything, but just as I finished, somebody or something brushed past me.' Dropping heavily into the chair, he confessed, 'I just barely had enough strength to make it out the door.'

"I asked Fred, 'What should we do about what is in the tree?' He said, 'I don't know. What would you do, George?'

"I replied, 'If they'll leave me alone, I'll leave them alone.' Fred said, 'That goes for me, too.'

"That being settled, we pretended to sleep, but neither of us did. At daybreak, we yawned, stretched, and pretended to be waking up.

"Fred asked, 'George, are you up to it?' I replied, 'I am.'

"Fred said, 'Let's go out and open the grave. It is already dug.' Seeing my look, he quickly explained, 'I dug it for a spring. Water failed to come in, so it is more a grave than a spring.'

"We went out under the oak tree. Fred removed small logs and brush and soon had a grave-sized gaping hole.

"We went into the house. Fred gently took the head end, and I took the feet end. We moved slowly to the grave. Fred had a rope fastened at head and foot to lower Fannie carefully into the grave. We pitched the rope in, also. I moved to the side of the grave breathing hard from exertion. In the process, I got careless and allowed Fred to stand directly behind me. Bruno began to take wild, haphazard laps around the grave. At first his laps were large, but then he closed in and came directly toward me. My hand was on my pistol. Bruno's intention was to clear the grave and knock me flat. I shot him in mid-air. Who would believe that he fell into the grave?

"I wheeled around to see what Fred thought of what happened. There he stood with his knife drawn and murder in his eyes. He tried to smile and said, 'George, if you hadn't gotten him, I would have.' I said in return, 'Bruno didn't have a chance, did he?'

"I knew Fred thought that he had pulled that off slick. But he didn't know how to let well enough alone.

"Afterwards, I closed the grave and covered it with brush, logs, and leaves until it bore no appearance of a grave. Just as I finished, I heard the most blood-curdling sound I had ever heard in the tree. I saw nothing, but heard the sound of wings going toward the tall timber.

"I sat alone for the longest time, lamenting what I had been forced to do, feeling that I had broken one of the commandments. Eventually I thanked God that I was still alive and slowly made my way home."

George asked softly, "What do you think of that, Kess?"

"George, you leave me speechless. For that story, I owe you a big dinner or an introduction to a good-looking woman."

George grinned, "Oh, gee, golly-durn—thank you, Kess; I'll take both."

Sister Diller and Me

C hurch going in the late 1920s and 1930s was very much in style. My father was a member of the Herod Springs Missionary Baptist Church. He attended revivals and associational services at Blue Springs, Bethel on Eagle Creek, and Macedonia at Mitchellsville, all of which were said to be of like faith and doctrine.

My mother's church preference was the Church of God, with headquarters at Anderson, Indiana, but she didn't hesitate to attend church services anywhere she had an opportunity.

A great deal of our early Sunday School and church-going was at Rudement Social Brethren Church. Our means of conveyance was a buggy driven by my mother and pulled by our black mare, Maude.

Mom in her buggy scene was somewhat like the "old woman who lived in a shoe," or at least it appeared so when she and five children ranging from one or two to nine or ten years of age crammed in or on a one-seated buggy. This only lasted until around 1930, when the traffic on Route 34 increased and caused it to appear too dangerous to be on the road with a buggy.

During a great deal of the 1930s, Mom stayed at home and cared for my ailing father and the younger children. The older children, including myself, walked with other young people and attended evening services at Rudement, Mitchellsville, Herod, and Spring Valley. At revival time, it made little difference to us young people whether the church was Baptist or Social Brethren. We turned out in large numbers for the religious and social aspects.

From the mid-30s on, most families had a good car, or at least some kind of an old car. Church-going continued while dating among young couples stepped up to a livelier pace.

In 1940, with mixed emotions, I left this never-to-be-forgotten era, as did so many other young men, to do factory work in Michigan. While there, Uncle Sam extended an invitation to serve in the U.S. Navy as an amphibious sailor. During this time, my father died. It was my good fortune in 1946 to return to the home, hills, and haunts of my childhood.

On returning home, I bought a good used car and fully intended to start friendshipping and fellowshipping at the above-mentioned churches, but instead complied with Mom's wish to take her to the First Church of God on Charleston Street in Harrisburg. She had been attending there when she had an opportunity.

I was extremely well received by the fine people at the Church of God. The good-looking, single girls attending there caused me to think that I might take Mom up there once in a while, or even twice in a while. However, my girlfriend, Evelyn, had already captured my heart through our correspondence during the war years, even though it was many moons before wedding bells finally rang (in 1950).

On the third Sunday I attended, it was time to elect Sunday school teachers and a superintendent for the following year. My name was placed in nomination for Sunday school superintendent along with a couple of other people. Being new at the church, I was so sure of not being chosen that I didn't decline the nomination.

When the votes were counted, I was the newly-elected superintendent and started acting in that capacity the following Sunday. The confidence the church put in me wasn't taken lightly. Although I tried to serve with as much dignity and dedication as I could muster, I still feared if weighed in the balance, I would have been found wanting.

Attending the church at that time was a little old lady who was only slightly more than five feet tall and who appeared to be about eighty-five years old. We will call her Sister Diller (not her real name). That had been her church home for many years. The church accepted her as she was, and to my knowledge, didn't try to change her.

Sister Diller had the "old time religion" all the way down to her toes. She was far more emotional than any-one else in the church. Her children, who were then past middle-age, refused to go to church, so I've been told, because her shouting had a tendency to embarrass them. Please, don't get me wrong. I'm not opposed to shouting in church. Nevertheless, I thought she overdid it. Lively singing or inspirational preaching would turn her on, and she would walk around slightly springing up and down with both hands in the air. Her expressions of elation clashed harshly with the singing or the preaching. However, looking back on the positive side, she helped keep the congregation awake, boosted the ego of visiting ministers, and caused me to realize that I had a case of war nerves.

At a Sunday evening service, a few of us decided to tape a certain quartet. As we expected, we also taped Sister Diller as she shouted, giving expression to her inward joy.

Thinking that it might be enlightening to her to hear her input, we asked her if she would like to hear the tape. She did, and she enjoyed it even more the second time around, shouting at the exact same places as before.

It was my impression that Sister Diller was poorly educated. The reading of Matthew, Mark, Luke, and John may have been a challenge for her even when she was younger. She impressed me as being senile in some ways, but in other ways, she seemed to have the power to look into a person's innermost being.

One Sunday as we shook hands, she told me that she was praying for me. Instead of thanking her as I should, I asked her why she was praying for me. I just wanted to know what she would say. She answered, "Because you are my superintendent and I love you."

Not long after the quartet-taping incident, she told me that she was still praying for me. Thinking I would try a little humor on her, I asked, "Are you fearful that I'll make a monkey of myself and allow the old Devil to grab me by the tail and drag me down to the bad place?"

She didn't laugh. Her expression told me that what I had said wasn't funny. She replied, "Son, I see I'm gonna hafta pray harder than ever for you."

Not wishing to be deprived of her prayers, good will, and respect, I decided to do an about-face and send out waves of friendliness and good will in her direction.

...

Along about then, in the early summer, I took a job at a house on Barnett Street in Harrisburg, removing the loose wallpaper, plaster, and plaster lathe from the ceiling joists and the studding, and replacing it with sheetrock. It turned out to be as dirty a job as working in a coal mine.

Ralph Yocum promised to help me do the job for a dollar an hour. I was never around a better worker. His work pace was faster than average. He never complained once the whole week it took us to do the job.

On Friday afternoon, when we were sure we would be finished by 5:00 p.m., I accidentally turned my right ankle and injured it so severely that placing the slightest weight on it caused a spasm-like pain that was almost unbearable. Continuing to work standing on one foot was impossible. Swelling was soon noticeable. Ralph suggested that I sit down and take it easy while he finished the job.

Instead of sitting, I decided to hobble out to the car and go across town and borrow a set of crutches from my uncle. On the way, I was about to pass Sister Diller's house. Suddenly, thinking that it would make her feel good without slowing me down too much, I decided to stop and have her pray for my ankle. The call would show my confidence and respect for her and speed up my redemption in her sight.

A picture formed quickly in my mind how I would hop in her house and sit on her leather-bound foot-stool, which would make us about the same height. In my mind's eye, she would put her hand on my head and would say a humble little prayer, for which I would thank her kindly and hurry on to get the crutches. It didn't turn out that way.

With my shoe and sock removed from my injured foot, I went hopping into her house. Sister Diller's look was one of great astonishment. I wasted no time in telling her of my sprained ankle and asking her to pray for it.

I did sit on her foot-stool, but all else that I imagined was different. She dropped down on her knees and started calling mightily on the Lord to touch her dear superintendent's ankle. I was still in no way affected by this most sincere prayer. Not until I felt her cheek on my dirty foot and felt her tears running off my ankle did it dawn on me that this lovely little woman was knocking on Heaven's door on my behalf. Her tears moved me to tears also. In my heart and mind, I said, "Amen, Lord, grant her prayer in the name of Jesus."

When she said, "Amen," I got up and checked the results. I walked back and forth across the room without pain. She started shouting like I had never seen her shout before. When she stopped, I decided to spring up and down a little on the foot that was sprained just to make sure. That turned her on again. I did quite a bit of testing while she was shouting. Later, she told the church-folks that the Lord had healed my sprained ankle, and that I had shouted all over her living room.

I didn't go on after the crutches as I had planned, but instead went back to work. Ralph showed neither surprise nor emotion as he commented, "My mother believes in prayer for the sick, too."

When I reflect on my life's many phases, including the one just mentioned, my reaction is much the same as the one expressed by Sergeant York at the close of a movie that bears his name. It is as follows: "The Lord sure does work in mysterious ways."

The Making of a Teacher

O n my 20th birthday, August 31, 1940, our home, in which I was born, burned. Fortunately, nearby on Wallace property was an old one-room building, which was formerly used as a store that had closed around 1910. It served as home for our family of eight for three months while we rebuilt.

Because of my dad's age and poor health, the task of rebuilding lay heavily on my shoulders. (Dad died six months later.) Five brothers and sisters were still in school.

In my mind, I can still see Mom picking up and stacking bricks from two chimneys while they were almost too hot to handle, in preparation to rebuild. Mom was unbelievably cheerful, partly because it was her nature, and partly to keep me from being unhappy.

Mom asked if I thought we could have a basement in the new home. I told her we could, since we could borrow a slip scraper from a neighbor, and we had a team of mules to pull it.

Handling the mules and loading the scraper was a job. It was made easier on a couple of weekends when two of my younger brothers could take turns handling the mules while I manned the scraper.

Rebuilding went like magic. I hired two good carpenters for 50 cents per hour and worked with them. A few hours were donated by friends. The house was framed out of fine white oak sawmill lumber that I bought for the low price of $20 per 1000 square feet. To pay for the building materials, we were forced to place a small mortgage on the farm.

Around November 20, 1940, we moved into the new house. We were proud of it. The electric line came through that fall, so we had electric lights and a radio. One hurdle was down, but a big one, that of paying the mortgage, lay ahead. It seemed that my going to Michigan to work was the answer to that problem.

On a cold November 30th, I was invited to ride with Orvil Gribble to Pontiac, Michigan. He planned to lock up his home, put farming on hold, and give factory work a try. Orvil's wife, Dovey, and son, Valgene, were along on this trip to Pontiac. The day after we arrived, Orvil and family rented an apartment, and I got room and board at a boarding house. We parted ways and lost touch until we saw each other six years later back in Southern Illinois.

My first job in Pontiac was at a bakery. It was a good holdover job for a few weeks until I started to work at Jig Bushing.

The man owning controlling interest in Jig Bushing was on the draft board. He told me that he was running a non-union defense plant, and that if I fit in, when I got my call to service, he could get me three six-month deferments. Those extra eighteen months were a blessing, for they allowed me to pay off the mortgage on the farm.

At the end of my third deferment, I was sworn into the Navy in Detroit. I had five weeks of boot camp training at the Navy base at Great Lakes near Chicago. I was in a company that got advanced amphibious training at Fort Pierce, Florida. We were put in five-man crews and taught to operate LCMs, which were used as landing crafts. After much island-hopping, we were sent to Saipan, a small island in the South Pacific. There we were assigned to the Harbormaster to service large ships anchored offshore when they couldn't get in to the harbor.

I was on Saipan when the war was over with Japan. But it was 1946 before I got off the island. Men were dismissed on the point system. Points were given for age, dependents, time in service, being married, etc. All of the above put me low on the totem pole. So I continued on Saipan on into 1946.

In my favor while remaining on Saipan, I took two courses at the University of Saipan, one in business law and the other in psychology. Both were taught by U.S. lieutenants. By my request, my credits were recorded at Southern Illinois University in Carbondale.

It was a pleasure leaving Saipan on a slow-moving troop transport. I had much time to meditate what the future might hold. However, my plans were to return to my job in Michigan.

After being discharged from the Navy at Great Lakes, I returned home for a week to visit with family and friends. It was grand to spend quality time with Mom.

Then I went to Pontiac to visit with some church friends and to report to Jig Bushing and let them know that I was back and available to work. My foreman was happy to see me. He suggested that I first spend a couple of weeks with my mother and then come back, and a good job would be waiting for me.

...

Those two weeks were zipping by. I began to dread leaving home again. Having come from a family of teachers, I pondered becoming a teacher myself. With time running out, I applied for a teaching position at Pierson School, about four miles south of Harrisburg.

The clerk of the Pierson board told me that the board would be meeting the following night, and that they would discuss my application then. He suggested that I check with him the following morning. The next day, I contacted him. To my disgust, he told me that he had forgotten the meeting and had gone fishing instead. I decided that I would forget Pierson School and go back to my old job in Pontiac.

Two or three days before I was to leave, I saw Orvil Gribble at a social at Rudement Church, about ten miles south of Harrisburg. We were glad to see each other. He told me that he had stayed in Pontiac only two years and was back home farming. He said that he was never happier in his life.

Orvil asked if I was going back to Michigan. I told him that I would be leaving in two or three days. I went on to tell him about the Pierson School fiasco. Orvil was quick to reply, "I'm clerk of the school board here at Rudement. If you want to teach our school, we can get together tonight."

We left the community get-together without so much as a "By your leave, Sir." We picked up board member Virgil Ewell and went over to the home of the third board member, Lee DeNeal. By virtue of a gentlemen's agreement and a handshake, I was hired to teach at Rudement School starting the fall of 1946. We got back to the social without being missed.

The next day, I went to the County Superintendent of Schools and told him that I had been hired to teach

Rudement School. I told him of my courses and training beyond high school. When I finished bragging on myself, he told me that he would issue me a certificate with the provision that I earn a certain number of quarter-hours of college work every four years. (I took my schooling seriously. Over the next few years, I earned a bachelor's degree in science and a master's degree in administration and supervision, and got a supervisory certificate to teach or supervise in grades kindergarten through junior college.)

It had been ten years since I had been in a one-room schoolhouse as a student myself. Now, suddenly hired as a teacher of grades one through eight, I realized I was facing a challenge.

Two or three days before school was scheduled to start, I was at Rudement General Store, just across the road from the school. A little ten-year-old barefoot girl wearing a round-top straw hat appeared from a gravel road to the south. She had a basket of eggs on her arm to trade for groceries. (The merchant bought eggs, butter, and cream.)

I thought to myself, "One of my pupils." I greeted the girl and introduced myself as the new teacher at Rudement School. Her name was Deloris. I admired her because she was neither forward nor bashful. She told me that her dad was Walter Wilson, a man I knew well.

I asked Deloris whether there was anyone among the pupils who could lead singing for opening exercise of mornings. She lowered her eyes for a split second and replied, "I can." That came as a huge relief, because I knew that I couldn't.

Next I asked if anyone could play the piano. She quickly answered, "Yes, Billy Paul Ewell plays well."

I rejoiced within myself, and said, "Thank you, Lord, for answering my prayer before I got around to asking it."

The first day of school came, and I stood before twenty-four pairs of eyes. Some shown with happiness and some with fear lest they would foul up. My board member, Virgil Ewell, being a big tease, had told a number of the children that he had made me promise that I would "whup" the kids and make them mind. (He wasn't lying about that—I had promised.)

I told the students that I knew most, if not all, of their parents and had great respect for them. "They call me 'Kestner,' but I want you to call me 'Mr. Wallace.'" No one had any problem with that, for which I was thankful.

I asked the students if they would like to sing each morning. They eagerly indicated that they would. No one was surprised when Billy Paul seated himself at the piano, and Deloris stood before the group and called out "The Battle Hymn of the Republic."

At the end of the singing, I told the students that we would do well to pause for a brief prayer asking God's blessings on the school year, the parents, and each student. I asked God to give me the wisdom to do a good job. Afterwards, assigning seats and handing out books took us to the first recess around 10:30 a.m.

When we were back in session, a brave boy serving as spokesperson asked, "What is it we can't do?"

I replied, "There are many things you can't do. You can't spell 'hippopotamus' backwards, you can't make a silk purse out of a sow's ear, and you can't jump over the moon."

The children laughed. I remarked, "I'm teasing. It is a good question. You certainly have a right to know.

In reality, my rules will be few. If I make a rule, I'll try to enforce it. Too many rules might work me harder than I want to work. These three come to mind. They were rules when your parents and grandparents were in school: no bad language, no smoking, and no fighting beyond horseplay."

This boy was hard to satisfy. He exclaimed, "I thought there would be more rules than that!"

"From time to time there will be suggestions."

"Like what?"

"Like 'Straighten up and fly right or off comes your head!'"

The children took on a serious look. Again, I had to admit that I was joking. Then, in all seriousness, I suggested that we enter into an agreement, "You don't give me a bad time, and I won't give you a bad time. Live by the Golden Rule and try to make this the best school year possible."

That first month of school went smoothly. I wanted to do something with the children to celebrate—like giving each one a candy bar. A box of 24 sold for 90 cents at the store across the road. I gave a student a dollar and asked him to get a box plus two extra bars.

I spent a lot of time on my feet, so it was a pleasant change to sit and do nothing. I told the students that we would have to get back to our lessons as soon as we ate, since it wasn't quite time to go home. It would have amazed you how the students used sign language to slow down the eating process. I realized that it was the end of the month, the end of the week, and the end of the day, so I slipped my chair back and a little to one side of my low desk and propped my feet on my desk—comfortable and not too unsightly under the conditions. What do you think happened next?

Sam DeNeal, who was almost as wild as I was at his age, scooted down in his seat until he was sitting mostly on his shoulders and cocked his feet on his desk. He looked right and left at his classmates with a big smile on his face. I showed no alarm—I just made as if that were normal behavior. One by one the students, boys and girls alike, followed Sam's lead.

I almost had a heart attack when I took in the scene. I asked myself, "What would the County Superintendent of Schools think if he were to bob in at this moment?" I tried not to let alarm show as I slowly put my feet on the floor where they belonged. One by one, the students did likewise. However, they remained upbeat and continued very slowly to eat their candy bars. Their candy lasted until time for them to go home happily.

One day about five minutes before the first recess, I observed that the students were just waiting out the clock. Windows lined the north side of the building, high enough that the students couldn't see out when seated. I took a look out the windows and saw a common black and white housecat walking across the field a good way off.

I decided to check on the power of suggestion. I exclaimed, "Never in all my born days! I want you to come over here and take a look for yourself."

The students nearly ran over each other getting over to the windows. Short children climbed up on desks to see.

I asked, "Do all of you see that cat?" After a few seconds, I said, "Back in your seats."

When they were all seated, I asked, "How many of you think that was a big cat?" Nearly all hands went up.

I asked, "Did any of you ever see a bigger cat?" No hands went up.

I inquired if anyone had ever seen a bobcat. None had. I quickly added, "That wasn't a bobcat. It had a long tail." I asked, "How long?" It would surprise you how long that they said.

I asked different ones to stand and tell me how high that cat would come on them. At first it was knee-high, and then it got higher. I figured that I had had my fun, but inquired of one more student, "Cecil Ray, what do you think about that cat?"

"I think it was a plain old housecat."

Sam stood up quickly. His eyes sparkled, and he had a big smile on his face. I read his mind. He was thinking, "If you want a big cat, I'll give you a big cat."

I asked, "Sam, what do you think?"

He answered, "I think it was as big as a calf!"

I asked, "Boys and girls, do you know what I think? I think it is time for recess."

The year was unique in many ways. Rather unusual, as it happened, I had both a boy and his aunt, who were the same age, in the 6th grade. They were "A" students, gifted and fun-loving. Much of their time at noon and at recess, they preferred each other's company. They did comical art and wrote silly verses. Despite their friendship, however, they fussed and bickered at times almost to the point of unbecoming behavior. I knew that, in time, I would have to have a little talk with them.

One afternoon, following the noon intermission, all was quiet. However, the girl's nephew was evidently being particularly trying that day. The girl slammed a book on her desk with a startling bang. The students expressed their shock under their breath in various ways, such as "Oh, my God!" and worse.

This student came up to my desk, with arms slinging and feet stomping in an unladylike manner. She came to attention after pounding down first her left foot and then her right.

In a high-pitched voice, equally out of control, she shrieked, "He has aggravated me this live-long day! I'm fed up with him. I'm not going to take any more of it! Now what are you going to do about it?" She returned to her seat stomping out her anger.

The room was as still as death. All eyes were on me. The students wondered what I would do. What would you have done? I knew that I had different options. The Navy quip crossed my mind, "The right way, the wrong way, and the Navy way." I decided that I'd take care of it *my* way.

A paddle lay on top of an upright piano in the corner of the room. I arose from my chair more slowly than usual, removed the pencil from behind my ear, put another turn on my upturned cuffs, and crossed the distance to the piano. On the way, I heard some students catch their breath.

Reaching the piano, I placed my elbows and lower arms on it, with my forehead between my hands. I sounded off with a loud "boo-hoo, boo-hoo, boo-hoo," loud enough to frighten the pigeons in the bell tower. I turned and walked back to my seat with a grin on my face.

The children, realizing nothing bad was going to happen, burst out in joyful, hilarious laughter. That is, all except the one little girl. She sounded off with tears falling like rain. Had I not been a big boy, I would have entered into her unhappiness and shed tears with her. We quickly got back to the afternoon classes. My observation at the last recess told me that all was well once more. That incident was never mentioned thereafter to my knowledge.

One Monday morning, during my second year at Rudement, I went to school early to write a letter to my girlfriend, Evelyn, who lived in East Prairie, Missouri. I had been introduced to Evelyn just a few days before I was drafted into the Navy. Five months later, I wrote her from Fort Pierce, Florida, just prior to shipping out. Her answer reached me months later on Saipan. Impressed as I was with Evelyn, however, that courtship was traveling along at a snail's pace, by correspondence only.

I was always a bit tense when writing to Evelyn. Her letters, penmanship and all, fell in the realm of perfection. What I had learned in the school of hard knocks didn't help much in letter writing.

The pen I was using should have been replaced. It alternated between writing too dimly to feeding out the ink too freely. Despite that, things were going pretty well after the third start.

Jimmy Williams, who lived nearby, came early most mornings. That day, he came up to my desk. I was so pleased that my pen was working and so engrossed in what I was writing that I was barely aware of Jimmy's presence. He put his hands on the desk in a leaned-forward position, with his feet a ways behind him. He bounced off the floor about six inches and announced, "I got baptized yesterday."

I wrote on. At the next attempt to get my attention, he sprang off the floor about a foot and said a little more loudly, "I got baptized yesterday!"

I was about ready to place a period at the end of the sentence when Jimmy kicked back with both feet like a young mule and shouted, "Mr. Wallace, I got baptized yesterday!!"

He moved the desk toward me and caused my pen to lose its bladder of ink on my letter. I did what no teacher should ever do—I lost my cool.

In an elevated tone, I exclaimed, "Jimmy, the preacher should have put you under three times and brought you up twice!"

The look on Jimmy's face told me that his heart was broken. That look put a dagger in my heart.

I put my letter in the waste can and came around the desk. I put my arm around him and said, "So you got baptized yesterday? I wish I could have been there." I asked for and received the details. He was happy, but I felt only a little better.

Later that same day, three little girls about Jimmy's age, who were sharing the same jar of paste in their artwork, came up for me to remove the lid from the jar. Often they were hard to remove. I was always pleased to display my strength. The lid was frozen tightly, and it was with difficulty that I turned it a half turn.

Jimmy came up just as I reached out to return the paste to the girls. He snatched the jar from my hand. He clutched it with all his might with his left hand and twisted with his right. He went down on one knee with a pretended attempt to remove the lid.

Then he brought up one knee like a baseball pitcher getting ready for the pitch. Finally, he removed the lid and handed it to the girls.

"Ooohs" and "ahs" were sounded by those who were tuned in. Jimmy's antics amused me. I felt of his muscles and winked at him, thereby telling him that I'd tell no one.

...

Jimmy was fearful to defend himself on the playground for fear that he would be in trouble with me. I observed that he was being somewhat mistreated by another boy. When I spoke to this boy, he assured me that it was all in play. In my opinion, it was a borderline case.

Later, Jimmy came to me on the playground and said, "This boy hit me in the jaw, and it hurts."

I asked, "Jimmy, what did he hit you with?"

"He hit me with his fist."

I put my hand on Jimmy's shoulder to make sure that I had his attention, and said, "You don't have any fists, do you?"

I saw the enlightened look on his face as he quipped, "Oh, I getcha."

Jimmy went over to this boy and kind of carelessly bumped into him. The boy came up with both fists. Jimmy flew in on him like a woodchicken on a June bug and built instant respect for himself. I walked over to them and asked, "Is this a fight or is it horseplay?"

They both responded at once, "Horseplay."

I said, "Good, because you both know I don't allow fighting on the playground."

One of my pupils, Ray Tarlton, held a certain fascination for me. He was the son of Virgil Tarlton, a mechanic and plumber. Ray was eight years old in the 3rd grade. He projected warmth and friendliness. Ray's dad bragged on Ray's interest in mechanics and what a good helper he made. I later used that piece of information to my advantage.

Ray needed motivation and extra help in reading. Lack of sleep was part of Ray's problem. His dad and mom attended revival meetings far and near and kept him up late. Ray would often fall asleep at his desk.

One day, I called him up to my desk to work with him on reading. He wobbled up almost too sleepy to stand. It was obvious that he had no interest in what I was trying to teach him.

I asked, "Ray, do you know how to 'time' a Model A Ford?"

He snapped awake as if I had dashed him with a cold cup of water. "Do you have a Model A Ford? How long have you had it? How did it get out of time?"

Before I could answer his questions, Ray said, "I don't know how to time a Model A Ford, but I'll ask my dad tonight and tell you tomorrow." We quickly turned to the reading assignment. I was surprised at how well that went.

The next morning Ray wanted to know whether I was ready to hear him read. I was surprised and told him to come on up. He didn't break open his book, but instead asked, "Do you still want to know how to time a Model A Ford?"

His directions were clear and concise. When I later followed them, I got my Model A in time without any problems. The reading went much better day after day following our talk about some old car. A warm feeling developed between us.

However, on occasion, Ray would revert to his former self. One of those times, he wobbled up to my desk all sleepy-eyed and asked in a whisper if he could leave the room—meaning, go to the john. I felt that a walk and the fresh air would be good for him. But I felt cantankerous and wanted to have a little fun out of him.

I took a deep breath, let it out with a heavy sigh, and asked in a loud whisper so as not to disturb the room, "Ray, if I let you go, will you come back?"

Ray took a deep breath and let it out with a heavy

sigh, also, and answered, "Lord, God, yes, Mr. Wallace, I'll come back."

Neither of us smiled. I nodded permission. Ray went to the door. With his hand on the doorknob, he paused, looked back at me, and grinned. His grin said, "I know we were pulling each other's leg." I smiled back and gave him a wink.

One day, in my third year at Rudement, two men walked up to my desk when classes were in session. They asked to be excused for the interruption and stated that they would take only a minute of my time. They said that they were appointed by the P.T.A. and the Board of Education at Pierson School to see if I would teach their school the following year. They said that they were willing to give me $50 more on the month than I was getting. Their concluding remark was, "Think it over and let us know."

The students pretended that they didn't know what was said, but when I asked them, they admitted that they had heard. They wanted to know whether I planned to go to Pierson. I told them that in the morning, I would let them vote whether I should go or stay.

The following morning, I gave slips of paper to the students in the five upper grades. I asked them to write "STAY" if they wanted me to stay or write "GO" if they wanted me to go. They all voted "STAY" except one. That person wrote "GO, GO, GO."

I knew it wasn't the little foot-stomping girl because she said, "If you go to Pierson, I'll go, too." My gut told me who the "go, go, go" person was. Today, well over 50 years later, I have no better friend.

I wrestled over whether it would be wisdom to go or stay, even after the promise of more money. I asked the Good Lord to lead in making my decision. He may have helped me recall what an old-time milk cow trader told me. This man couldn't read or write, but he knew cows and how to trade. I had asked him, "Amos, what is your secret to making good trades most of the time?" His answer was simple. "You know what you got, but you don't know what you are getting."

That helped me make up my mind to stay. I asked myself, "Why should I move from the Garden of Eden to the region of the unknown?"

The first year at Rudement School we had a good softball team. We played Spring Valley, Somerset, and Pierson, about three weeks apart. As I remember, we won all the games that we played. We had the size, and we made serious preparation before games.

Following that first year, our better ballplayers went to high school, and it took us two years to grow and motivate another team with the ability to challenge another school. That team from the third year was the team I'll never forget. To round out a team, we used two girls—Deloris Wilson and Betty Gene Gibbs—who were good and were anxious to play. We played schools that we had previously played. We won some and lost some, but always played well.

The last game that we played is the one that I remember the best. It was with Winkleman Hill. Hereafter, I'll call it the "Hill School" for short. A small caravan of cars carried Rudement's players and fans to the Hill School. We arrived about one o'clock and were greeted by the competition and their fans.

As I had warned our players, the Hill team was a half to a full size larger than ours. That meant that we would have to outplay them, stay on our toes, and always be on the lookout to make a double play. Our players were all keyed up like racehorses ready to leave the chute. The playground was the diamond. It was undersized and bordered with trees.

Our lineup was as follows: Sam DeNeal, pitcher; Billy Paul Ewell, catcher; Deloris Wilson, first base; Billy Earl Gribble, second base; and Betty Jean Gibbs, third base. We were first to bat.

As the game progressed, everyone was soon astonished at the closeness of the game. All the onlookers were getting their money's worth. The umpire, furnished by the Hill School, was fair and seemed to please everyone. Each team had its enthusiastic backers and still behaved in a neighborly, rural school manner.

When we had our turn at bat the last time, we were one run ahead. The Hill players were up to bat last, since we were the visiting team. I can still see Sam on the pitcher's mound, Billy Paul punching his fist in his catcher's mitt, and all of the other players anxious for the game to finish in our favor.

The first batter hit a grounder that went between the pitcher and third base. He got on first base.

The second batter up got a hit that went high over Sam's head. Billy Earl caught it on the first bounce about two steps from second base. He quickly tagged second base and slammed it over to first base ahead of the runner, thus making a double play. Rudement fans went beside themselves with joy.

As the Hill's last batter, a fourteen-year-old almost grown in size, came to the plate, tenseness gripped the group. The batter may have been nervous, but he tried not to show it. He pecked the plate three or four times with his bat and made a powerful fake swing as though he had in mind to put a softball into outer space.

Sam seemed calm and even professional. He had to have been under pressure. The batter was ready and anxious for the pitch. Sam delivered it about ten feet over the batter's head.

The umpire called, "Ball one!"

Sam took his time in deciding what the next pitch would be. The batter became more impatient. He tried to say, by tapping on the plate, "I'm ready—come on and pitch to me!"

Sam made as though he planned to throw a fast ball. It was a fast ball, but too far outside for the batter to step in and get a hit.

"Ball two," announced the umpire.

Again Sam took his time while the rest of us sweated it out. By now, I had decided that Sam planned to walk the big boy and hoped to put the next batter out one way or another.

Next Sam came up with his slow ball. It really was slow. It rolled over the plate.

"Ball three" was the umpire's call.

Sam took no time deciding on the next pitch. He fired one down the center of the plate. The batter put his weight behind his swing and caught the ball on the end of his bat.

Two thoughts raced through my head—"ball to kingdom come" and "home run." The Hill students, teacher, and fans went wild.

That ball flew just barely fair past third base about thirty feet high. It hit a tall pignut tree and ricocheted toward first base, where Deloris scooped it up on the second bounce and tagged first base. That ended the game with Rudement ahead by one run. It was Rudement's time to rejoice, but the nature of the out turned out to be a big joke. Congratulations for a good game went both ways.

...

What I have written concerning my five years at Rudement is only a fraction of all the interesting things that took place there. In spite of my initial prayer for wisdom, I made some mistakes that I won't mention in hopes that they have been forgotten. My sojourn at Rudement was largely a success due to the cooperation of the wonderful people that made up the community. Those Rudement years gave me a good jump start for the 35 years that followed, at Pankeyville and then at Independence School.

(And, for my readers who have been left wondering, despite Jimmy Williams' interference with my love letter, I did marry Evelyn on August 22, 1950. We're still living happily ever after more than 54 years later.)

Water High, Cotton Sack Dry

A long about dark on a rainy Sunday evening of 1948, my sister, Mabel Baldwin, became greatly concerned when her husband, Wallace Baldwin, hadn't arrived at Mom's. Wallace and Mabel were finishing their master's degrees at S.I.U. in Carbondale. Both of them had taught for several years. On coming home periodically, it wasn't unusual for Mabel to visit with Mom and for Wallace to visit with his elderly parents in the Hicks Branch community of Pope County.

When Mabel's anxiety increased, I volunteered to check on my brother-in-law. While I was putting on a water repellent jacket and reaching for a flashlight, my sister, Hazel, offered to go with me. She was assured that it would please me to have her go along.

Hazel and I had a great deal in common. We were both teachers, we were both single, and we both lived at home with Mom.

There were some differences, also. She was six years younger than I. (Now she would probably say at least twelve years difference.) She got a head start on me in teaching while I was in the Navy. Hazel was popular with a number of young people. I was more reserved; however, I could have married anyone I pleased. The trouble was I didn't please anyone. Anyway, we made a good team and were helpful to each other.

[Now for the benefit of anyone who doesn't know me, I've been happily married for about a hundred years. (Just kidding, Evelyn, you big beautiful doll.) It's only been since 1950.]

Anyway, in keeping with an old family saying, Hazel and I took off with our hair blowing back in our old Dodge car we called "The Blue Goose." As we crossed from Saline into Pope County and rounded the curve just north of Herod at Rocky Branch, we could hear the water in the creek roaring quite loudly. We commented that it had surely rained more than we had realized. In fact, by the time we were a mile or so south of Herod, the rain became a cloudburst for a few minutes with occasional low rumbles of thunder and flashes of lightning.

We turned right off Route 34 on a gravel road that went into the old J. D. Barter Farm, later known as the Cavaness Fish Farm. It was a mile more or less back to Hicks Branch, a rather good-sized creek. Just beyond the creek stood a large, well-kept white barn. The road into the Baldwin Farm curved around this barn on the west, then turned north to cross a bottom, and then made a gradual incline before reaching a beautiful ridge farm.

Our first surprise was to learn that the water in Hicks Branch was too high to cross even though many tons of concrete had been dumped into the creek and smoothed out to make a crossing.

Just below the crossing was a footbridge swung from side to side by steel cables. It swung slightly four feet above the water. It was agreeable with Hazel to remain in the car on the east side of Hicks Branch while I crossed on the footbridge and went on foot to check on Wallace.

In record time I made it through the rain to the Baldwin farm house. Mr. and Mrs. Baldwin and Wallace were pleased and surprised to see me. Wallace explained that since he knew the creek would be up, he had decided to wait until morning to go back to Carbondale.

Without much delay, I took my leave to return to the car where Hazel was waiting. Shortly after leaving the house, it began to rain hard again. In fact, it rained so hard that it was difficult for me to see my way. Water was half a knee deep across the bottom. The continuous lightning made using the flashlight unnecessary. At the creek my heart sank on realizing that the water was over the footbridge. Following the cables and extending one foot cautiously into the water, I learned very quickly by the way my foot shot downstream that attempting to cross would be unwise. My dad had commented a number of times to always respect fire and water. That advice wasn't wasted on me.

With considerable difficulty because of the roar of the water, Hazel received my message that Wallace was okay and that she should take the car, go on home, and come back at 6:00 a.m. to pick me up. By voice and sign language, I indicated that I would go back to the Baldwin's to spend the night. Hazel cautiously turned the car around. Soon the taillights were out of sight.

My attention turned immediately to the barn, since I knew that crossing the bottom toward the Baldwin's by now would be unsafe, also. On passing this barn in the past, I had seen horses, cattle, and hogs. The realization that they might not take too kindly to an unannounced guest wasn't a pleasant thought.

Pulling from the recesses of my mind the famous quote from the late President Franklin D. Roosevelt, "We have nothing to fear, but fear itself," I splashed my way to the entrance of the barn. A hallway ran from one end of the barn to the other, with stalls on either side. Sounds of horses, cattle, and hogs could be heard. In the far end of the barn were some horses. There was probably at least one stallion, judging from the kicking and squealing. About midway of the hall lay a big bull chewing his cud.

Standing just inside the barn with flashlight in hand, I searched for a ladder or stairway leading into the hay-loft. In addition to being concerned about being pawed, kicked, or bitten by the horses, gored by the bull, or having a leg taken off by a savage sow or boar, I just remembered that the owner of the place had a hired man who had been instructed to shoot trespassers first and ask questions later. The owner had been losing livestock to rustlers and gasoline and farm machinery to thieves. So it was with a high level of concern for my own safety that I walked down the hall.

About one-third way down the hall, what looked like a stall door turned out to be the entrance to a stair-way that led to the hayloft. In a very short time, with the help of the flashlight, I made an inspection of the loft. Now that the hurdle of being injured by the animals was past, my next concern was getting out of my wet clothes lest I get pneumonia from exposure. The search revealed that there were no blankets, quilts, bedding, old clothes, or anything. The hay was too rough of texture to be used next to my bare skin. There was no straw, either.

All of a sudden my heart leaped with joy because, out of nowhere it seemed, there appeared a white sack on a bale of hay. I knew at once that it was the type of sack, about seven or eight feet in length, that was used in the South when cotton was picked by hand. It was a godsend. Its appearance led me to believe it had been used in the cotton fields; however, it had been washed and folded and was ready for me to unfold, shake out, and put to use.

After laying a thick layer of hay on the loft floor, I spread the cotton sack on it and placed a pile of hay on either side. Next I stripped to the skin, wrung out my clothes, hung them in a breezy part of the loft to dry, and then backed into the cotton sack. When about two-thirds way into the sack, I placed the piles of hay over the sack and snuggled further down into the sack. Of all the sacks I've hit in my time, this one stands out most vividly. In trying to show my appreciation to my Maker for small blessings, I was about to quote the Twenty-third Psalm, "He leadeth me beside the still waters," but when I heard the creek roaring, I changed it to "He maketh me to lie down in a clean cottonpicking sack. Thank you."

Since it was too early to go to sleep, I decided to think of some great and profound philosophical thoughts. Inasmuch as I'd never thought any of those kinds of thoughts before, or since, for that matter, I soon gave up the idea.

Next I tried to identify with Old Testament characters such as the Hebrew children in the fiery furnace, Daniel in the lion's den, Jonah in the belly of the whale, and Job and all his troubles. The parallel I drew was that God was with them and, had He not been with me, I would not have survived to the present time. But this again took only a very little time.

Then deciding to come farther down the ladder of nobility, I decided to recall some of the humorous incidents of by-gone days. There would be enough of these to hold me all night. Among these was my first experience with a revolving door.

One day, at the tender age of twenty, I was shopping in a downtown store in Pontiac, Michigan. I had gone into the rather large store by a regular entrance. On leaving, the crowd led me to the most strange, frightening, and elaborate device for letting people out. Approaching it suddenly, without paying much attention, I was taken by surprise. I had to stop and take notice before getting in, or on, whichever the case was, and in so doing, blocked the way for others. This caused mass confusion. The people behind me began to push. A woman who looked to be about thirty and who in height came up to my shoulder, gave me the most dirty, impatient look that I'd ever seen. Her look said, "Get in or get out!" She barged in ahead. This caused me to think that I should do something even if it was wrong. And wrong it was. I followed her example and crowded into the same compartment with her instead of moving the contraption up one space. If she was angry before, you should have seen her then. The two of us made it so crowded that the only way she could move was up. She began to go up and down like a jumping jack. She would look over one shoulder to glare at me. I couldn't stand the glare and would move my head to the other side so far she would quickly turn the other way to see me. This was repeated throughout the ordeal.

For her the worst was yet to come. When that modern contraption got in motion, it began to strike my heels each time I attempted to take a step. That would cause my knee to come up and catch the woman in the back end in almost perfect rhythm with the jumping she was already doing. The only difference was that, instead of coming off the floor about six inches, she was clearing the floor about a foot. When we finally got to the outside opening, she shot out of there like a bat out of the bad place. I chose to go another round. Wonder why? In my reminiscing, my sympathy for this unfortunate woman still kept this incident from being really funny to me; however, there were others that caused me to smile to myself.

After who knows how long, I sleepily came to myself and realized that the rainstorm was over and the creek could barely be heard. Knowing that if I said my prayers before falling asleep, I'd better get at it, I began, "Thank you, Lord, for the way you have watched over me all my days. You have led me by the hand and guided me with your eye." Then a slap-happy streak hit me and I added, "Thank you, Lord, for backing me into this cottonpicking sack." I smiled a little to myself and said, "You know what I mean, Lord. Thank you." That was the last I knew until after 5:00 a.m.

On awakening, I quickly dressed in almost dry clothes, folded the cotton sack, replaced it on the bale of hay, and was bobbing up and down on that swinging bridge (which was well out of the water), when the Blue Goose driven by Hazel came into sight.

On the way home, Hazel told me that Mabel had a good night's sleep after learning that Wallace was okay. In turn she was briefed on my experience.

Later Mabel asked me how it felt sleeping in a cottonpicking sack in a barn. I told her my feelings concerning it were about like those of the man who was tarred, feathered, and ridden out of town on a rail. When he was asked how it felt, he replied that if it weren't for the honor of it, he would just as soon have walked. I assured Mabel that aside from the honor of it, I'd rather have spent the night in my own bed.

By now you are surely beginning to wonder what is the point, the moral, or the lesson to be gleaned from this story. I'm sorry to say that there is no point, there is no lesson, there is no moral in this story. However, it is my sincere wish and desire in your behalf, if you find yourself in a similar predicament, you will find some cottonpickin' way out.

My Big Splash

My fishing began around 1950, shortly after Evelyn and I married. A razzing from two good friends, Bill Butterworth and Raymond Gibbs, helped to get me started. They told me that they were sorry I couldn't go fishing with them the following Friday night, since I was married.

Heretofore, my busy schedule hadn't permitted me to go fishing, but the thought of not being able to go stuck me in the craw. I told Evelyn of my invitation to go fishing and suggested getting my mom, who lived nearby, to spend the night with her. Since Evelyn had been a town girl, I thought that she would be afraid to spend the night alone in the country.

Evelyn's reply still rings joyfully in my ears: "You go fishing with your friends if you wish. I won't be afraid to stay by myself."

Bill, Raymond, and I found a fishy-looking spot on Saline River, which had deep holes and drifts on each side of it. We chose it for our campsite. Then we gathered enough driftwood to keep a campfire burning brightly all night.

Immediately after dusk turned to darkness, by the light of carbide lamps, we baited the hooks with chicken liver or large wiggly earthworms. As darkness crept around us, we put the last of our thirty bank poles in likely places up and down the stream from the campfire. We stuck the sharpened cane poles firmly in the creek bank in such a way that the bait dangled about a foot under the water.

Bill had brought an extra long stringer so that he could get a picture of all of our catch the following morning. We fastened one end of a light dog chain to the stringer and tied the other end to a sapling on the creek bank, which was well illuminated by the campfire.

We felt joy and satisfaction as we checked our bank poles about every thirty minutes and took off four or five fiddler cats, which we called "jumbo cats" because they were bigger than the pan size we were expecting to catch. We had to rebait on each round because of the "bait stealers." Some of them wound up getting caught, but we let them off with a warning and didn't count them.

After the first time or two, we took turns checking the bank poles, rebaiting, and bringing the fish back to the stringer in a bucket. I noticed that Bill and Raymond tossed the fish slightly into the air after adding fish to the stringer. It made for a gratifying splash. Added to that were other interesting night sounds of owls, frogs, bobcats, foxes, whippoorwills, and cattle lowing in the distance.

The night passed quickly. We talked, told jokes, and laughed. Throughout the night, we ate fried potatoes, scrambled eggs, bacon, and hot dogs prepared over the campfire.

Just after daybreak, we decided to gather our poles and equipment and go home. While Raymond went upstream and I went downstream to gather the poles and fish, Bill proceeded to load his 1936 Chevrolet. Raymond got back before I did, but I heard the splash as he returned the stringer of fish to the water.

As I added my catch—the final two or three fish—to the stringer, Raymond, in preparation to leave, unsnapped the dog chain from the stringer without my seeing him. We all three beheld the fish and glowed with satisfaction.

I took the stringer of fish and thought to myself, "He who splashes last, splashes best. Hurrah for me; I'll make the biggest splash of all."

With those thoughts in mind, I heaved that heavy stringer of fish into the water. I will never forget the splashing sound of the fish hitting the water, because at that same moment I realized that the dog chain had been unfastened from the stringer. They landed near the middle of the creek and were seen "nevermore."

I was heartsick, ashamed, disgusted, and angry. All that saved the day was the fact that it struck Raymond and Bill as being funny. That was the biggest laugh of the night to them. I was glad that they saw humor in my action, even if I didn't. In an effort to lift my spirits, they told me that the fish would be a feast for the turtles, and that they would tell no one what I had done.

Shortly after that all-night fishing trip, my sister Hazel and her husband, Stan, Evelyn, and I decided to set a trotline from Stan's 12-foot aluminum boat in the Ohio River near Rosiclare—a new experience for us.

We went out into the river about 300 yards and set a short line with about thirty hooks that we had already made up and baited with dough balls. Each end was held down by a window weight. To one of the weights we tied another line from which we floated an empty, gallon plastic jug so we could easily locate our trotline later.

While this line was fishing for us, we took a boat ride. It was a delightful afternoon for boating. The clear water complemented the blue of the sky. It wasn't too hot and the water was calm—ideal for amateur adventurers.

After about two hours, we decided to check our line and take it up and go home. We felt a hefty tug as soon as we lifted the window weight from the riverbed and knew that we had at least one good fish. In a short time, as Stan helped keep the boat parallel with the line and Evelyn and Hazel looked on, I lifted a beautiful blue catfish into the boat. A conservative guess of its weight was about five pounds.

Evelyn exclaimed, "Oh, isn't it pretty! Let us give it a dough ball and let it go."

I promptly and respectfully vetoed that suggestion on the grounds that it would interfere with my eating. However, a new family saying came into existence. To this day, "give him a dough ball and let him go" is given as a solution to various problems.

The tug on the line seemed to be just as great after the catfish was removed. It turned out to be a 12- to 15-pound carp. Had anyone suggested it, I would have given it a dough ball and let it go, but the others thought it would be a good idea to show it off back at Herod on the way home. I'm glad we did because we gave it to a man who was glad to get it.

After that renowned two-fish catch, I got the boat fever and bought a four by eight foot plywood boat and a used seven-and-a-half horse motor for creek fishing. Evelyn and I promptly took it down on Big Creek to try it out. We slid the boat down the steep bank into the water about a hundred yards from the Ohio River and with some difficulty embarked.

The motor cranked up easily, but it idled so fast that no additional throttle was needed. My weight and the weight of the motor caused Evelyn to ride high in the bow, while the stern was only four or five inches out of the water.

After a short trip up the creek, my gut feeling told me that we had a deathtrap set up, and the quickest way we could get out of the creek would be too slow.

On returning, as we neared the spot where we put in the water, I shut off the motor and sculled up to the bank. Evelyn carefully crawled off the bow on to the steep bank. The moment she left the boat, it reared straight up into the air and fell back. I got baptized heels over head backwards without the benefit of a ceremony. The only fishing we did that day was fishing out the boat and motor.

The late Reverend George McClusky and I enjoyed several trips fly fishing together in the Hardin County sinks. We were always anxious to know how the other was doing, but still needed to keep our eyes on our own floating line. I told George that I would let him in on a little secret if he would faithfully promise me that he would not tell anyone. He gave his word of honor.

I told him that it was extremely important to extend sincere courtesy to fish. I said that as soon as we saw our line straighten out and felt the first pull as we responded, we should ring out with a resounding, "How-do-you-do."

Time after time we hilariously called out, "How-do-you-do," with the courtesy of a southern gentleman. I have let close friends and family members in on this secret, and it is still used today.

...

One day while fishing from the bank on Big Creek at the Old Iron Bridge, I had a humiliating letdown. I had just landed a pole-bending catfish and was proud of myself. A man who was fishing nearby without success dryly said, "If you had a dozen like that, you would have a good mess wouldn't you?" I swallowed hard and grunted in agreement.

This man left and was soon replaced by two boys about 10 or 11 years old who appeared to be twins. They wore cocky hats and had new equipment—rods, reels, tackle boxes—the works. Among the questions they shot at me were: "Why are you wearing a big old straw hat like that? Why aren't you fishing with a rod and reel? Why are you using a bucket instead of a tackle box?"

They got under my skin a little so I fibbed a little. I told them that I was a poor man and couldn't afford any better. I got no sympathy from the boys. One of the boys snapped back, "You ought to save your money and buy some better equipment."

My guardian angel smiled on me and allowed me to get back at them. I hooked a big carp—at least a ten-pounder. I landed it after playing it for a good while, as the boys looked on wild-eyed. I unhooked it and made as though I was trying to judge its weight while holding it out before me with both hands. All of a sudden, I tossed it into the water.

The boys shot the same question at me: "Why did you do that?"

My answer as I prepared to leave was, "I don't keep little fish."

Evelyn has never forgiven me for making fun of her suggestion that we "give the catfish a dough ball and let it go." This is an example of how she gets back at me:

Our daughter, LeAnn, who lives in North Carolina, was home the Fourth of July for a week's vacation. She, Evelyn, and I were finishing breakfast. We were talking about the day's fishing trip LeAnn and I had planned.

In an attempt to escalate LeAnn's anticipation of a good catch to a higher plateau, I commented that the last time I had fished at the Old Iron Bridge on Big Creek, I had come home with a stringer of really nice fish—with plenty of emphasis on the "really nice."

With a mischievous look in her eyes and mirth in her voice, LeAnn asked, "Mom, did Dad bring home a stringer of 'really nice' fish?"

Evelyn's reply was, "Yes, he did. I didn't hear a curse word out of any of them—not even while they were being skinned. He and I ate *all* of them for supper."

All of my exciting adventures did not take place in the long ago. The next and last incident that I'll relate at this time happened in May of 1989. Should any of you have concern for my future safety, please don't, because I have added this experience to a long list of things that I don't plan to repeat.

The scene of this particular fishing trip was near the bridge that crosses Bay Creek just north of Bay City. Several times in recent years, I had fished from a little flat spot at the water's edge that was adjacent to a steep concrete slab that furnished reinforcement for the bridge abutment.

On this trip, the water was over my favorite fishing spot and a few feet up on the steep supporting concrete, leaving no available place to fish from the bank. I was disappointed, because at that spot at one sitting I had caught keepers of sunfish, bluegill, crappie, and fiddlers. So my mind began to devise a way to fish from what looked like an impossible incline.

I usually fished with two 12-foot telescope poles. On one, I used a float; with the other, I fished on the bottom, which increased my chances of getting a fiddler or a blue cat. Quite often I took along an inflated inner tube and anchored it in the water near the shore to lay the poles on at times.

This inner tube loomed in my mind as a possible answer to my predicament. I decided to sit in and on the tube and scoot down the incline near the water's edge and fish with one pole. A little willow growing out of a two-inch expansion joint in the concrete about four feet from the water would serve as a scotch for my tall, five-gallon, plastic fish bucket and spare pole.

I put on a nail apron that I carried in my tackle box. It was laden with extra hooks, line, leader, lead, knife, etc. I put a covered coffee can of worms in the bib of the apron.

With the bucket on my arm and the poles across my lap, I inched my way on the incline. The first half of the 15 or more feet to the water was wild. I could almost feel myself splashing into the water like a huge bull-frog—feet first on my back. However, by using my heels for brakes and by exerting pressure on all parts of the tube, I managed to get it stopped about halfway down. Then, by using my heels, elbows, and rump, I managed to inch down to about four feet from the water.

With the light rope that I usually use to anchor the tube, I managed to get about two gallons of water in the bucket and get it behind the willow scotch. Just then, I recalled that at a prior time from the bridge, I had seen a snake in that expansion joint. That caused me to position myself about four feet from the fish bucket.

The tube and the concrete adhered to each other, and I found, to my surprise, that I was more or less comfortable in a reclined, sitting position.

The fish began to bite from the very first. The first two were bluegill—the 10- to 12-ounce size. A little toss with my steady right and they were splashing in the bucket. The next fish was a big-mouth perch, sometimes called a rock bass, which bit harder and was more exciting to hoist into the air with the limber telescope pole. I carefully removed the hook. As I was about to toss the bass into the bucket, the tube and I made a sudden slip of three or four inches. Then the tube became as stable as ever, but my nerves were not. I missed the bucket with the rock bass.

Just as I put my next catch—a chunky sunfish—into the bucket, I saw about four inches of the head end of a grayish brown snake emerging from the expansion joint, between the bucket and the water. The head was bluntish and about the size of an English walnut.

We looked each other over pretty well. I don't know what it was thinking, but I was thinking thoughts of coexisting—you leave me alone, and I will leave you alone. However, under the circumstance, I departed from my noble goal and with my pole, I slapped the concrete, just missing him a few inches on purpose. This didn't excite the snake. Ever so slowly he drew back into the expansion joint. I went on fishing successfully, but never for a moment did I forget that he posed cause for concern.

The snake never became aggressive, but he was curious throughout the time that I was there. I laid my spare pole behind the bucket with one end in my lap. When the snake peeked out at me, I would lift the pole over the bucket and let it down to the concrete and swish it down the expansion joint. In that manner, I fished on until I got a total of 32 fish, not counting the ones that missed the bucket. They always seemed to be the big ones.

That was a great fishing trip. I will never forget it. You can bet your life that I will never repeat it.

Sometime, Somewhere

It was in the mid-fifties, and I was driving to Pankeyville, where I taught grade school. Somewhere between Thacker's Gap and Mitchellsville, a man wearing a cap appeared at the edge of the road. Tall, lank, and lean, he was standing there with his thumb high in the air. I judged him to be in his mid-sixties.

My quick reflexes, for which I've always been thankful, made it possible to come to a screeching stop exactly even with him. Although it was easy to see that he was not impressed by my wild, juvenile type of stop, he opened the door and piled in quickly. He wore overalls, a blue jacket, a blue work shirt, and a flimsy railroad worker's cap.

My "Good morning, sir," didn't impress him much, either, for he immediately corrected, "The name is Bill Drayton."

"How are you, Mr. Drayton?" I replied.

To this he responded, "Call me Bill."

Not being in a very serious mood, I told Bill that I was superintendent, principal, teacher, and custodian at Pankeyville Grade School. Without giving him a chance to comment, I went on to say that down in Mountain

Township, I was Justice of the Peace, but he wouldn't have to call me "The Honorable Kestner Wallace." He could just call me "Kess." For the first time Bill's rather solemn face took on a grin. I smiled and then we laughed together. From then on we greeted each other with a friendly "Bill" and "Kess."

In the few miles we traveled together that first morning, Bill told me that he lived in a little trailer that belonged to one of the finest men that he had ever known. He said that the trailer was a poor excuse for a place to live, but the man didn't charge him any rent and was always doing nice things to make life a little more pleasant. I further learned that Bill was going to John and Ruby Nelson's store in Pankeyville, just a stone's throw from the driveway that went into Pankeyville School. Bill expressed his appreciation for the ride. I voiced my pleasure for the opportunity to make his acquaintance. We parted ways.

Over the next several weeks Bill rode with me a number of times to the Nelson Store. He explained that, since he didn't have an ice box and was to some extent on a milk diet because of stomach trouble, he had to go to the store daily. I hesitated to ask him about his past for fear that he would tell me that it wasn't any of my business. After I knew him better, we had plenty to talk about and it didn't seem to matter.

One morning when I overtook Bill, he was walking without looking back or indicating that he wanted a ride. However, his gait was most unusual. About every third step, he took a little hop. He got in as soon as I stopped.

I said, "Bill, you seem to be in a bigger hurry than usual."

In his usual tart way he replied, "If the doctor told you that you had only six months to live, you would be in a hurry, too." He went on to say, "There are so many things I have planned to do, and now there is such a little time to do them."

I told Bill that the doctors didn't always know and, after his six months were up, he would probably just live on and on and on.

Bill further said that even though the doctor didn't say, he knew that he had cancer. Very little could be said to cheer him up that day.

One evening I picked Bill up as he was on his way home from Harrisburg. After we had gone a little ways, I told Bill that I'd have to leave the highway for a short distance to pick up my mother, who was visiting with friends, and if he wished, he could stay with me and I'd take him on down the road. Bill said that would be fine since he was a bit tired. We picked Mom up and were on our way back to the highway, when a woman ran out from a house in an excited manner and waved us down. She told me that she recognized the car and thought my mother might be along. She said that she wanted to talk to her. I informed the woman that she was in luck and that Mom was in the back seat.

Since the car didn't have air conditioning and the weather was hot, the windows were down. The poor woman had a serious problem, as was later determined by a doctor. A misunderstanding on her part was more than she could cope with. She cut loose with a tongue-lashing you wouldn't believe. Her vocabulary was rather small, but what a turnover she had! I watched Mom in the rearview mirror. I'll have to admit, I was enjoying it a little. Realizing that if Mom could pick blackberries all around a big, rusty coiled rattlesnake and then walk off and leave it undisturbed because she couldn't see anything handy to kill it with, she would handle this okay, too. I watched Bill out of the corner of my eye, but mostly we sat there and looked straight ahead. I had heard Mom pray many times, "Lord, help us know when to speak and when to be silent. Help us to speak those fitly spoken words that are as apples of gold in pictures of silver." I couldn't keep from wondering whether she was going to speak or be silent.

Finally, when the woman ran down or ran out of breath, I asked if that was all she had to say.

She said, "Yes, that was what I had on my mind."

Then I asked Mom if she wished to make any comment.

She replied, "No, I think not."

Bidding her farewell, we continued on our way.

After waiting a good while and realizing that no comment was forthcoming from Bill, I pleaded, "Bill, say something."

He said four words that still help me today and further prove that a college education won't hurt a man if he is willing to learn something afterwards. Those four words were, "Least said, easiest mended."

More and more in the process of time, Bill complained of pain. One day he asked if I had a good .38 Smith that he could buy. He said he wouldn't use it unless the pain got unbearable. I told him that I didn't have a .38 and would hate to let him have one for what he had in mind.

I asked Bill if he was a Christian and if he had ever asked the Lord to give him strength to hold up and spare him too much pain. His reply was that he was a non-believer and would not or could not become a

Christian, because he couldn't bring himself to forgive a man who had done him wrong.

I asked Bill if I could come over to his trailer and talk to him about the Bible and the Lord. He told me that I was welcome to come any time. We agreed on the following evening. When I arrived, Bill gave me a warm reception. No time was wasted in coming to the point. Bill was given the admonition that Jesus gave Nicodemus when he told him, "Ye must be born again." That was explained and other scriptures were quoted. I told Bill that I was there to help him put his life in harmony with the Lord. He was assured that he didn't need to tell me or anyone else about his sins or shortcomings or the man that he couldn't forgive. God knew about it and still loved him, the other fellow, and all mankind. I instructed him to the best of my ability, prayed with him, and took my leave after receiving his sincere thanks for coming. The next time I saw Bill he made my heart rejoice by shaking my hand and saying, "You're the one man who has been able to tell me how to have peace of mind."

It is too bad that my story doesn't end here. The next time I saw Bill was at an ice cream social at Rudement Church on a Friday night. Even though I didn't talk to him immediately, I studied him from a distance. He seemed very alert with periods of deep thought.

After a while I shook hands with Bill and asked if I could buy him some ice cream and cake. At first he refused; then on second thought he said that I could. On accepting the ice cream and cake, he said, "This will be the last ice cream I'll ever eat." He went on to explain that he had it all planned out. He was intending to ride on a bread truck to Cave-In-Rock the following morning. Every so often he had been riding down with this driver as he made his way up the river from Cave-In-Rock to a cabin that he referred to as his other home.

Bill explained how he intended to place some heavy stones in his row boat along with some strong cord and row out where the water was deep. Then he would bind the stones to himself and cast himself into the water. He was sure that he would never be found.

Even though I had a feeling that he wouldn't be satisfied until he had taken his life, I tried to talk him out of it. I asked him to spend the night with Evelyn and me. We would talk until late, and then we would sleep late. I assured him that Evelyn would fix us a good breakfast, and since school was out, we could make some fishing plans. When I could think of nothing else, he quietly said, "My mind is made up." We said what we thought was our final goodbye.

The next day, Saturday, Evelyn and I had an early lunch about 11:00 a.m. and took off to go fishing at the ferry landing down the river from Elizabethtown. Just before we reached the Humm's Wye at Route 146, we overtook Bill. We stopped. He got in and commented that he was running behind schedule. He said that since it was raining when he should have gotten up to catch the bread truck, he just stayed in bed longer. My first comment was, "Bill, you are traveling light."

He gave me a knowing look and said, "This is a one-way trip." We explained to him that we were going to the ferry landing to fish and invited him to go with us.

"I have other plans," he replied.

When we neared the road that led to the ferry landing, I told Bill that we needed some extra lead for our fishing lines and would take him on as far as the hardware store. I parked some 35 feet or more away from the store so that we could have our last walk together. In front of the store

I stopped. He stopped. For the longest time we looked each other straight in the eyes. Then suddenly Bill put out his hand. The last words Bill ever said to me were, "I hope to see you again sometime, somewhere."

Fishing was good at the landing. When Evelyn and I could no longer see our floats, we went home.

On Monday Evelyn and I went to Bill's cabin. The door was open. From the door I saw the cap that Bill had on every time I saw him. The one time I saw him without his cap was the time we prayed together. We then went down the path to where his boat should have been docked. There was no boat. We saw what might have been his last footprints. Looking out over the clear, deep water, in my mind I said the last words Bill said to me, "I hope to see you again sometime, somewhere." Then we went home.

Days later Bill's body was seen afloat by a passing boat captain. It was a number of days after his burial that, by chance, I read an account of his death, which in part stated that he was never married and was laid to rest beside his father and mother.

Summer Stresses

While teaching for nine years in two different one-room schools, I attended college part-time at SIU. In the summer of 1955, I registered for enough classes to complete my Bachelor of Science degree in Elementary Education. One of those classes was an elective in speech.

While I hoped that the course would be of some benefit, my main motivation was the credit. Then, too, the scheduling of the speech class fit well in the daily Harrisburg-Carbondale car pool.

The class was made up of twenty or more juniors and seniors who accepted me really well even though I was several years older than they. We all seemed to have one thing in common—a fear of making fools of ourselves.

The speech teacher, whom we will call Mr. Joe, was tall and slender, with black, wavy hair, brown eyes, and a sad smile. He tried hard to put us at ease, but in spite of his efforts, throughout the course we stayed keyed up like the strings on a banjo.

At the first class session, Mr. Joe asked each of us to stand and introduce ourselves, add a few enlightening remarks, and tell why we were taking his class.

When my turn came to speak, I made no mention of being a teacher for fear that Mr. Joe might expect my performance to be on a higher plane. My remarks touched on the following: graduation from Harrisburg High School, work in a defense plant in Pontiac, Michigan, Navy experience in World War II, mining, and farming. My stated reason for taking the class was to "learn to speak without sputtering."

Had the class been graded on their applause, we would have all made an "A." We made each other feel good by laying on the "glad hand" when a speaker finished. The applause given me was generous, but to save my life, I couldn't tell whether Mr. Joe wanted to laugh or cry.

From day one, Mr. Joe emphasized that we put in practice the techniques that he would explain and demonstrate. He told us to forget about grades; he said to listen carefully and improve our speaking ability, and the grades would take care of themselves.

He stated that he would be mindful of the many short talks that we would make in class, but the only one that would really count would be the last one—the final speech. He liked the adjective "powerful." Time and again he told us that the last speech was to be a "powerful speech"—one that would incorporate voice intonation, eye contact, hand and body movements, and many other techniques.

Tension began to build within me and reached its climax two weeks before the final speech, when Mr. Joe told the class that we would have to turn in a "letter-perfect" outline of our final speech just prior to giving it. He told us that we could make a carbon copy and use it while making our final speech—not to read, but to use as a guide.

Being poor in the art of "perfect outline-making," I called on a close family member to make me an outline on any good subject for a speech. That help would give me more freedom to do well on my other exams. I had confidence in the ability of this person, being an English major and a high school English teacher. There was no money involved directly. We will say that this person owed me a big favor.

This person spent hour after hour in the library, supposedly doing research and taking notes for a "powerful speech." However, my nervousness began to increase on hearing statements such as the following: "I can hardly get anything done for talking to former students and friends in the library."

The day before the final speech arrived and still no outline. I began to feel desperate. I didn't know whether to pray, "cuss," or cry. I didn't cry. I don't remember about the other two. Still I was assured that I had nothing to worry about. The outline would be in my hands—complete and easy to follow.

The speech day arrived. I was on my way to class pondering what incident in my past to use as a powerful speech. Suddenly this "outline writer" met me on the campus about 300 yards from my classroom and handed me what appeared to be an outstanding outline, without a carbon copy.

My speech was second of two that fell on the last day. The turmoil of my mind made it impossible for me to make sense out of the outline. It was completely foreign to me. So I listened to the speech being given, smiled my support, nodded my understanding, and applauded the conclusion.

When my name was called, I walked over to the instructor, who was sitting in a student chair near the back of the room on the right side, and handed him my outline. I looked deep into the instructor's eyes and gave him a trace of a smile before going to the podium in the front of the room. After properly addressing the group, I began as follows:

Upon finishing my sophomore year of high school, I went to Ypsilanti, Michigan, to get summer work. After paying five dollars to the fellow who hauled passengers to and from Harrisburg and Pontiac, Michigan, I had seven dollars.

I went to the address of a friend from Harrisburg and was told by the landlady that this person had moved to Pontiac. Before the impact of this statement fully hit me, a young lady, who lived in the same building from which my friend had moved, approached me. She was attractive, with blue eyes and blond hair.

Even though I didn't recognize her, she said with emotion, "You are from Harrisburg. I knew you as soon as I saw you."

Going on she told me that her present name was Mrs. Emma McWorth, the former Emma Leak—married for three months and homesick enough to die. On a hunch, I asked her if she was kin to Aunt Em Killman (no relation to me, but a name by which everyone called her).

Emma threw wide her arms, and with a little cry of delight, exclaimed, "Am I kin to Aunt Em Killman! She is my grandma!"

It took a little self-control on my part not to fall into my dear cousin's arms, but the realization that we weren't really kin and the fact that she was "Mrs." caused me to restrain myself.

In a short time, as Emma and I sat on the apartment steps, her husband came bounding down the sidewalk swinging his lunch bucket. He was tall with an athletic build and a quick, pleasant smile.

Emma, still filled with enthusiasm, said, "Mike, this is my cousin, Kestner Wallace. Kestner, this is my husband, Mike."

As we shook hands, Mike said that it was good to have company from home. He told me that he was from Southern Illinois also—several miles north of Harrisburg.

By this time I felt that I had my speech off the ground. One thing that bothered me was the difficulty Mr. Joe was having in locating where I was on the outline. I tried to distract him by slightly exaggerating my arm and hand gestures and by slapping my open hand on the podium a time or two. Finally, he gave up on flipping the pages on the outline and settled down to listening. That made it easier on me. Still the pressure was on throughout. My goal was to make the speech so powerful and interesting that he would forget that it didn't go along with the outline.

You can take my word for it that I displayed all the techniques that Mr. Joe had taught us—eye contact, facial expression, palms up, palms down, body movement, voice intonation—the whole bit. I threw in one or two of my own for good measure.

It was Mike's opinion that the only available work would be farm work. He suggested I spend the night with them and said that Emma could help me look up and call about "help wanted" ads in the morning paper.

The first farmer I called was Fred Parsons, who lived two miles southwest of Ypsilanti. He told me that he and his sister lived together, and the person they hired would live in the home with them. The wages would be $30 per month. Room, board, and laundry would also be included. With pride in his voice, he said that he and his sister were college people and they wanted their hired hand to have at least a high school education.

When I got a chance, I said, "Let me tell you about myself. I'm 16 years old, but would probably pass for 18 or 19. I'm strong, healthy, and don't drink, smoke, or use bad language. I know how to work with or without supervision. I have just finished two years of high school and plan to continue school in September." I added that I had in mind a wage minimum of $40 per month.

There was a pause before Mr. Parsons asked where he could see me. We made arrangements for him to meet me at Emma and Mike's house. While waiting for him to come, I expressed my appreciation to Emma for her and Mike's kindness. She said that they were happy to be of help and hoped we could visit again soon.

I learned a great deal about Fred and Sarah Parsons the summer I worked for them. He was 65 and she was 67 back in 1937. Neither of them had ever been married. She had taught some in her younger days and had a great love for art and music.

Fred was interested in politics, the stock market, and big league ball games. He relied heavily on the county farm advisor for advice on the latest trends in farming.

Neither Fred nor Sarah was lazy. Even though they lived in a large, country mansion, drove late-model vehicles, owned much cattle and land, and were thought by their neighbors to be very wealthy, they put in long days at work.

Sarah was concerned about Fred's health and feared that he worked too much. She fussed at him about first one thing and another, and it appeared that she had the bluff in on him. He would tip me off when she was in a bad mood, and we would both be careful.

Fred and Sarah liked me as a farm hand. They engaged me in card games and worthwhile conversations of evenings. They invited me to return and work for them the following summer.

The Parsons were fine people in spite of the fact they were ultra-conservative and verged on being selfish. However, they were most generous in spreading a good table. At the noonday and evening meals, there were always one or more kinds of meat, a variety of fruit and vegetables, home-baked bread, and pastries. A small pitcher of whole milk was by my plate at each meal.

Fred and Sarah had three or four hundred acres of high-grade farm land in a crop rotation that included corn, wheat, hay, oats, and pasture for a fine herd of beef cattle. They also had a 20-acre apple orchard in which Fred took great pride.

In addition, Fred had 80 acres of wheat that was harvested the old-fashioned way—neighbor helping neighbor. Fred sent me with a team and wagon to return the help his neighbors had furnished him. From the neighbors, I learned more about Fred and Sarah Parsons than I wanted to know. I tried to conclude that their critical attitude stemmed from their being jealous of the Parsons' prosperity, which was considerable. However, that summer an incident occurred that gave me a different perspective.

One day Mr. Parsons and a relative of his, whose name was also Fred, and I were taking up loose, sweet-smelling hay and loading it with long-handled pitchforks onto a large horse-drawn hay wagon. Things were going so well it hardly seemed like work.

About eleven o'clock that morning, I saw a black man considering his steps as he walked slowly toward us across the stubbled hay field. I made no mention of his approach, but observed that he was well along in years, slightly stooped, but still blessed with class, dignity, and pride. He wore brown dress trousers and a vest to match, a necktie, and a clean, well-fitting shirt. His brown shoes were probably shined for the occasion.

Before Mr. Parsons knew he was around, the man greeted Mr. Parsons by saying, "Good morning to you, Fred."

With a surprised grin, Mr. Parsons responded, "Hi, Fred. We are well blessed with Freds today." Nodding at his relative, he said, "This is my cousin, Fred."

Mr. Parsons nodded at me and said, "This is Kess. He has the job you had when you worked for me."

The black man and I shook hands firmly as he remarked, "Kess, you are working for a good man."

I sensed a sincere concern when Mr. Parsons inquired about Fred's health. In response, Fred told him that he had been in the hospital for surgery and had been out only a few days. He felt the walk from

Ypsilanti out to the farm would be good for him if he walked slowly and rested along the way.

I liked Fred from the first word he spoke. He seemed to have a clear, pleasant voice, keen eyes, and an alert, cultured mind.

Mr. Parsons looked at his watch and said, "By the time we get this load to the barn and unloaded, it will be dinner time." Then Mr. Parsons looked at the black man and asked, "Fred, you will eat dinner with us, won't you?"

His reply was, "Yes, Fred, if you think it will be all right with Sarah."

After the hay was unloaded and the team fed, the four of us went trooping off to the house with Mr. Parsons in the lead. I brought up the rear just behind the black man. I was happy he had been invited to eat and was looking forward to seeing him enjoy a good meal to the fullest. I couldn't keep from wondering if Fred had been accepted as warmly as a family member as I had. It was my desire to play the part of a family host, still realizing my limited role as a hired hand.

Washing for meal time was done on a closed-in porch just off from the dining room. I realized that Mr. Parsons had had time to inform Sarah that another plate would need to be set. I peeked in through the door to try to read Sarah's mood and reaction. There was no question in my mind about her having enough food for all of us.

When I got a glimpse of Sarah, she was standing rigid, arms flared out and palms down. It was clear to me that she was saying: "No way, Fred, I won't stand for it."

I was holding a paper towel to hand Fred as soon as he washed. I can still see those long black fingers *as they extended into the water to the first joint, at the same time that Mr. Parsons walked up and said regretfully, "Fred, Sarah says she won't be able to serve you today."*

Fred's quick reply, after the initial shock, was, "Oh, well, Fred, that's all right."

With a heavy heart, I handed him the towel as planned and observed as he rubbed it over his already dry hands. I watched his stooped, dejected form as he started his long trudge back to Ypsilanti.

The meal was extra special. My dessert was a large piece of apple pie with a piece of cheese on it and a half of a large cantaloupe with the center filled with ice cream made from pure cream. I had a little trouble eating at first because of the lump in my throat. However, I ate and tried not to let my feelings show. Still, that was my least enjoyable meal with the Parsons.

I stepped back and gave a little bow to indicate that my speech was over. The group gave me a good applause which lifted my spirits some. I went to Mr. Joe, as the others had done, to pick up my outline and to be told my term grade.

Mr. Joe said confidentially, "Your speech went over well with the class. I liked it, too. I'm giving you an 'A' on your outline, but I'm giving you a 'B' for the course because your speech didn't follow your outline."

I said, "Thank you, sir. I recognize your generosity." We shook hands and, to my surprise, he gave me a smile.

My dear friend and "outline writer" was waiting pale-faced and anxious to know how I'd done on my speech. I smiled my answer as I said, "Take a look at this big fat 'A.' In fact, I want you to have this outline for 'show and tell.'"

It was accepted with pleasure. To this day, I have no idea what was in that outline.

Lonnie Hyden and Me

S ince Lonnie Hyden was 27 years my senior, I called
him Mr. Hyden. Almost everyone called him Lonnie,
so in this story, I'll call him Lonnie, also.

On a pleasant June morning in the early 60s, I was
working in the garden with a hoe, picking up an earth-
worm now and then to use on my next fishing trip. Around
mid-morning, Andrew Duncan, a man with whom I had
hunted and fished, drove up in our driveway and told
me that he wanted me to meet his brother-in-law, Lonnie
Hyden. Andrew added in an undertone, "He is about to
fish me to death."

Lonnie and I shook hands. I showed him my can
of worms and asked, "Does this look like I'm a fisher-
man?" Lonnie's blue eyes sparkled through his thick-
lensed glasses.

Lonnie was about five feet six inches tall and weighed
around 160 pounds. My wife, Evelyn, walked up from
working among her flowers and spoke to Andrew and
was introduced to Lonnie. Lonnie's tip of his hat and
handshake, along with a slight bow, spelled out a touch

of culture of a bygone day. He didn't seem to mind showing his bald head.

I told Lonnie that I fished from a 4' x 8' plywood, fiberglassed boat that I carried on the top of my car. Lonnie's eyes shone with excitement as a new plan popped into his head. He explained that we could haul the boat around in his Dodge pickup and fish far and near.

That afternoon Lonnie and I headed to Long Lake north of Shawneetown, with me at the wheel. Our first fishing trip was our best number-wise. We caught 77 bluegill.

Another fishing trip soon thereafter in Hardin County was a near failure. On the way home, neither of us said anything for the first two or three miles. Then with great enthusiasm and a big smile, Lonnie said, "We had a good time, didn't we?"

I disguised my surprise and swallowed hard and replied, "We sure did." I gradually caught on that, fish or no fish, one can have a good time fishing. Still today, more than forty years later, I give Lonnie credit for teaching me that there is more to fishing than the number of fish caught—for instance, the enjoyment of nature and all of its fullness.

Little by little on fishing trips, I learned about Lonnie's past. He had volunteered for the Army at the beginning of World War I. He never missed an opportunity to tell people that he was gassed and shell-shocked during the war—it was his badge of honor.

On Lonnie's 80th birthday, he told me that since he was 21, he hadn't missed a month getting a check from the government. He was sent to college by the government and specialized in agriculture, while taking other courses in math and engineering. Lonnie said that the doctors gave up on schooling as a means to help him get over being shell-shocked and gassed in the Army. Lonnie made sure that one and all knew that on dismissal, he was instructed by the Army doctors to take life easy and fish at every opportunity.

Looking amused, I asked Lonnie one time if he thought that I could write a letter to the Veteran's Administration and get them to recommend fishing for the stress that I had suffered in World War II, along with a monthly check to show their appreciation for my contribution toward world peace. Lonnie smiled and replied, "I think you are an intelligent man, but not sharp enough to pull it off."

Over the years that I knew him, Lonnie barely mentioned his first wife and two daughters—they were a part of his life hidden to me. His second wife, Sarah, along with her two brothers and two sisters, were born two miles south of Rudement to Elijah Gibbs. Sarah worked in Evansville at a cigar factory and remained single until she was perhaps in her fifties.

After Sarah and Lonnie married, they moved to Texas, where Lonnie went into construction, as he proudly told people later. His equipment consisted of a pickup truck, two wheelbarrows, a portable cement mixer, and some hand-powered finishing tools. He put in walks and driveways, using cheap Mexican labor. He did well until his health forced him to give up on construction.

After Lonnie quit construction work, he peddled peaches for a while. He asked me once if I had ever tried negative selling in my hobby, car-trading and selling. I told him I hadn't and asked him how it worked.

He told me that he would go to the orchard and get some fairly good peaches that he could sell for $2.50

a bushel and some extra good peaches that he could sell for $5.00 per bushel. Lonnie said that he would go up to a mansion-type farmhouse, park in the driveway, and slowly walk toward the house. About halfway to the house, he would stop and wait for his shell-shock and gas attack to pass. Often a friendly dog would announce his arrival. Usually a man would come out.

As soon as he got his breath, Lonnie would tell the man that he wanted to show him some fine peaches for $2.50—just right to eat raw, can, or make delicious cobblers. Then he would give him the negative sales pitch. "I bet you wouldn't be interested in a bushel of the orchard's best at $5.00 per bushel."

Lonnie explained that the old farmer would reason, "What makes you think I wouldn't be interested in a $5.00 bushel of peaches?" Lonnie said that the man would then buy one or two bushels.

If you, my readers, will bear with me, I'll tell you a little about two of my trading cars and my own attempt at negative selling. I drove a trading car when I taught school at Pankeyville. I also furnished transportation for my mom to and from Duncan School, a one-room schoolhouse where she taught.

Mom had more than a passing interest in my car trading. She was brought up in the horse and buggy days, so she felt that anything that would run was an improvement over the old days. However, her knowledge of operating a car was nil.

This particular trading car ran like a striped snake. One day, after I had picked Mom up from Duncan, we were coming home with our hair blowing back. Suddenly something was terribly wrong. The car bounced and shimmied. It reminded me of a time when I was driving and an earthquake occurred. I wondered whether the drive shaft had come loose and I had run over it. I looked in the rearview mirror and realized that the battery had fallen out, and I had run over it in the loose gravel. It lay in the middle of the road.

The engine was running on fast idle, meaning that the car was continuing to run off the generator. I backed up and put the battery in the trunk, and we came on home.

I later heard Mom recounting the incident to some friends. She told them that we were coming home from school when the motor fell out of the car, and I had stopped and picked it up and put it in the trunk, and we came on home. Mom's story amused me so much that I never told her otherwise.

On the way home, after the battery fell out, I told Mom that it was about time that I gave that car a good trading off. She gave me her usual lecture about misrepresenting and cheating people. I gave her a Lonnie Hyden grin and said, "Maw, you know me better than that." I didn't get rid of that particular car with negative selling, however. I traded it to an Eagle Creeker for a coon dog and then sold the coon dog to the man's brother-in-law.

One Friday evening just near dark, I bought a car. It looked good under a pole light, but I had failed to see some sideswipe damage on the passenger's side. I drove the car the half mile to Mom's on Saturday morning to take her to town to do her shopping. She gave the newly purchased car a good looking over. Neither of us said anything at first as we took off for town. Then she said, "You're driving a different car, aren't you?"

I answered, "Yes, I bought it after dark." Her reply with amusement in her voice was, "You may have to sell it after dark."

It occurred to me that this sideswiped car would be ideal for me to try my hand at negative selling. I improved its appearance by doing some bodywork on it. I got a prospect lined up and said, "I bet you wouldn't be interested in a good buy in a quiet-running car that is easy on gas and doesn't use oil."

This bird's reply set me back a bit. Without hesitation he said, "That is a safe bet. I wouldn't be caught dead in that trap." I came to the conclusion that what will work for one person might not work for another.

Now, back to my story. Sarah Gibbs came into ownership of her homeplace before she married Lonnie. She looked forward to retiring there. When Lonnie's health failed, he and Sarah decided to move to Illinois and live in her homeplace.

Lonnie loved the homeplace. It reminded him of his old Kentucky home. The outside had been sided, but the inside displayed huge, hewn white oak logs and a fireplace that rounded out all he could wish for.

Suddenly Lonnie had an extended family. He had two sisters-in-law and four brothers-in-law. He was blessed with a large number of nieces and nephews, who proudly called him "Uncle Lonnie." He took an interest in each one and encouraged each one to get the best education possible.

Lonnie had a brother-in-law, Ira, whom I never met. Ira, who was blind, complained to Lonnie that he liked to fish as well as the next one, but no one would take him. Lonnie told me that he had taken Ira fishing a short time before he died. Lonnie set him in a likely place in a lawn chair, with a baited hook and a pole in hand. If Ira didn't feel a pole movement, Lonnie told him when to pull and how to lift the fish out. Ira had a grand time, and Lonnie got a blessing out of doing a good deed.

Even though I never met Ira in life, I attended his funeral at the Gibbons Funeral Home. My attending was mostly to please Lonnie. However, he was lamenting the fact that Ira's funeral fell on a time when we had planned to go fishing.

Lonnie hatched a plan how we could do both. He said that we could put the boat and fishing equipment in the truck and park a little ways from "close up." We could wear a tie and a jacket and shed them as soon as we got to the truck. He explained that Sarah would want to sit with her brother and sisters, and that we could sit on the non-family side that would be first in the final viewing march. That way, we could be on our way sooner.

During the long eulogy, Lonnie and I refrained from sighing, but we silently prayed that the message would move along a little faster so the dear brother could be laid to rest. At last the final viewing began. I followed Lonnie. As we neared the casket, Lonnie took out his handkerchief. I took out mine in case I needed it. As I viewed Ira, I recalled how Lonnie had taken the poor blind man fishing. My eyes filled with tears. We both moved along dabbing at our eyes. Afterwards, making our escape, we went on and fished, well pleased that things had turned out so well.

Sarah's health failed and she spent her final several days in the hospital. Lonnie was heartbroken over her death and said that he couldn't continue living in her home knowing that she wouldn't be back.

He moved in the farmhouse that was the old Wallace homestead, which I owned. The house was old-fashioned and fully furnished, with a large fireplace and a shady

"L"-shaped porch. Lonnie was happy with the arrangements we worked out concerning his well-being.

Every so often, Lonnie would check himself into the Veteran's Hospital in Marion. I visited him midweek and Saturday afternoon. During one of his hospital stays, Lonnie was telling his nurse what a wonderful landlord he had. His nurse said that she would like to meet me sometime.

Lonnie and I agreed that my next Saturday visit would be at 4:00 p.m. So that I could make a good impression on his nurse, Lonnie wanted me to dress up in my best "go-to-church" clothes—white shirt, hair groomed, and shoes shined, etc. I promised to do as he requested.

Being the practical man that I am, I drove my old, faded red International pickup truck to bring back a load of lump coal. Lonnie would need it when he got out of the hospital.

I pulled into the Harrisburg Mining Company, located a few miles west of Harrisburg. The mine appeared to be closed for the weekend. Two well-dressed men stood about a hundred yards from where I stopped near a pile of lump coal. I got out of the truck, and perhaps appeared to look important. One of the men started toward me. As he was walking, he said over his shoulder, "I guess he is here to try to buy us out." However, he was kind and friendly, and upon learning my true intent, got on the end loader and guessed at a generous ton of coal.

At the hospital, the nurse was waiting in Lonnie's room. Since Lonnie was out of the room, the nurse and I introduced ourselves to each other. She bragged on Lonnie's being such a kind, polite man.

In a short time, Lonnie came into the room with his hand outstretched to shake hands with me. He smiled broadly and patted me on the back. I did likewise to him.

Trying to make me look important, he asked, "Did you drive over in your Buick or your Olds?" He was careful not to ask in a way that would indicate that both were my old trading cars.

Whatever image he had carefully painted in the nurse's eyes was quickly marred when I announced, "I drove my old pickup to pick up a ton of coal on the way over." The nurse peeped out the window, where she could see my poor excuse for a truck loaded down there in the parking lot. Showing his disappointment in me, Lonnie was only slightly mollified when I hastened to explain that the coal was for his fireplace when he returned home, to supplement his gas heater. Trying to cheer him up, I told him to just imagine how that coal burning in the grate of his fireplace would warm the cockles of his heart.

Not long after he was released from the hospital, Lonnie took a trip over to Kentucky to visit his kinfolks for the first time in many years. He had a brother, Ben, and a sister, Alma, who was born after he went off to war. They had never seen each other. Alma told me later that she knew Lonnie as soon as she saw him, because he looked so much like their father.

Lonnie told me that his folks treated him like a king. They had a church called the Hyden Church. He was asked to take charge of the Sunday morning service. That was one of the high points of his life.

Alma and her husband, Fred Barnett, came over and visited Lonnie. Evelyn cleaned house for him and put the spare bedroom in good shape. She also catered in their evening meal, with my help.

The Barnetts were well pleased with how happy Lonnie was with his living setup. But it was their opinion that he should spend the rest of his days in Kentucky with his blood kin. Lonnie hated to go, and Evelyn and I and his friends hated to see him leave, but it appeared that the hand of God was in the move.

Alma kept us informed concerning Lonnie's well-being. When he died, she sent me a clipping of his obituary from the hometown paper. I put some personal touches with it and had it put in the Harrisburg Daily Register.

It would be an injustice to leave the reader feeling that Lonnie's only interest in life was fishing. He was also interested in science, education, religion, and politics, and we had many interesting discussions over our friend-ship. His deepest desire was to meet his Maker with clean hands and a pure heart, and I believe that he did. Lonnie, I'll always be thankful that for a pleasant period of time, our paths ran parallel along this uneven journey of life.

4-0-3 to Beech Hollow

In an effort to recall the fascination of a trip to Beech Hollow in the mid-1930s, I recently retraced my steps of long ago. I was not trying to live in the past, but to recapture and preserve a part of that past for posterity.

This trip was both alike and different from those of earlier years. As I started out on this and previous trips, Womble Mountain was at my back. The hills, ridges, and valleys were surprisingly about the same after the passing of more than fifty years. Different was the increased difficulty in crossing the same terrain.

In the '20s and '30s the first half of this acreage was fenced. A few head of horses and cattle grazed on it. Paths and trails crisscrossed the pasture land then, making it rather easy to walk across. Gates, gaps, or some means of passage were provided from one fenced area to another. Now, there are no fences and no paths, and once cleared land is overgrown.

This trip was also different in another way, as it was my first to Beech Hollow on foot. Before, I had ridden Sampson, our easy-riding, sure-footed mule. Two or three times I had gone alone, but usually the trip was made with others along.

For a number of young men who lived around Womble Mountain from Rudement to Herod, a trip to Beech Hollow was the therapy used for a broken heart. The heart of the young man was usually broken by his girlfriend quitting him.

A number of names were given in those days for a courtship being terminated. Among them were as follows: "getting sacked," "having the boom lowered on them," "getting walking papers," etc. But the one that was closely associated with Beech Hollow was a "4-0-3."

The "4-0-3" was a term associated with terminating a period of work on the W.P.A. It was with concern and anxiety that the 4-0-3's were received by any who were working.

The term "4-0-3" was picked up in our area as a way of saying that one of the "Good Old Boy's" gal had quit him. Since I had not yet reached my middle teens, I had never received a 4-0-3 from the Works Progress Administration or from any other source. But I saw the sad look in the eyes of some who received both kinds.

The first person to my knowledge to use the Beech Hollow therapy was a fellow we will call O.E. Jones. O.E. had been engaged for some time to an attractive young lady who, for reasons best known to herself, gave him a 4-0-3. He had a broken heart that affected soul, body, and mind. The sympathy of the community was with him. He asked his good friend, whom we will call H.D. Walls, to walk with him over to Beech Hollow the following Sunday.

In those days there were no telephones in the community, but there was a "grapevine" that reached all around Womble Mountain, with one branch that ran up toward Rudement and another that ran down to Herod. Famous animals that assisted in spreading the news were Jack, Kate, Queen, Prince, and Sampson.

According to informed sources, as O.E. and H.D. walked from south to north in Beech Hollow, a young man, "Private Eye," had already concealed himself on the west slope near the center of the hollow, close to a low flat rock. He merely wanted to observe firsthand the action of a man with a broken heart.

O.E. and H.D. were talking very little. On reaching the large flat rock, O.E. sat down on it and motioned H.D. on as he said, "I'll be ready to go back in fifteen minutes."

O.E. put his elbows on his knees. He cradled his head in his hands and sat there almost as motionless as a statue. The only movement was that of his head and shoulders, which "Private Eye" thought was a result of weeping. It was also his opinion, and later quoted as fact by others, that O.E. was asking God to lift the load from his shoulders and the burden from his heart.

When H.D. returned, O.E. was on his feet standing taller and less tense. He was smiling and talking freely as they began to retrace their steps. Private Eye went quickly to his mount, which was tied at some distance, and was back home in time to eat noon-day dinner with the family.

In a few weeks, H.D. called on O.E. to walk him to Beech Hollow. H.D. wanted to get in on some of the publicity that O.E. had gotten out of his trip. H.D.'s girlfriend had given him a 4-0-3 for seeing another girl on the sly. It pleased her to think that he was that concerned, and they were soon back together.

As an outgrowth of the two mentioned cases, several boys, on getting 4-0-3's, also took trips to Beech Hollow. The trips were usually made on horseback or muleback. The number of comforters increased to five or six or more. They whooped and hollered to drive away the lingering blues of the sorrowing friend.

They would also keep a sharp lookout for a bumblebee's nest to fight out. There was nothing like two or three bumblebee stings to cause a fellow to get his thoughts off his girlfriend long enough for his mind to become clear.

On this most recent trip, the first quarter of a mile was richest in memories. More than a hundred years earlier, this land belonged to Jonathan Wallace. Now it belongs to his great-grandson, Ray Jonathan Wallace, my son.

A wooded valley runs from east to west on the second half of this quarter of a mile. Smaller valleys or ravines angle off north and south from the larger valley. From these valleys, ravines, and ridges as a boy, I took squirrels for food and coon for food and pelts. Here, too, a number of years later, I tagged my first deer.

Farther west I crossed over on land that years ago was known as "The Grant Place," but for the past good many years is DeNeal land. I crossed this land a few hundred feet south of Gary and Judy DeNeal's home.

From this ridge, I eased off down into Sally Hollow, which is not without its charm and beauty, and very slowly climbed the west side to the ridge above. Since this ridge is rather narrow, I was soon descending a steeper incline that leads to the heart of Beech Hollow.

On previous trips to Beech Hollow, I had ridden Sampson north and south in the hollow on the dry rocky creek bed without difficulty. But this had changed. Trees had been blown across the creek bed and others had fallen because of their age, making passage difficult even on foot. Water stood in the creek bed in places because of dams formed by fallen trees, limbs, and leaves. In spite of these minor inconveniences, the hollow was just the same, in that stretches in the creek bed had no obstructions.

Only seconds after arriving, even though I was breathing heavily and leg weary, I felt well repaid for my efforts. My heart was light and my spirit gleeful. I couldn't help wondering, "Why had I stayed away so long?"

Unable to determine which rock O.E. sat on, I made myself comfortable on a stone with a tree close enough to furnish a backrest. Around me were large smooth-barked beech trees. One only a few feet from me had a number of initials carved on it. More plainly than a number of the initials, the year 1930 was carved. That put me in deep meditation for some time. The date was before my first trip over there more than fifty years earlier. Since that time, I had been as far from that place as one could go without being in outer space. Some folks that had their initials on that tree would be quite old, and others had quit the walks of man.

Fortunately for me before my up-beat mood became too sentimental, a couple of squirrels began barking at each other or at me. That caused me to space out again and wonder about the wildlife population presently and in the past. It even caused me to consider to what extent the Indians had used the hollow to secure food and protection.

Time passed quickly. I found myself wishing I could sit there until almost dark and then be lifted out by helicopter. Knowing that to be wishful thinking, I slowly retraced my steps.

There was not more than fifteen minutes of daylight left when my sweet wife, Evelyn, met me at the door and told me that she was glad I was back. Over a good dinner, I reported the trip with so much pleasure that she wanted to know when I could go back and take her, too.

On the Mountaintop

T he past paraded before the eyes of my memory as I recently sat on the top of Womble Mountain in Southeastern Saline County. More pondering of the past took place than on many previous trips up there.

I walked the few hundred feet from the scene of my birthplace east of Illinois Route 34 to the foot of the mountain. Here on the west side the terrain made a marked turn upward.

At this point a little brook flows. Since childhood it was known by our family as the "Spring Branch." The brook is fed by two springs. One was called the "Tent Spring." The other was called the "Big Spring." Both are on the land of my son, Ray J. Wallace.

Ray's great-grandfather, Jonathan Wallace, made corn whiskey and peach brandy legally beside the brook with a federal license he held in the years around 1880. Old records show that the license was issued at Paducah, Kentucky.

As a child, I asked my dad why the smaller of the two springs was called the Tent Spring. His reply was that a long time before he was born in 1868, Indians lived in tents near the spring. He said that their chief may have been Chief Womble. He was the first person to be buried in the cemetery that is now known as the Wallace Cemetery.

After talking to older people, Dad formed the opinion that Chief Womble was an honorable man. He was the father of a number of daughters who married in the area. Based on the names mentioned, some of his offspring have blended into the Saline County population. For fear my zeal to inform would exceed my knowledge, I'll say no more about Chief Womble.

After a slow, steady ascent of perhaps three-fourths of a mile, I was on top of Womble Mountain, where I sat almost exhausted.

I sat motionless for a while, and my mind wandered back several years recalling things that had happened on that mountain, as it concerned me or fell within the scope of my knowledge.

In 1900, Aaron Lambert bought a sizable number of acres of Womble Mountain. For the next three decades, he provided well for his family by filling contracts for railroad cross-ties, mining ties, and mine props. During this same period of time, the mountain held a great attraction for young people. Oftentimes they would take picnic lunches and spend the day. This was particularly true on Easter Sunday.

At the time of Mr. Lambert's purchase, about twenty acres on the very top of the mountain were less wooded than the surrounding acres. Mr. Lambert told my dad that he would give him all the corn that he could raise on this plot for a certain number of years if he would put it in cultivation. My dad was pleased with the corn crops he took off the mountain.

Off and on through the years, crops were taken off the mountain. I knew of some good red clover hay being grown there. The last crop grown there was produced in 1936 by Verdon and Douglas Lambert, sons of Aaron Lambert. However, a crop I still remember was grown in 1930, when I was ten.

Many things stand out in my mind that took place that year—some good, some bad. From good to bad were the following: a happy family life, the birth of my baby brother Gaylord, the birth of a pair of twin mules, the birth of my famous riding mule, Sampson, the Great Depression, and a year of little rainfall—a drought.

The man that rented the mountain that same year borrowed $10 from my dad with a promise to repay it with corn at harvest time. True to his promise, that fall he put the corn in our barn based on the going price of corn, 20 cents per bushel.

The same day that the corn was delivered, another man stopped on his way home from the store at Rudement. He had bought three pairs of black dress shoes made of genuine leather for 15 cents per pair. They were sizes 6, 7, and 8. Shoes of that quality were selling for four or more dollars a pair. But because of a mix-up at the factory, all six shoes were for the right foot. With full knowledge of this, my dad traded three bushels of this mountain corn for the three pairs of shoes. Even yet when I think of the shoes, I think of the mountain corn.

Being the oldest of three brothers, I got the size 8. They were too large, but they laced up fairly well. The same was true with my brothers two and four years younger than I.

On that day, our sense of humor had not yet been dulled by the hard knocks of life. We looked at each other's feet and became hilarious with laughter. The full impact of Dad's action had not yet come to rest on our tender spirits. We more or less agreed that for 20 cents a pair, they were a bargain. However, it soon became clear that Dad had fallen short of using his usual good judgment and foresight.

Whatever humor we saw on that eventful Thursday evening vanished on Friday at school. It didn't take us long to realize that the fine kids weren't exactly laughing with us. If you think life is rough for a boy named "Sue," try wearing your shoes on the wrong feet. The thing that saved the day, our reputation, and sanity, was the fact that this measure of conservation was short-lived.

My mood was one of gloom on Saturday morning. I put on my new black shoes, but instead of moving around like a ten-year-old boy, I got around like an old man with the weight of the world on his shoulders. There was a cloud over my dad's countenance also. He willingly gave me permission to take Old Maude, the mother of the twin mules, for a ride. The twins were now weaned.

Dad watched me carefully as I left in an aimless mood. However, my destination was the top of the mountain. I followed the rough wagon road that led to the top from the northwest side.

Once on the top, I seated myself on the ground at the edge of the corn field and removed my shoes. I stood up and turned around a few times with my eyes closed and threw one shoe as far as I could. I turned around a few more times with my eyes still closed and let the other one go. Without looking to my right or my left, I returned home.

Dad was aware of my returning. He asked, "How was your ride?"

"It was fine. Your next question is 'where did you go?' The answer is on the mountain top."

"Why did you go up there?"

"I went up there and threw those dreadful shoes away. I would rather be dead than to wear them this school year."

"Did they really make you feel that bad?"

"I didn't only feel bad for myself, but I felt bad for you and my two brothers."

"You felt bad for me? Why did you feel bad for me?"

"I have heard you say that many large families have at least one 'odd-ball' in it. With our wearing those shoes, people would get the impression that you have more than your share of oddballs."

"Why didn't you take the other boys' shoes along also?"

"You don't need to say any more. Their shoes will turn up missing too."

That afternoon Dad hitched the black mare to the buggy and had Mom take all three of us boys to the store to be fitted for new shoes.

Somehow three brothers have remembered that episode longer and talked about it less than other things that happened in 1930. We have had our disagreements through the years, but when we were last together, we agreed that money isn't everything, but it is a pretty good cure for poverty. About the only advantage we could come up with in favor of being poor was that it didn't cost very much. We also laughed about our meal-time choices in 1930s—it was take it or leave it.

I don't really know how much time was spent running the events of 1930 through my mind. When I came to myself, a squirrel was about six feet up on the side of a sapling no more than fifteen feet from me, barking his head off.

Seeing the squirrel reminded me of how hard I had tried to make a squirrel dog out of a dog, Tige, we had in 1934. He was a good watchdog—lively and young. His papers, if he had had any, would have shown mostly mutt and stray dog.

Tige was with my two brothers and me about half-way up on the side of the mountain one summer day, while we were cutting our next winter's heating wood. We hoped Tige would tree a squirrel and by and by turn into a squirrel dog. It was understood that in case he treed, one of us would go to him as quickly as we could to honor his effort and further encourage him.

About the middle of the morning, Tige began barking in rapid succession. We were sure that he had a squirrel treed. His location was a long distance from us. In fact it was just over the bluff a short distance from where I sat recalling the past. I suggested that my brothers rest while I ran and checked on *my* dog.

I took off in a run and didn't stop until I got to him. He was easy to find because he didn't stop barking. He was on a flat rock about four feet high and twelve feet across. My heart sank when I saw him slapping the rock with first one big black paw and then the other. I was familiar with dogs having fits, but Tige appeared to be completely off his rocker in a different sort of way.

Not knowing what else to do, I climbed up on the rock with him. Then I saw what he had bayed. It was a big black ant, known as a—oh, never mind what he was known as. Tige was a little afraid of the ant. He would slap his paws down about two inches from it and kept it in a spot no bigger than a foot in diameter.

Back at the wood cutting, I didn't beat around the bush. I just up and said, "Boys, I'm sorry to tell you, but *your* dog Tige will never make a squirrel dog."

However, later Tige became *our* dog again when he turned into a good opossum dog.

One night when my brothers and I were hunting, Tige bayed a possum not far from where he had barked at the ant. It was the biggest possum that I've ever seen. His head was as big as a big man's fist. He must have weighed ten pounds. Hunters call that kind an old "residenter."

When we got to Tige, the possum was on the ground playing dead. In other words he was sulled—nature's way of protecting him, since he doesn't move too quickly. Tige was a softy, unless he needed to be otherwise. He knew how to keep the possum sulled by slapping him now and then with his paw. This kept the hide and carcass in good shape. This "big boy's" hide would bring more than a dollar, and I could trade the carcass pound for pound for sweet potatoes.

Tige was too excited to hunt for a while. He just pranced along beside me as I carried the sulled possum by the tail. If he could have talked, Tige would have told us how proud we should be of him. We were proud of him and told him so, and he understood. He was no longer a "dumb dog."

When Tige started hunting again, we sat down to wait for him to tree or bay. We could tell the difference by the way he would bark. We laid the possum near us.

When Tige barked treed, we sprang to our feet. I reached down to pick up the possum. We couldn't believe our eyes. There was no possum to be seen. He had slipped away through the dry leaves without our hearing him. We were amazed as well as disappointed.

When we got to Tige, he was barking up a big den tree. We thought it might have been a coon. We went home empty-handed, but we didn't blame Tige. We thought that he had performed well.

...

Realizing that I had reminisced long enough for one trip on the mountain, I slowly got to my feet to find that I was almost too stiff to walk at first. My lament that I couldn't speed down the mountain as I once could was soon replaced with a thankfulness for being able to get down under my own power. After the passing of an hour, I lay on my stomach and drank from the Tent Spring, mostly to prove to myself that I could.

In another fifteen minutes, I was back home with my heart strings vibrating with happiness. It was partly because I had been on the mountain top, but more so because I had returned safely and was standing in the living presence of the one who has and is making life really delightful—my lovely, charming wife, Evelyn.

Memories Relived

Upon hearing a reunion of students and teachers of Sadler School was being planned, I became immersed in deep thought. I recalled hearing my father say that he had attended a one-room school built of logs in the same vicinity.

He often mentioned the fact that grown young men and women attended Sadler in the 1870s and the 1880s. That practice continued through the first two decades of the 20th century. It wasn't uncommon for some of the students to be as old as a young teacher.

Dad recalled that one of his teachers, an older man, treated his students on the last day of school by giving them each a stick of peppermint candy. He also gave the boys who were old enough to shave a snort of whiskey from a gallon jug. That was probably the exception rather than the rule and may have been frowned upon by some of the parents.

Dad's younger sister, Aunt Florence, remembered her teachers as being good, godly men who began school each morning by reading a chapter from the Bible and then offering a prayer. Therefore, the impression on people's minds left by the one-room school would vary from person to person and from school to school and from decade to decade as much as the impression that was made on the three blind men who went to see an elephant—you know the story.

My eight years of schooling at Sadler began in a one-room, frame building that replaced the log school my father had attended. It sat on high, vertical stone pillars. In the latter part of the 1920s, this building was replaced by a more modern building on a solid foundation.

While attending Sadler School, I walked the mile path, which was mostly wooded. The path crossed two hollows and a rocky branch.

On the morning of July 20, 1990, I made known to Evelyn, my dear wife, that I planned to visit the Sadler School site. I could have driven over there in five minutes by following the Mountain Grove School Bus Route, built by the W.P.A. in the 1930s. But I planned to follow the old trail that had been out of use for more than fifty years.

To my surprise, Evelyn wanted to go with me. My mentioning the ruggedness of the trip—underbrush, saw briars, thistles, snakes, chiggers, and ticks—didn't seem to dampen her desire to go. With some reservations, I extended a welcome and my blessings on her going. At the same time, I realized that part of her desire to go was her love for adventure, but perhaps foremost in her mind was her being along in case my steps faltered and I needed someone to lean on.

Prior to our making the trip on foot, our son, Ray, followed me in his car to the school site, where I left a car so that Evelyn and I would have transportation home.

Evelyn and I set out from Ray's home just off Route 34, on the same site of my childhood home near Womble Mountain. We went about 300 yards north to the site of the original Wallace homestead. That building was razed several years ago. Another 300 yards east put us in the front yard of my cousin, Kenneth Wallace. Back in the '20s, '30s, and '40s, this was the barn lot of Kenneth's father, Uncle Courty Wallace. We passed a few words with Kenneth, who expressed surprise at our desire to attempt such an undertaking.

We circled Kenneth's house and set our sights in a north-east direction and were soon beyond the area that had the appearance of civilization. It was then that we began to ponder our steps more carefully. We would smite the ground and part the grass and weeds with the long snake sticks that we carried.

At this point, I paused to display my skill as a narrator of a guided tour. I said, "If this grown-over field could talk, what a story it could tell! Among other things, it would probably point out the exact location of a 10-acre peach orchard owned by my grandfather, Jonathan Wallace. He used the peaches more than a hundred years ago to make peach brandy in his whiskey still that he operated with a federal liquor license."

My narrating was interrupted by a deer bounding off from near at hand, as though he had no intentions of stopping until he had crossed the County Line road into Gallatin County, but then he stopped about a hundred yards away to look us over.

Somehow seeing the deer caused my mind to go away back to the time that the Indians had used that ridge for a hunting ground. I pointed out that about twenty-five years earlier, when the field was last cultivated, Ray had found a perfect arrowhead near where we were standing.

As we faced northeast, I pointed out that just over our right shoulder was Womble Mountain, the home of the legendary Indian, Simon Womble, and over our left shoulder, under the large cedar, Womble's bones lay peacefully waiting for the final resurrection.

Then fearing my narrating would exceed my knowledge, we began to take in the beauty all around us. First we took notice of the many shades of green. I stopped counting on eight. Next to catch our eye was the sumac. Many bunches of hundreds of seeds, each in various degrees of maturity, displayed colors from an eye-catching pale yellow to a color between an auburn and some shade of red. The maturing sour dock was taking on a rich brown. Last year's crop of sage grass, still standing and interlaced with the pale green new crop, made a habitat that all but hid a chameleon-type lizard. The leaves of the sassafras had not begun to turn, but the tops of the persimmon bushes displayed a yellow and red.

We then went on to what had been a fence row. There was no fence or posts, but there was an east-west growth of trees in the right location. I told Evelyn that the school path had crossed there fifty feet one way or the other. I also told her about the time Uncle Courty sat there flat on the ground with his feet drawn up close and crossed in front of him. He was watching honeybees working on some sweet clover. He would locate their bee tree by watching them make a bee-line for it. After finding the bee tree, he would set an empty bee box near and hope that when they swarmed they would accept the box as their new home.

On this particular day, Uncle Courty was trimming his fingernails with his pocket knife and watching the bees. Suddenly he saw a huge, coiled rattlesnake about four feet in front of him.

When asked what he did, he said, "With almost no display of motion, I closed my knife and slipped it into my pocket. I drew my knees up under my chin and slowly did a back roll—my first. I sprang to my feet. My first step was a six-footer."

...

An episode that involved a neighbor boy also took place at this fence crossing. This boy and I had been bickering all the way home from school to this point. We each carried a heavy snake stick. But we were far too well-disciplined to use the sticks on each other. We helped each other crawl through the barbed wire fence. Then our quarreling seemed to grow more bitter. He set his gallon syrup bucket, which he was using for a lunch bucket, on the ground in front of me and dared me to hit it with my stick. He went ahead to double dare me. Then he said in a hateful tone, "You are chicken with feathers on your legs if you don't. I double-dog dare you to hit it."

At that point I drew back with my stick and let drive with the velocity of a golfer. He picked up his sorry-looking bucket, and we walked on together as though nothing had happened.

This boy's mom told everyone, including my mom, about my rude behavior. Mom believed my version of the story, but her response was in keeping with her nature. Shortly thereafter, she sent this woman a gallon syrup bucket of freshly churned buttermilk and told her she could keep the bucket.

After leaving the fence row, we headed for the Rocky Branch. Never at any time was I sure that we were within a hundred yards of the original path. Deer trails helped us some, but too often they led us off course.

When we got to Rocky Branch, the banks were far too steep to be our old time crossing—far too steep to cross with a team and wagon as I one time did.

Still, I told Evelyn about a neighbor girl, Eva Dean Milligan, who fell on a sharp rock in the Rocky Branch as she and her brother, Marvin, were going to school. Marvin helped her up and tied his handkerchief around her knee. They went on to school. School was in session when they arrived. The teacher almost fainted when she saw an inch-and-a-half cut exposing the knee cap.

I offered to run home and get a team and wagon to take Eva Dean home. In record time I was on my way back with a team of mules hitched to a light farm wagon. It was a thrill to see those mules perform, as I sat high on the spring seat. They seemed to sense that we were on a serious mission. In rough places, they were slow, sure-footed, and cautious. Where conditions permitted, they would trot or even gallop.

I really felt important as I pulled the wagon horizontal to the school steps. A number of helping hands assisted Eva Dean into the seat beside me. To minimize the shaking and jarring, the mules were forced to walk all the way to Eva Dean's home.

Mrs. Milligan was admired by all who knew her. She showered Eva Dean with great love and kindness as I carried her into the house. Later she complimented Mom on having a wonderful son with such a tender touch.

Years ago, just beyond Rocky Branch, on the left, was a house place—with all buildings long gone—and two old-fashioned pear trees, which never failed to bear sweet, yellow pears. These trees seemed to be on no-man's land, so all the ten to fifteen children from south of school helped themselves. We thought of the pear trees as being halfway to school.

Nothing looked natural throughout the trip. My passion to tread the old trail hindered my drinking in the scenes from nature to the fullest. However, Evelyn and I pointed out to each other den trees, squirrels, wild flowers, and some lovely ferns with lacy fronds.

We marveled at the melody made by a woodpecker. We concluded that he surely knew that he was more than just a woodpecker—he was an accomplished musician.

We came out on the road about half a quarter mile west of where our car was parked near the school site.

The former school ground had its surprises also. Trees had reduced the play area to about one-third of its former size. Not even a stump was left of a huge white oak that once stood on the north edge of the playground. When I attempted to point out to Evelyn the hickory saplings from which we boys had swung from one to the other, I was surprised that there was no hickory of any size. They had probably been removed for firewood, and oak trees had replaced them.

I pointed out to Evelyn where a freak accident had taken place. I explained how Howard Tuttle and I, after tiring of riding through the trees, doubled up on one last sturdy sapling. Our plan was to ride it from the top to as near the ground as we could and then drop.

Lucille Simpson, in an effort to be helpful, rushed in and grabbed the tree by the top just as we turned it loose. She was thrown about ten feet into the air and made a wild flip before coming down on her back end with her feet straight out in front of her. Howard and I were two happy boys when we realized that she wasn't seriously injured, but just addled for a short time.

As Evelyn and I walked to the car, in a temperature we learned later to be 92 degrees, Evelyn said with a great deal of enthusiasm, "If we didn't have the car, we could walk back and see where we would come out—at Glenn Logan's or on Womble Mountain."

Trying not to show any surprise, I replied, "Yep, we shore could."

Brother Jay Bird and Brother Chin Whiskers

For the benefit of you who are unaware of a close friendship that existed between Jay Bird and me a few years ago, I'll give you an update.

Yes, Jay Bird was a two-legged creature with feathers, and he could fly. What made him most unusual was that he could talk, and talk he did. He didn't realize that I liked to talk, too. However, I mostly listened.

He called me "Chin Whiskers," since at that time I wore chin whiskers. My desire to nurture a strong friendship led me to address him as "Brother Jay Bird." That title pleased him.

Our first meeting was most unusual. This jaybird was flying along beside me as I was returning from the Herod post office. For fear that he didn't have my attention, when I pulled into my usual parking place, he fluttered before my face and pooped on my windshield. He then perched on my side mirror and made signs to roll down my window.

274

That is a brief sketch of how our mutual friendship began. Over the years, we've had many encounters and shared many laughs. More recently, however, several months had passed since I had seen Jay Bird, until he popped up again one day last week.

I was sitting in our pickup while giving our little dog a chance to exercise. The window was down. Suddenly Jay Bird lit on the truck door. I gasped for breath and exclaimed, "Brother Jay Bird!"

In turn, he made a little flip in the air and said, "Brother Chin . . .!" But when he saw that I no longer had chin whiskers, he quickly said, "Brother Bird Brain!"

When Jay Bird picked up on the fact that my expression was somewhat pained, he hastened to explain, "I meant 'Bird Brain' as a compliment, being a bird myself. I had in mind a great big beautiful bird like you never saw before."

My countenance changed and said, "Bless you, Brother Jay Bird. It is just like old times having you back."

Jay Bird said, "I think I'll shorten your name from 'Brother Bird Brain' to 'Brother B.B.'"

I smiled and said, "Thanks, Brother Jay Bird. I like that better."

"Brother B.B., do you remember the time I snuck down from the top of a tree when you were fishing and got into your bait can and ate all your worms?"

"Yes, I remember that I had to go home with a half a catch of fish."

"Stop griping. You went home with a pretty good string."

"You are just saying that to make me feel good. But now that you mention it, it was one whale of a good catch."

"Not that big, Brother B.B.—just enough for your and Evelyn's supper, if you weren't too fish hungry."

"Brother Jay Bird, you know how to jerk a body up and slam him down hard."

"Just trying to keep you from stretching the truth."

"Do you remember how I got even with you for eating my bait worms?"

"No, that has slipped my mind, or let me say, I'm still trying to forget."

"Allow me to refresh your memory. I tied a nice big juicy worm on the float of my fishing line and got my hook caught on an underwater log on purpose. I put all the pressure on the line that I dared. I had my fiberglass pole bent almost double. Then I waited. Soon you were perched on the float trying to get the worm loose. I applied a little more pressure on the line, and the hook snapped. That slung you in the air like a shot out of a cannon. You went up through the leaves on the overhanging tree. Two or three leaves and a blue feather came floating down."

"What did you think when I didn't come back down, B.B?"

"I just patted myself on the back and exclaimed, 'Praise God! I put a Jay Bird in orbit.'"

"B.B., just reliving that experience leaves me weak."

"Sorry about your weakness. Would you like for me to go to my worm bed and get you a handful of worms?"

"No, I was just fishing for sympathy. It doesn't seem that I'm going to get any."

"When I get through feeling sorry for myself, I don't have any sympathy for anyone else."

"Brother B.B., it grieves me that you are so critical of yourself. The truth is that you are the gentlest, kindest, most sympathetic and goodest bird brain that God ever put guts in."

"Brother Jay Bird, you sure know how to give me a

lift. Come to think of it, you could be right."

"Now, Brother B.B., if you can stop crowing and listen, I can tell you something you might be interested in."

"I can hardly wait. Blaze away."

"This took place while you were in the Navy. You probably never heard of it. Your mother acted as midwife many times—three that I was in on. I'll tell you of the other two some other time. They were humdingers, too.

"During the War years, I hung around your mom's place. Your brother, Gaylord, who was about fourteen years old then, held my attention like a vise. However, we never learned to talk to each other as you and I do. He never passed up a chance to throw a corncob at me. You know what I did to him every chance I got? Even at fourteen, Gaylord was a big, strapping boy and made a good target!

"Anyway, on to the story . . . Gaylord broke that beautiful, high-spirited bay you left when you were drafted. He kept good heavy-duty steel shoes on the horse and delighted in seeing the sparks fly when he rode the rocky and gravel roads at night.

"I learned that on occasion, I could fly along behind him at night and light on the pad just behind the saddle and get a joy ride."

"Did you enjoy the ride?"

"No, B.B., it was horrible, but it did something for my craving for adventure. It was hard on my gizzard, and gave me gizzarditis for a day or two.

"Soon after that I had another adventure. I was at your mother and Gaylord's when an old wreck of a car without a muffler whizzed in. A man jumped out and ran in like a madman and said, 'Miss Verba, my wife is having a baby. Come as quick as you can!' He was gone before your mom could say anything. Your mom was disgusted that the man didn't wait for her to go with him.

"Miss Verba, as everyone called her, gave orders to Gaylord to saddle his horse. I said, 'Hooray—more gizzarditis!'

"Gaylord said, 'Mom, you can't ride that horse alone.' She said, 'I don't plan to ride alone. I plan to ride behind you.'

"Gaylord said, 'That horse is too high-strung to ride double.' Your mom told Gaylord that in her time she had ridden high-strung horses sidesaddle.

"Gaylord rode his horse up to the porch, which was the right height for easy mounting. Your mom wasted no time in landing on behind Gaylord. The horse threw back his ears. Gaylord kicked him in the ribs, held a tight rein on him, and let him turn around a time or two before cracking him with the end of the rein. He headed him off toward the region near Eagle Creek.

"I flew along close enough to hear everything that was said. At first they moved along in a trot. Then Miss Verba asked, 'Can't we go any faster?'

"Gaylord nudged the horse to a very impressive short lope—sometimes called a 'cat lope.' Made me wish I was on with them.

"Your mother surprised the heck out of me when she asked, 'Can't we go any faster?'

"Gaylord let out a war whoop like a mad Indian with one drink too many. That horse stuck his nose out like a wild goose in flight. They really covered the ground with sparks flying. Fortunately they were close enough that they arrived before the horse got too winded.

"I perched on the windowsill with both eyes open. Gaylord was about to go in when the man stepped in front of him and said 'Wait in my car. You don't know anything about what is going on in here.'

"It was getting on toward morning when Miss Verba came out and found Gaylord asleep and told him she was ready to go home. That was all she said all the way home. She locked her arms around Gaylord and was in and out of dreamland all the way."

"Thank you, Brother Jay Bird, for telling me that story, which was almost lost on the wings of time."

"Brother B.B., that's just one of my stories! Nothing would please me more than to tell you what I observed another time while sitting on the windowsill at Rudement School, where you ruled with an iron hand."

"You almost give me the nervous jerks for fear you will show me up in a poor light."

"Don't you worry, Brother B.B. Remember—we are friends!"

"Brother Jay Bird, let's save that story for another time!"

Excitement on Big Creek

Can you stand one more fish story? If so, read on!

Years ago, my son, Ray, got permission from John English for me to drive on an all-weather road across his farm in Hardin County to Big Creek, two miles more or less from Elizabethtown. Ray must have told Mr. English that because of my age and operations, I had trouble getting in to good fishing places. The word came to me, "Go in and fish as much as you like."

At the creek, a road ran close to and parallel with the creek for more than a quarter of a mile. Over the years, I had fished many different spots and found them good and better. Some days, fish started biting early on for two or three catches. Then for the longest time, the only action would be that of the turtles stealing my bait. Other days it was a half an hour before I'd land the first keeper.

Mr. English's stretch of Big Creek must not have been open for public fishing. In all the times that I had fished there, I saw no other fishermen.

Why Mr. English took a liking to me, I'll never know. My ages old straw hat and lonely appearance may have touched a tender spot in his heart. He checked on me from time to time and was always pleased to see that I had some take-home, pan-sized fish. He was free with his compliments when my catch was somewhat larger. He told me to use his Jon boat if I wanted to. He further showed his generosity by saying, "Get you a mess of roasting ears when they are in season." I was grateful for his offers; however, I never took him up on either of them.

I had had some good fishing trips to Big Creek in the past, but this particular trip is one that I will never forget. The day's set-up was typical of many other fishing trips. As usual, a third of a five-gallon bucket of ice water, taken from home, served as my holding tank—this method was much safer than trying to dip from the steep bank of the creek. On this fish bucket, I placed a padded piece of plywood, which made a comfortable seat.

I started fishing about two hours before sundown. The only catches for the first hour were throwbacks. The small fish and turtles kept me busy pulling in my line and rebaiting.

Then, all of a sudden, it happened. My float went totally out of sight. The tip of the 12-foot extension pole slapped the water. I was fishing in more than twelve feet of water. Odds were against my landing that fish on a bluegill hook and a crappie pole. The fish swam up the creek. In response, I pulled down creek. Then the fish headed downstream. I applied pressure up creek. When the fish tried to go across the creek, I set my pole perpendicular and played give and take.

Repeats of these same procedures went on for what seemed like a long time. Finally, that fish allowed me to draw it in to the water's edge of a plateau about four feet wide and thirty feet long. The plateau was around eight feet lower than where I was standing. From that distance, I wasn't sure whether the fish was a catfish or a bass. All I could see was that it had a mouth big enough to put a fist in.

I knew that my hook, line, or pole wouldn't stand the pressure of drawing the fish up the steep bank. Standing the chance of losing that fish was out of the question. Without a second thought, I held the pole in my left hand to keep the pressure on the fish, turned my back to the creek, grabbed a tough limber bush, and slid down the steep bank.

I carefully slipped my fingers into the fish's gills. At last I knew it was a bass, probably around six pounds. The hook came out easily. Knowing I would need both of my hands free to scramble back up the bank, I took the fish in both hands and flung it far back on the bank. Although my breathing was hard, my heart was filled with pride.

I then turned my thoughts to how I might scale the bank. In preparation, I gave my pole a javelin throw up to the top of the bank. I sailed my straw hat up there, also. I then inspected that little plateau more closely and, to my dismay, found it all equally steep.

In my first attempt to scale the wall, I used a lot of energy clawing and pawing, trying to climb the wall, only to slide back down each time. I quickly realized that I needed to have a little talk with myself to help evaluate the situation.

Staying calm when I realized I was trapped wasn't easy. My repeated attempts to climb the soggy, steep bank that had become my prison wall had resulted only in muddy hands and skinned knees. My slick rubber shoe soles kept me sliding back when I got up two or three feet. Taking off my shoes, I flung them up to the top, to join my pole, hat, and fish. Digging with my toes and clawing with my fingers got me higher up the bank, but then it was farther to slide down when my attempts failed, working murder on my knees.

I hunkered down with my back to the bank for a rest, lest I'd have a heart attack. I was starting to think that, at the age of 82, this hadn't been such a smart idea.

Darkness came on quickly. Fortunately before it got really dark, a full moon shone through the trees on the east side of the creek. Night sounds took over. Swamp owls sounded off. Beavers startled me even more by slapping their tails against the water. However, what concerned me most was something swimming near me without my knowing whether it was a water snake or a muskrat.

In spite of my predicament, I stayed fairly calm throughout the ordeal. I told myself that Ray would come looking for me when he got off work at 10:30 p.m. To pass the time, I decided to do a little meditating. Before I got started, two barge pilots sounded off at each other out on the Ohio River. It reminded me of messages on ships at sea when I was in the Navy: "Passing on your right—passing on your left." I thought that if I had a bull-horn, I'd scream, "I'm passing out up Big Creek!"

Things soon got too quiet for comfort. Was it the lull before a tragic happening? A rustling behind and above me broke the stillness. The words "wampus cat" and "Hardin County cougar" came to mind. Fear took over when something bounded a couple of times over that bank, barely missing me and plopping at my feet. It was that bass! Too paralyzed to move, I watched that prize catch wriggle off into the water. As if to mock me in my situation, it paused a moment in the moonlight, then, like a miniature submarine, it slowly went out of sight and was seen "nevermore."

Was I disappointed? Yes, but I tried to console myself by saying that that is one I will not have to clean. Eventually, I returned to my attempts to meditate. The question became, "About what? Jonah in the whale's belly? The three Hebrew children in the fiery furnace? Daniel in the lion's den?" None of the above grabbed me.

I gave a little more serious thought to Moses, as he stood before the burning bush. You know the story. The Lord asked Moses, "What do you have in your hand?" Moses replied, "A staff." The Lord told Moses to throw it down and it became a snake. That staff became a magic worker over the next forty years.

I asked myself, "What do I have in my hand?" The answer came quickly, "Nothing."

I looked down and saw within reach what looked like a sturdy stick about sixteen inches long and about an inch in diameter. I at first refused to pick it up for fear it would turn into a snake and cause me to jump in the creek and drown. However, observing no movement, I eventually picked up the stick. It felt good and strong in my hand—smooth and sun-seasoned.

Again, the question came to mind, "What do you have in your hand?" The answer revived my spirits—"a hand and toehold digger." I decided that with my remaining strength, I would make one last-ditch effort to get back up the bank.

With my stick, I dug holes slanting in and down. Roots in some of the holes made good handholds. My ascent started slow and easy. Each step seemed to be the last I could possibly make. Finally my right hand grasped the bush that, hours ago, had helped me down the bank. A last little burst of energy put me on top. I lay flat on my stomach for a brief breather, which revived me enough to get to my hands and knees and on to my feet.

Nothing looked familiar to me. It was much darker under the trees on the bank. It had become cloudy, or the moonlight wasn't penetrating the trees that lined the bank. In the dark, I could see no fish bucket, straw hat, shoes, or pole. The fear of poison ivy and snakes kept me from feeling around. I walked in my sock feet in the general direction of my car, and soon came upon it. With a thankful heart, I was soon on my way home. My wonderful wife, Evelyn, was much relieved that I was safe at home, since she had been frantic with worry.

My clothes were so muddy I had to leave everything at the door. Evelyn helped me clean up and bandaged my knees, shins, and hands. While she worked on me, she listened to my whopper of a fish story.

One more unsolved mystery remains. My good friend, Cletus Killman, and I had already had plans to fish the Three Mile Creek the next day. Despite my previous day's ordeal, I decided to go ahead with the plan. We had to go to Big Creek first and get my hat, shoes, and fishing equipment. When we got there, it took less than two minutes to gather up everything.

Then I asked Cletus to take a look at the plateau on which I had been stranded. However, as I gazed down the bank, there was no plateau to be seen. The creek didn't appear to have risen. We hardly gave it a second thought at the time, but I've turned the matter over in my mind since then. I still look for that plateau. My conclusion is that it submerged, dissolved, and sank to the bottom of the creek. I'm just thankful that I got off before it happened.